Java 2

PEARSON EDUCATION LIMITED

Head Office
Edinburgh Gate, Harlow, Essex CM20 2JE
Tel: +44 (0)1279 623623 Fax: +44 (0)1279 431059

London Office
128 Long Acre, London WC2E 9AN
Tel: +44 (0)20 7447 2000 Fax: +44 (0)20 7240 5771
Websites:
www.it-minds.com   www.aw.com/cseng

First published in Great Britain 2002
© Pearson Education Limited 2002

First published in 2000 as *Java 2 Nitty-Gritty* by Addison-Wesley
Verlag, Germany.

The rights of Florian Hawlitzek to be identified as Author of this Work have been
asserted by him in accordance with the Copyright, Designs and Patents Act 1988.

Library of Congress Cataloguing Publication Data
Applied for.

British Library Cataloguing in Publication Data
A CIP catalogue record for this book can be obtained from the British Library.

ISBN 0-201-75880-6

10 9 8 7 6 5 4 3 2 1

Translated and typeset by Berlitz GlobalNET (UK) Ltd. of Luton, Bedfordshire.
Printed and bound in Great Britain by Biddles Ltd. of Guildford and King's Lynn.

The publishers' policy is to use paper manufactured from sustainable forests.

Contents

Part III – Go ahead!   353

Past history

The author has worked for many years using C++ and since 1996 has been working increasingly using Java. He was in overall charge of the development of several courses and style guides and, in the fall of 1999, published the text book *Java Programming using IBM VisualAge*. This book has been written as a response to the positive reactions of its readers and many enquiries.

Many sections have their roots in the VisualAge book, where step-by-step learning of the language and the development environment are at the fore. *Nitty Gritty Java* is rather more a practical introduction with tips and a reference for looking things up.

The text book accompanied the author through a turbulent phase both in Java and in his professional field. Sun published Version 1.3 of Java, which has already found its way into this book (as well as information on the upcoming Micro Edition). Professionally, the author became self-employed during this time, as he took the step from managing an applications development department to founding the company of Hawlitzek IT Consulting.

Thanks

I would like to give my warmest thanks to all of those who have contributed to the preparation of this book:

Firstly, I would like to thank my girlfriend Kirsten Literski for her valuable suggestions and for her great patience with me in the last few months, which she has provided for a second time. Again, I underestimated the effort required in writing a book. Thank you for your devotion and love.

I would particularly like to thank Wernher Bien for his work on the content, his many suggestions for improvements and his splendid commitment. Many thanks also to Tilmann Ochs for good documents and graphics. Naturally, my thanks also go to all of those who helped in the preparation of the VisualAge book, as well as the management of my former company ARS, who made it possible for me to write this book.

Most sincere thanks to the publishers Addison-Wesley.

Part I

Start up!

Basic Java concepts

The first three chapters in this book provide an overview of the *Java* programming language and also explain the use of development environments and some important concepts of object orientation. The intention is that you get to know the key concepts and terms involved. We leave the finer points of syntax and standard libraries to Part 2.

The first chapter presents the architecture of Java and the potential applications offered by the language. Using a short example we illustrate the structure of a Java program, conversion of the source code into the platform-independent binary format, and its execution in the runtime system.

I have chosen to leave out the history element common in other books. True to the "nitty-gritty" motto, I concentrate on the essentials instead, namely the following questions:

- ➜ What can I do with the language?
- ➜ How do I do it?
- ➜ How does it work?

1.1 Areas of use

Java is a universal language, meaning that in principle it can be used for any type of application. This is where it differs from script languages, which are particularly efficient in one field, for instance JavaScript for controlling web browsers, Perl for web servers, or macro languages such as VBA for interfacing Microsoft applications.

There are, however, certain applications for which Java is particularly well suited, and others where I would not recommend it so strongly.

One of the strengths of Java is the Internet connection. Java has proved very useful both on the client side in the web browser and on the web server. This is thanks partly to Java's platform independence, partly to the standard classes that already provide convenient support for web protocols and technologies.

Numerous e-commerce and banking applications, for instance, are implemented in Java in this way.

Java is versatile, modular, and easy to learn, and includes a large number of standard programming libraries and interfaces. This means that Java is a popular choice for projects requiring high development efficiency or where changes are highly likely. Demand for these features used to be limited to the hobby programmer and the academic sector, but now the professionals expect them too. Another factor in Java's popularity is access to excellent development environments, some of which you can obtain for free.

Java runs anywhere. Runtime environments range from palmtop to mainframe. This is why Java is preferred when it is not known in advance what platform the future user will run it on. Another reason for using Java is that it lets you keep your options open in case you need to move the server onto more powerful hardware or a better operating system to cope with an unexpected rush on the application. This is also known as scaling.

Java is particularly popular in distributed, object-oriented systems. Whenever an application relies on using the computing power of different computers simultaneously or on task sharing – for example display, processing and data storage – then it requires an infrastructure or middleware that ensures communication will work and then provides reliable secure access without risk of conflict. Java actually provides its own mechanisms for this purpose, and also integrates established technologies such as CORBA (*Common Object Request Broker Architecture*, standardized infrastructure for object communication).

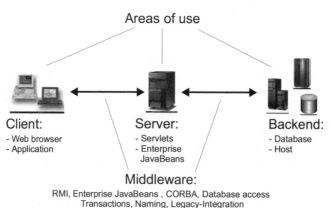

Figure 1.1 *Areas of use*

There are also areas, however, where Java is less well suited.

Java cannot access the hardware directly. This means that you cannot program drivers in Java, nor can you use Java to operate special devices such as scanners or force feedback joysticks. In addition, all applications that are programmed very close to the hardware for efficiency reasons, for example action computer games, are problematic, unless you are lucky enough to be able to use the Java 3D API, which enables access to OpenGL or DirectX on some operating systems.

Hard real-time requests are also not feasible. "Hard" in this context means that an operation – for instance a machine control action – must guarantee a response time, say 10 milliseconds. In this case Java cannot be used. This is because the run-time environment is very complex and performs occasional memory clean-ups, which occur at "random" intervals and must not be interrupted.

1.2 Java as language and platform

Java actually has two meanings: the first as a programming language, the second as an environment providing all possible services and interfaces.

1.2.1   The Java programming language

Java is an object-oriented language whose syntax is similar to C++. The following example programs a simple class:

```java
class Account
{
    int    number;
    double balance;

    void payin (double amount)
    {
        balance = balance + amount;
    }
}
```

The Account class describes what attributes characterize an object in this class – here the account number and balance – and what functions the class provides, in this case just paying in.

The language offers everything you are used to from other programming languages such as BASIC, C etc., i.e. variables, loops, conditional statements and so on. But Java is fully object oriented, so that everything is packed in classes and objects. Items of data are saved as states of objects, i.e. as values assigned to variables. For example, an account could have the number "08154711" and the balance "2,500.68". The functions are available in the form of methods for these classes. Another option in object-oriented languages is inheritance, i.e. reusing common codes and specialization of classes. Thus, for instance, you could have the more specific types "Giro account" and "Savings account", which both inherit all the attributes of the account, but also have additional attributes.

Compared with C++, Java is slightly simpler and thus easier to learn and understand. This is because the programmer no longer has to bother about memory management, and also because complex language tools have been left out. For instance, in Java there is no multiple inheritance, no templates, and no overloading of standard operators.

1.2.2　The Java platform

Since 1998, Sun Microsystems – the inventor of the language – has also referred to Java as a platform. What do they mean by this?

Java provides a host of off-the-shelf class libraries. The full spectrum covers classes for creating graphical interfaces, database access, encoding and data compression. In a similar way to operating systems, e.g. Windows, in which there is a set of programming interfaces for all possible areas and devices, the libraries in Java provide the functionality as an *API (Application Programmers Interface)*. In this case, however, the same interface is employed for all operating systems used, with the function calls being converted by the runtime environment on the actual platform itself. The environment, which is abstractly defined in this way, together with the associated emulator is called a *virtual machine*. Since Java behaves like a stand-alone platform as far as the programmer is concerned, the term has subsequently been adopted to express that Java is more than just a language.

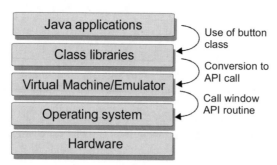

Figure 1.2　*Conversion of an API call*

Figure 1.2 shows an example in which a button (*Button* class) is used in a graphics application. Each call is converted in the virtual machine into a call to the Window API of the host operating system, for instance that of Windows or the motif library under UNIX.

Editions

It would not be logical, however, to provide all the libraries on every platform. After all why would you need support for application server components on a palmtop? It would be prohibitive for space reasons anyway. Sun has therefore defined three different editions aimed at different sectors:

1   Standard Edition for desktop client or PC

2   Enterprise Edition for application servers

3   Micro Edition for miniature devices such as palmtops and embedded systems, e.g. video recorders

This book deals primarily with the *Standard Edition*, which is also the most widely used version. Figure 1.3 shows the areas that this collection of class libraries is concerned with.

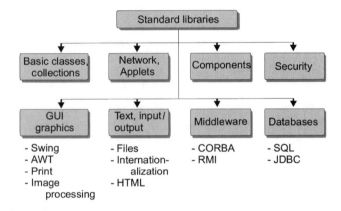

Figure 1.3   *Java 2 Standard Edition*

The *Enterprise Edition* (see Figure 1.4) is a larger version of the Standard Edition, containing extra functions for an application server. This kind of server provides services to different types of users and integrates back-end systems. One example might be an e-commerce application in which a customer can order via a web browser, and which also accesses mainframe databases and a merchandise information system. Reliable middleware plays an even greater role here, for instance name and directory services or transactions.

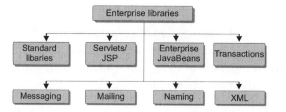

Figure 1.4 *Java 2 Enterprise Edition*

Unlike the Standard Edition, the Enterprise Edition is not a runtime environment but just a set of programming interfaces and compatibility standards that an application server must comply with to receive the relevant certificate from Sun. The Enterprise Edition originated from various optional upgrades to the Standard Edition.

The *Micro Edition* is a lower spec version of the Standard Edition intended for miniature devices, and has been optimized for low hardware requirements.

1.3 Runtime environment

The Java runtime environment essentially consists of the *virtual machine* mentioned above, adapted to the target platform. What does this actually mean, and what advantages does it bring?

1.3.1   Platform independence

Java was designed to run on the widest possible range of systems. This meant it was not possible to make assumptions about the target hardware or the properties of the operating system on which the applications were to run. Instead, Java is run on a system that is defined in the abstract and emulated in the target system, in other words the *virtual machine*.

Interpreted languages

Many interpreted languages like BASIC or REXX share a similar concept. In these languages the source code is read directly by a runtime environment and converted instruction by instruction into machine code (or operating system API calls). This process is not particularly efficient however.

Virtual machine

Java's virtual machine (*Java VM*) on the other hand is actually defined as a machine, i.e. as hardware that can interpret specific opcodes (machine instructions). In fact, chips have already been developed that implement this machine in hardware. Normally, however, a runtime system emulates the machine on the target platform concerned.

But why the added complexity of installing a runtime system on every target platform? Surely you could provide the code in the correct form already?

Compiled languages

Figure 1.5 shows the sequence for comparison.

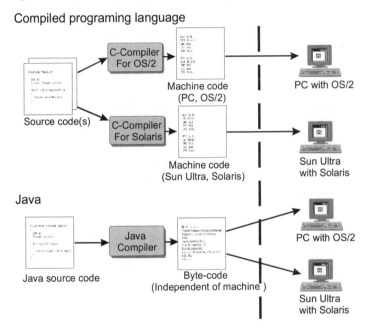

Figure 1.5 *Comparison of compiled and interpreted programming languages*

In a compiled programming language like C, a separate binary code must be generated not only for each piece of target hardware, but also for each operating system (or even every operating system version!). This means that developers must have systems plus development and test tools for all these configurations. Since these are normally incompatible with each other, you almost always need to manage different versions of the source code as well.

In practice this normally means that only one or two platforms are covered, since the time and effort involved in a non-mainstream system would be too great.

START UP!

BASIC JAVA CONCEPTS **23**

Java

In contrast, Java developers generate a universal source file (*Source*) on just one platform, which they compile there into binary code or *bytecode* for the Java VM. The runtime system – known as the *Java Runtime Environment*, or *JRE* for short – consists of the emulator and a series of class libraries, and this is what executes the bytecode. Sun themselves provide it for Windows and Solaris, but there are lots of other producers, such as IBM, HP or Microsoft. All of these should be identical, but unfortunately the small things sometimes cause the problems.

1.3.2   Java versions

The main differences lie in the Java language version supported and the associated libraries. Sun uses a three-digit number to identify the version, the second digit being the most important. The last digit usually just identifies the fixpacks (set of bug fixes) or minimum function upgrades.

The first version 1.0.x is completely obsolete and is hardly ever used now. You are safer using 1.1.x, for instance 1.1.8, which is supported by practically all environments and browsers. The language took a great step forward with Java 1.2.x, in particular in the area of graphics, security and middleware. This is why Sun also refers to "Java 2" after this version. Unfortunately, many users still have no corresponding virtual machine installed, and things don't look that promising for browser support either. Often, however, the new facilities justify its use. Version 1.3 is totally new. Admittedly it only offers a few new programming interfaces, but it does provide a more convenient and faster runtime environment.

1.3.3   Variants

There are four versions of the runtime environment, two for the client side and two for the server side (see Figure 1.6).

1   Client JRE for applications
2   Web browser with applets
3   Web server with servlet engine
4   Application server as EJB container

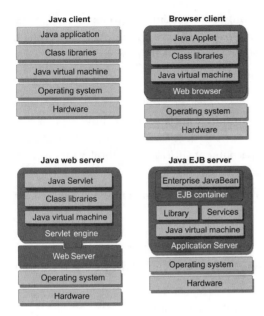

Figure 1.6 *Variants of the Java Runtime Environment*

All have a similar structure. The classes are executed in the *virtual machine* and use the class libraries supplied. The differences arise in the type of applications and the system on which the VM runs.

On the client, Java applications run either as applications in the traditional sense or as applets. These traditional-type *applications* do not constitute executables, however, but are run by passing to the Java interpreter a class that contains a *main* method.

```
> java Homebanking
```

Applets are special classes that run in a Java-compatible web browser. This already contains the runtime system; in Netscape Navigator/Communicator or Microsoft Internet Explorer however, the runtime system can be replaced by a current version using a Java plug-in from Sun. Applets are embedded in a web page using a special HTML command, and are usually loaded on a web server. Applets contain special facilities for communicating with the browser or web page in which they are embedded. They are also subject to specific security restrictions. These are meant to prevent unknown code downloaded from a web server from damaging your system or spying on it.

Java is also at home on web servers. *Servlets* are widely used. These are Java classes that generate dynamic HTML pages, and in principle work in a similar way to CGI applications. This type of runtime environment is called a servlet engine, and is typically available as a plug-in for standard web servers.

A Java *Enterprise Application Server* provides a runtime environment for specific Java components called *Enterprise JavaBeans*. These not only use the standard Java class libraries, but also a range of services provided by the server.

1.4 Example

This section shows how to write a simple application and how to get it running. We are using the Standard Java Development Kit here (JDK or Java 2 SDK), which contains both the runtime environment (JRE) and a compiler for converting the Java class into an executable form.

The class in this example is meant to read the current system time and display it on the command line.

Writing the class

To write the class, open any text editor and type in the following lines (without the explanatory comments):

The first line makes the system class for the date visible:

```
import java.util.Date;
```

The next line gives the class a name and opens a block.

```
class DisplayDate
{
```

When the interpreter is run it automatically executes the *main* method. It must be initiated exactly as shown below so that it can be found:

```
    public static void main(String[] args)
    {
```

Now we create a new date object that is automatically set to today's date unless we specify otherwise:

```
        Date currentDate = new Date();
```

Then we convert the date into a character string (String class):

```
        String output = currentDate.toString();
```

and output this on the standard output, the console:

```
        System.out.println(output);
```

Now we must close the method and class blocks:

```
    }
}
```

An experienced programmer would have written these steps slightly more compactly, resulting in the following shortform notation:

```
import java.util.Date;
class DisplayDate
{
    public static void main(java.lang.String[] args)
    {
        System.out.println(new Date());
    }
}
```

Save the class under the name *DisplayDate.java*.

> **Tip** The .java file must have exactly the same name as the class, including upper and lower case letters, for instance not *Displaydate.java*.

Compiling the class

In the command line switch to the directory in which you saved the class. Make sure that the Java compiler *javac* is in the path, or enter the fully qualified path:

```
> javac DisplayDate.java
```

or

```
> %JDK_HOME%\bin\javac DisplayDate.java
```

This produces your executable class as a file called *DisplayDate.class*.

Running the class

If the working directory "." is contained in the environment variable CLASS-PATH, you can run the application as follows:

```
> java DisplayDate
```

Tip If you get an error message saying that the class or main method was not found, the likely reason is that the runtime environment only looks in CLASSPATH and the working directory is not held there. Correct the problem by entering the following under DOS/Windows:
```
> set CLASSPATH=%CLASSPATH%;.
```
If you get a NoClassDefFoundError with the comment "wrong name", you have probably not observed the upper/lower case notation.

When you use packages later, you must not switch to the directory containing the class, but must work in the base directory from which the package name starts. There you enter the full class name including package, e.g. `java com.nittyGritty.DisplayDate`.

It is often difficult – especially for Windows users – to make these entries in the command line. Associating the ".class" extension with the Java interpreter does not help either, since then the working directory is not set correctly. It is therefore best to create a simple ".bat" file that contains the Java interpreter call and the correct class name.

Development environments

One of the reasons for Java's wide popularity is not least the availability of ultra-modern programming environments for the language. These simplify the day-to-day work of the developer and reduce work in general. Some of these tools are even available for free!

2.1 Java Development Kit

We have already introduced a simple development environment, the Java Development Kit from Sun Microsystems.

2.1.1 Components

The *Java Development Kit* from Sun, *JDK* for short, is a runtime system and development platform in one. The runtime components are also available separately as the *Java Runtime Environment (JRE)*. Since JDK version 1.2, it has also been called the *Java 2 Software Development Kit (Java 2 SDK)*.

The JDK for Windows and Solaris can be obtained from the Sun subsidiary JavaSoft (www.javasoft.com/) .

Contents

In addition to an HTML documentation system, the JDK contains a virtual machine and a series of simple command-line tools for software development under Java.

The JDK should not be confused with full, integrated development environments, which we describe in Section 2.2.

2.1.2   Tools

Procedure

Firstly write the source files using an editor; no editor is included in the JDK by the way. Every (public) class must be saved in a file having the exact class name and the extension .*java*.

Then compile the file using the compiler, so that the applications can then run in the runtime environment of the JDK. You can either run applets in a Java-compatible web browser (not included) or in the limited applet viewer of the JDK.

2

■ START UP!

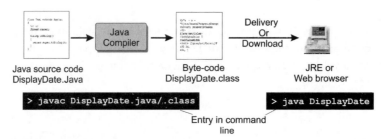

Java source code   Byte-code   JRE or
DisplayDate.Java   DisplayDate.class   Web browser

> javac DisplayDate.java/.class   > java DisplayDate

Entry in command
line

Figure 2.1 *Procedure for writing a program using the JDK*

javac

The compiler is called *javac*. To run the compiler, enter javac in the command line together with the java file as parameter.

```
javac DisplayDate.java
```

If there are no errors in the source files, the compiler generates the bytecode file *DisplayDate.class*.

> **Tip** You need to enter the file name when compiling, i.e. usually the class name plus the extension "*.java*". The file could have a different name, however, or contain more than one class. The result will always be "*.class*" file(s) having the correct name of the class(es), each class being held in its own file.
>
> After installing the JDK, the Java compiler (unlike the interpreter) is not located in the system path. Enter the bin directory of the JDK under the PATH environment variable, or use the following notation whenever you run the compiler:
> ```
> > %JDK_HOME%\bin\javac DisplayDate.java
> ```
> If a class references other classes, then these must exist in the CLASSPATH either as source code or binary code. In our example the class *java.util.Date* is referenced. As this is part of the standard library it is found automatically. If we had used a class of our own that only existed in source code until then, the compiler would have automatically compiled it at the same time.

You can get detailed status messages using the parameter -verbose. -classpath lets you overwrite the standard environment variable CLASSPATH to specify where the compiler should look for referenced classes. The table below shows the most important parameters.

Parameter	Meaning
-classpath	Specify path for locating other classes
-d <Directory name>	Specify other destination directory
-deprecation	Warning when using outdated classes and methods
-g	Generate debug information in class
-O	Generate optimized binary format
-verbose	Display detailed status messages

Linking is not necessary because the Java runtime system loads the required classes dynamically, i.e. only when needed, and links them at runtime.

Figure 3.2 shows two different Account objects in UML notation, where the dashed line indicates instantiation. Each instance is identified by a colon and underlining. The value is specified for each of the instance variables.

Objects are saved in the memory. Java's automatic memory management system makes sure that enough memory space is reserved, and that this space is released again when the object is deleted. It is no use storing the object just anywhere in the memory, however, because it needs to be accessed again. This is where references come in, which point to a particular object. You can think of object references as rather like the name of the object (as long as you do not assign this reference to another object). So a reference is a kind of intelligent pointer that always points to the object automatically, even if the object has moved in the memory.

Tip These are not real pointers like in C, however; references do not constitute a front for memory addresses, and you cannot play pointer arithmetic with them!

This is how you create an Account object in Java and assign it to a reference :

```
Account customerAccount = new Account();
```

The first *Account* here is the type of the reference with the name `customerAccount`; thus this reference can only point to instances of the *Account* class. A new object of the *Account* class is assigned to this (see Figure 3.3).

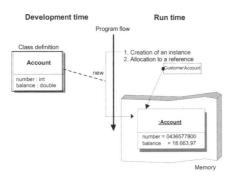

Figure 3.3 *Generating an instance of the Account class*

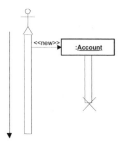

Figure 3.4 *Instantiation in UML*

Figure 3.4 uses the UML format to illustrate the process (sequence diagram). The left-hand arrow shows the time axis, with the vertical bars indicating the lifetime of objects. A cross indicates when the Account object is deleted, and the stick man symbolizes the user.

After referencing, you can access the object as follows:

```
int accountNumber = customerAccount.number;
customerAccount.payin (100.0);
```

Significance of classes in Java

As an object-oriented language, Java is completely class based. It differs from C++ however, in that there are no global functions, variables or constants. In particular there is no global `main` function either. An application starts execution with the main method of that class passed as the parameter to the interpreter. Since each class can contain its own main method, a group of several classes could for instance constitute different applications depending on which class you started with. Applets are also based on classes. As we will see later, each applet is a sub-class of the class *java.applet.Applet*.

Special features of variables and methods

In addition to instance variables, you sometimes get fields that are assigned to the classes as a whole, i.e. are used by all instances in common. These are called *class variables*. Similarly there are also *class methods*, which can be executed independently of objects. One example of this is the `main` method already mentioned.

Method overloading

Method overloading means that more than one method can have the same name. Which of the methods sharing the same name is called depends on the call parameters at runtime. Method overloading can be used to combine groups of semantically equivalent methods. For the programmer it is definitely clearer if all methods performing equivalent functions also have the same name.

```
void transfer(Account destinationAccount, double amount)...
void transfer(int destinationAccountNumber, double amount) ...
```

3.2 Inheritance

After *encapsulation*, i.e. the grouping of data and functions in classes, inheritance is the most important object-oriented principle. Objects can "inherit", i.e. adopt, properties from other objects or their classes, provided these properties are not defined differently in the object's own definition. This means that you only have to program identical code once, which is also useful for maintainability reasons.

3.2.1 Super and sub-classes

Additional classes can be derived from a *super class* (often also called a *top class* or *base class*). These classes then inherit the behavior of the super class. You can add specialization to the behavior of these *sub-classes* by adding extra variables and methods.

Example

We will take our account example a little further. In addition to the general account there are two derived account types:

→ a savings account, for which extra interest accrues.
→ a Giro account that can be overdrawn.

Super class

The properties (account)*number* and *balance* are not just properties of savings accounts, but of all types of accounts. So these properties are assigned to the *Account* super class. This class contains all the properties that apply to every account.

Sub-class

The *credit limit* property is a special property of Giro accounts. The *GiroAccount* class is derived from the *Account* super class, and inherits all its properties. Only those properties that provide extra specialization for this class are added to the *GiroAccount* sub-class. Using this technique you do not need to redefine general properties for each account type (e.g. savings account, credit-card account).

In the *UML* notation, inheritance is represented by an arrow with a non-solid arrow head pointing to the super class (see Figure 3.5).

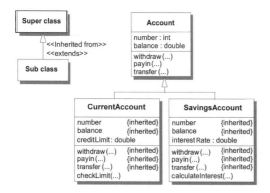

Figure 3.5 *Single inheritance*

Inheritance in Java

The example above is implemented in Java as follows:

```java
class Account
{
    int    number;
    double balance;
    void withdraw (double amount)
    {
        if (balance > amount)
        balance = balance - amount;
    }
void payin (double amount)
```

```
    {
        balance = balance + amount;
    }
    void transfer(Account destinationAccount, double amount)
    {
        withdraw(amount);
        destinationAccount.payin(amount);
    }
}
class GiroAccount extends Account
{
    double creditlimit;
    boolean checkLimit(double amount)
    {
        if (balance - amount> -creditlimit)
            return true;
        else
            return false;
    }
}
```

3.2.2   Overriding methods

Methods in sub-classes can *override* methods in their super class. You simply declare these in the sub-class using the same name and the same signature. Often an overriding method calls the shadowed method of the super class, and then adds its own functionality.

Our Giro account has had a problem up to now: you could withdraw money but only as long as there was some in the account; the credit limit was ignored. You could of course write a separate method withdrawWithLimit(), but the override facility makes it a lot easier:

```
class GiroAccount extends Account
{
    [...]
    void withdraw (double amount)
    {
        if (checkLimit(amount))
        balance = balance - amount;
    }
}
```

When we are working with accounts, the Java runtime environment automatically detects that it is dealing with a Giro account (i.e. the more specific type) and always calls the correct method. These are also referred to as *virtual methods*.

> **Tip** In the code example above I have left out the part that is irrelevant to the current issue being explained. Any omitted code is indicated by **[...]**

3.2.3   Multiple inheritance and interfaces

Single inheritance

Multiple inheritance means that a class is derived from several super classes. This can lead to ambiguities, however, if an attribute or a method with the same name occurs in the super classes of one and the same object. What is more, you can easily get lost in such a web of inheritance structures.

This is why Java only supports single inheritance, which means that each class (except for the original class *Object*) has just one super class.

Interfaces

Nevertheless, you might often want to define classes that comply with the interfaces of more than one base class. For instance, you might have written a "class" *InterestBearing* that provides common interfaces for securities and savings accounts. In our example, however, we could not derive anything else from this class, because the *SavingsAccount* is already derived from *Account*.

Java provides *Interfaces* for this purpose. These are purely abstract classes without instance variables or method implementations. This means that the methods are not implemented at this point, but just the signature is specified (the method header with the parameter list). This prevents ambiguity, while still guaranteeing the presence of methods. When a class complies with an interface, this is referred to as implementation. The class must then implement all those methods whose declaration is included in the interface.

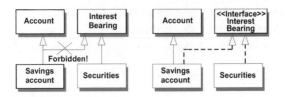

Figure 3.6 *Interfaces*

```
interface InterestBearing
{
    double calculateInterest();
}
class SavingsAccount extends Account implements
InterestBearing
{
    [...]
    double calculateInterest()
    {
        [...]
    }
}
```

3.2.4   Advantages/disadvantages of inheritance

Using inheritance offers some important advantages listed below.

Reusability

The behavior of a super class is passed on to sub-classes. The program code of the super class is then also used in the sub-classes, so there is no need to write it again. Nor do you need to maintain (and edit) several similar code sequences in parallel for all sub-classes – an unpleasant task and a likely source of errors.

Consistency of interfaces

Methods and variables that have already been defined in the super class are also identical for all sub-classes. This guarantees standard interfaces, at least with respect to the behavior defined in the super class. Thus these interfaces are also the same in all sub-classes.

Rapid prototyping

Employing reusable components that you can define by class hierarchies can confine the development task for new projects to the creation of new project-specific components. The "rapid prototyping" approach involves getting a basic set of software components running, and then adding extra components step by step.

Information hiding

The user of class hierarchies only needs to understand the public interfaces of the class hierarchies. The actual implementation remains hidden. The visibility of the class components within the inheritance hierarchy can be fine-tuned using various access rights.

In some cases, however, using inheritance can prove a disadvantage.

Efficiency

General methods held in super classes are often slower and less efficient than "tailor-made" methods designed for the individual situation. More elegant programming and more readable program code takes precedence here over fully optimized, but non-reusable solutions.

Complexity

Taken to the extreme, however, the inheritance concept can cause the opposite. Class and interface hierarchies containing endless branches through numerous levels are hard to understand and make the program code less transparent. This is where the programmer's experience and instinct comes in. It is quite common when starting Java programming that enthusiasm for an elegant inheritance design can cloud your vision of simple and clear class hierarchies. So before defining any class and interface hierarchy, you should think carefully whether a class hierarchy is really needed for solving this particular problem, or whether it might also be solved with simpler constructs.

Einstein quote

Bjarne Stroustrup the inventor of the C++ programming language (from which Java's inheritance concept is derived) had good reason to quote the mathematician Albert Einstein when discussing the design of C++ classes:

"Keep things simple: as simple as possible, but no simpler."

Part I

Take that!

Java syntax

4

The second part of this book looks at Java syntax and the standard class libraries. It is intended as a reference source when you need a short introduction to the individual topics and a description of the most important classes, methods and keywords. If you are more interested in tips on what Java options are available and how to use them, then you are better off referring to the third part.

In this chapter I aim to explain the keywords of the Java language. We will meet again the classes and objects already explained in the first chapters. Further options for influencing how classes and individual members behave are also explained, for instance how to assign access rights. In addition, the chapter deals with language constructs such as loops, conditional statements etc., as well as the equally important elementary data types such as *int* or *double*.

4.1 Language elements

Like every other programming language, Java contains a set of keywords recognized by the compiler as language elements. It also includes control structures, labels, (names or identifiers), constants (literals), operators (e.g. +, <, &, etc.) and comments.

4.2 Keywords

Java recognizes the following keywords:

abstract	continue	finally	interface	public
boolean	default	float	long	return
break	do	for	native	short
byte	double	if	new	static
case	else	implements	null	super
catch	extends	import	package	switch
char	false	instanceof	private	synchronized
class	final	int	protected	this

throw	transient	try	void
throws	true	volatile	while

Tip There are also two reserved words `const` and `goto`, but these are not used. Their main purpose at present is for the output of explanatory compiler messages (*"not supported"*), should a C++ programmer mistakenly use these keywords common in C.

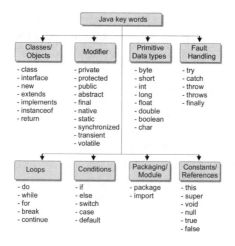

Figure 4.1 *Keywords arranged according to usage*

4.3 Comments

There are three types of comment in Java:

Single-line comment

Comments that apply to the rest of a line start with two forward slashes.

```
// Credit check
if (checkLimit(b)) // if limit not exceeded
```

Multi-line comment

These can contain any character except the final character (*/), which means that a multi-line comment can also contain a single-line comment. Nesting is not allowed, however.

```
/* Withdrawal is only possible if
   the credit limit is not exceeded */
if (checkLimit(b)) [...]
/* Nesting is
  /* not */
  allowed! */
```

javadoc comment

For purposes of generating code documentation, there is a special comment that the javadoc compiler converts to HTML format:

```
/**
 * method for converting Euro currencies
 * uses rounding and correct scaling
 * @return java.lang.String converted value
[...]
 */
public String calc(String value, String sourceCurr, String
destCurr)throws CurrencyTypeException, CurrencyFormatExcep-
tion
{
[...]
```

Method Summary	
java.lang.String	`calc`(java.lang.String value, java.lang.String sourceCurr, java.lang.String destCurr) method for converting Euro currencies uses rounding and correct scaling
java.lang.String	`getCurrencyName`(java.lang.String currency) returns long currency name for a 3 letter international currency code
java.math.BigDecimal	`getExchangeRate`(java.lang.String currency) returns exchange rate from given currency to Euro

Figure 4.2 *Extract from the javadoc documentation for JDK 1.2*

Sun's standard API specification for Java is produced using this tool.

Special control characters can be embedded in this type of comment, which are then highlighted or appear as links in the generated HTML documentation.

Tag	Meaning	Example
General		
@see	Hyperlink to referenced class or method	@see java.lang.String

Tag	Meaning	Example
In methods		
@return	Return type and description; used for highlighting in method documentation	@return java.lang.String converted value
@param	Name and description of a parameter, used for highlighting in method documentation	@param destCurr destination currency for conversion
@exception	Reference to and description of exceptions that may arise in the method	@exception CurrencyTypeException unknown currency for conversion
In classes		
@version	Version details for classes	@version 1.1.8C
@author	Class author information	@author Florian Hawlitzek

4.4 Class structure

As already explained in the previous chapter, classes are made up of members that can be either variables (fields) or methods. A class declaration in Java appears as follows:

```
<Modifier> class ClassName
{
    // Member definitions
}
```

<Modifier> stands for various keywords that are instructions for the compiler, for instance specifying an access right. We will look at these in the section on "Modifiers".

A class is derived from another using *extends*, and an interface is implemented using *implements*:

```
<Modifier> class ClassName extends SuperClass
                            implements InterfaceName
{
    // Member definitions
}
```

Tip According to the naming convention, class names are written with an initial capital letter, e.g. *Account, String, SecurityManager.*

4.4.1 Members of classes

Instance variables

The attributes of an instance are saved in *instance variables* (fields). A type must be specified for each variable. Any data types can be used, such as the primitive data types *int, double* or *char*, or even references to objects of any class. The general syntax reads

```
<Modifier> <Type> variableName;
class Account       // class Account
{
    int number;     // Instance variable for account number
    double balance; // instance variable for account balance
    Customer owner; // Instance variable for account owner
                    // Reference to another object
}
```

The instance variables are valid once the instance has been generated, i.e. they do not exist until a concrete object has been created. Each object of this class is assigned its own values for the instance variables.

Class variables

In addition there are also class variables that exist just once for the whole class. All instances then access the same value, and you can even read this value if there are actually no instances of it. Class variables are declared like instance variables, although identified with the modifier *static* (see Section 4.5.2):

```
<Modifier> static <Type> variableName;
```

Constants

Constants are values that are assigned at declaration and cannot be changed subsequently. They are identified with the modifiers *final* and *static* (see Sections 4.5.2 and 4.5.3):

```
<Modifier> final static <Type> constantName = <value>;
public static final double PI = 3.14159265897;
```

Methods

The *methods* in a class have full access to all variables and methods in the same class. The methods are part of the public interface of an object; they define its behavior and allow access to the instance for which they are called. They consist of a declaration section containing the names and the parameter list, and a block containing the method implementation. If applicable, some extra instructions for the compiler are added to the declaration, for instance access rights for the method or possible errors. We will look at this again later. Unlike other languages, the declaration and implementation are not separated in Java.

```java
<Modifier> <ReturnType> variableName;
class GiroAccount extends Account    // Class GiroAccount
{
    double creditlimit;                    // Instance variable
    void withdraw(double amount         // Method declaration
    {                                       // Implementation block
        if (checkLimit(amount))
        balance = balance - amount;
    }
    boolean checkLimit(double amount)// Method declaration
    {                                  // Implementation block
        if (balance - amount> -creditlimit)
            return true;                    // Method end
        else
            return false;                   // Method end
    }
}
```

The methods are executed until the end of the implementation block is reached, or the *return* instruction is performed. *return* terminates the method immediately, returning as the method return value that value present after the instruction (see `checkLimit()` method). This value must be of the type specified in the declaration. If a method has no return value then it is declared with *void*. The method is then terminated just with *return*, which in this case can be omitted at the end of a block (see method `withdraw()` in the example above).

Local variables can be declared within method blocks. Here's yet another version of the `withdraw()` method:

```java
void withdraw(double amount)
{
    boolean creditCheckOK = checkLimit(amount);
    if (creditCheckOK)
        balance = balance - amount;
}
```

> **Tip** The order in which methods and variables are declared within a class definition is irrelevant. For instance in the previous example it is allowable to call `checkLimit()` in `withdraw()` even though the declaration is not made until later. Of course it is usual for the variables to be declared first and then the methods, but this is not a stipulation. The Java compiler actually works as a two-pass compiler, reading the declarations in the first run.

> **Tip** According to the naming convention, variables and methods are written with lower-case initial letters, e.g. `number`, `withdraw()`, `setSize()`. This does not hold for constants, which are often written wholly in upper-case, but even this is not observed consistently within standard classes of the JDK.

4.4.2   Access rights and methods

Access rights

We will deal with access modifiers in detail in Section 4.5.1. Because they are of fundamental importance in modeling classes, however, we will give a brief explanation here.

Access rights exist for both classes and their members. The lowest access right is *public* (visible everywhere). Public classes, variables, and methods can be seen from any context. Often this is not wanted, so you can declare internal utility methods and variables as *private* (only visible within the class). As a result you can easily adapt and improve the implementation later without having to change the interface to the outside world. The access rights *protected* and "*default*" (no modifier specified) are special cases of private classes or members that are still publicly accessible for certain other classes, for instance their sub-classes or classes in the same package (see Section 4.10.4).

Our Account might then look as follows:

```
public class Account
{
   private int    number;
   private double balance;
   public void withdraw(double amount)
   {
      if (balance > amount)
      balance = balance - amount;
   }
   [...]
}
```

We could therefore call run and use the *public* elements from any class, no matter what library (or package, see Section 4.10) they are in. On the other hand, direct access to the internal data from outside the class *Account* would be blocked. If we had wanted to allow access to derived classes such as *GiroAccount*, then we could have declared them as *protected*.

Access methods

Now users of the classes no longer have direct access to the account balance, and can only manipulate it indirectly via the methods `withdraw()`, `payin()` and `transfer()`. This may be sensible in some cases, but normally you want to have selective access to the contents of fields in a class. Access methods can be used for this purpose. These provide public read and write functionality (where this is required for the variable):

```
public class Account
{
   private int    number;
   private double balance;
   public int getNumber()
   {
      return number;
   }
   public double getBalance()
   {
      return balance;
   }
   public void setBalance(double amount)
   {
      if (amount > 0)
      balance = amount;
```

```
        else
            // Error message
            throw new AccountLimitException(
                    "Not allowed to be overdrawn.");
    }
    [...]
}
```

Access methods and public instance variables

When analyzing the implementation of the **access methods (selectors)** `getNumber()` and `setBalance()` for the instance variables in the example above, you might wonder whether this additional programming complexity is necessary, or whether you might just as well set the class variables to *public*. There are some fundamental arguments against this however which are explained below.

→ Using access methods you can guarantee that objects of the class always contain valid values (by carrying out range checks say in the method). In the Account implementation above, the user of the class does not have direct write access to the variable `balance` for instance, because it was declared as *private*, and so the user cannot change it to an invalid value. When accessed via `setBalance()` or one of the other methods, you can perform additional validations – as is done in the example above – to ensure the object has a valid status.

→ You can set access rights selectively. For instance in the Account example, subsequent manipulation of the account number is prohibited; the variable can only be read (read-only). It is a different matter for the account balance, which can be read or written. Of course write-only variables are possible too.

→ Another reason is data encapsulation or data hiding, where a clear interface is presented to the user of the class. The user is no longer dependent on the internal implementation of the class, and need not be informed of the implementation details. Thus the programmer of the class can change the internal representation of the data when they feel like it without lots of code having to be changed at the user's end.

→ Concealing implementation detail also helps know-how protection, since only the public interface is visible to the outside.

→ The JavaBeans Components standard specifies provision of access methods, so that every tool can automatically identify the public attributes and generate "clean" code.

Naming convention

As we shall see in Section 10.4 on the JavaBeans Components standard, the standard also contains access functions, which must begin with the prefixes `get` and `set`. These are therefore called Getters and Setters.

> **Tip** If boolean values are involved, i.e. variables of type *boolean* that can only take the values *true* or *false*, then "is" is often used instead of `get`.

Variable	Get methods	Set methods
visible	isVisible(), getVisible()	setVisible()
private boolean visible;	**public** boolean isVisible() { **return** getVisible(); } **public** boolean getVisible() { **return** visible; }	**public void** set-Visible(boolean v) { visible = v; }

4.4.3   Constructors

Uninitialized variables

In C and other programming languages there is the problem of access to uninitialized variables. As an example, take the following extract of a C program that can be compiled without errors:

```
main()
{
    int x, y;
    y = x + 2;
}
```

Depending on the compiler, this gives a value in y that is two greater than the random value contained at the memory address for variable x, or a value that has been incremented after pre-initialization by the compiler. This action is worth noting, because it is often the source of undetectable programming errors.

Constructor

Java (and C++) provides the solution to this problem using a special method known as the constructor. The constructor is a personal method written by the programmer of the class, which is automatically called for each instance of the class as soon as this instance is created. It can therefore be used to initialize an object immediately at its creation. So amongst other things, the constructor can ensure that an object always contains "correct" values.

One difference from C++ is that when a new object is created in Java (using *new*), all member variables (fields) are automatically initialized before the constructor is called. References are initialized with null, boolean variables with false, numeric values with 0 and characters with "\0". This ensures that each object has a defined state after it is created.

> **Tip** Java compilers flag up an error for **local** variables that are not initialized explicitly:
> ```
> Variable x may not have been initialized.
> ```
> Instance and class variables are initialized as just described.

```java
public class Account
{
    private double balance;  // Instance variable,
    automatically

// pre-assigned with 0.0 for each instance
    [...]
    public void withdraw(double amount)
    {
        boolean creditCheck; // Error, since variable
                             // is local for this block
        boolean creditCheckOK = checkLimit(amount);
                             // So it is OK!
        if (creditCheckOK)
        balance = balance - amount;
    }
    [...]
}
```

Therefore the programmer only really needs to initialize those *fields* to which he wants to assign more suitable values. It makes for good programming style, however, if all values are initialized manually, since the code is then easier to understand.

A constructor takes the name of the class and no return type is specified. Normally constructors belong to the public interface and should therefore be declared *public*.

The following could therefore be added to the Account class:

```
public class Account
{
    private int     number;
    private double  balance;
    public Account()
    {
        number = Bank.getNextFreeNumber();
    }
    public Account(double newBalance)
    {
        number = Bank.getNextFreeNumber();
        balance = newBalance;
    }
    public Account(int newNumber, double newBalance)
    {
        number = newNumber;   // may need to check if free...
        balance = newBalance;
    }
}
```

With this code, whenever an object of the class *Account* is defined, its constructor is called to ensure that the instance variables are assigned valid initial values.

```
// Using a single constructor:
Account myAccount  = new Account();   // Account() calls a
                                      //constructor.
// Using a constructor with parameters:
Account anotherOne = new Account(453476800, 3000);
```

This also illustrates the notation for this instantiation. The part in front of the assignment is the declaration of a reference of the **class** Account (as type), whereas the second half creates a new object using the Account () **constructor**. The constructor call is a method call, hence the round brackets..

Tip The Account example was an example of overloading methods. The constructor exists in several versions but with different parameters. You can do this with all methods in Java.

Return value

Note that the constructor has no return value (not even *void*). This means that the constructor need not contain a return statement either. The constructor does not return a value but initializes an object.

Default constructor

If you have not written a class without any constructor (something I omitted in the Account example in the early chapters), the compiler adds a constructor without parameters and with an empty implementation block. This is called a *default constructor*.

> **Tip** This can lead to problems if you subsequently add a constructor with parameters to a class containing a default constructor. This is because the compiler then removes the default constructor, and all object instantiations of the type `new ClassName()` become invalid, since only the new constructor is valid!
>
> In this case you should write a constructor yourself without parameters and with an empty implementation block. This will avoid problems when running the code that was previously based on the default constructor. The best solution, however, is to think in advance about what types of constructors you want to offer the user of your class.

finalize method

Java differs from other programming languages in that the Java programmer need not bother about memory clean-up. This is done automatically by the runtime system. When an object is no longer referenced because all references are invalid (end of block reached or set explicitly to null), it can be disposed of by the system at any time (see Section 12.2)

Objects may not occupy memory alone, however. For example, an object might open a file or occupy a network socket. It must be possible to release these resources, which is where a special method `finalize()` comes in. Before deletion, this is called by the Garbage Collector and executed (see Section 12.2). This method can be added to any class, but must follow the signature precisely (method header as shown below):

```
protected void finalize()
{
    openFile.close(); // Example of freeing up resources
}
```

4.4.4   Internal classes

When programming a class you often find you need an auxiliary class that is only relevant in this context and should be completely hidden to the outside world. Such classes are referred to in Java as *embedded* or *internal classes*, as they are declared directly in the body of the main class.

```java
public class Account
{
   // internal class
   class CheckingRulesForTransfer
   {
      boolean checkAccount(Account destinationAccount) {...}
      boolean checkCover(double amount) {...}
   }
  [...]
void transfer(account destinationAccount, double amount)
   {
      [...]   // uses auxiliary class
   }
 }
```

Usage

You could replace internal classes with package-wide visible classes or private methods for the encompassing class. It is usually more elegant to implement with internal classes, however, firstly because it emphasizes that the internal class belongs to just one class, and secondly because an internal class encapsulates the functionality better than a set of methods.

Internal classes are a popular choice for programming graphical interfaces. For instance, there are auxiliary classes for handling particular events, or for displaying the cells in a table class in a particular way specific to the context of their surrounding class.

Tip It is even possible to create anonymous internal classes. These have no name but are defined inside a method call.

```java
new <Name of the super class or an interface>
{ <Implementation block> }
```

Unfortunately, anonymous classes produce code that is quite hard to read, so I do not advise using them.

Modifiers are keywords that influence the definition of classes, methods and variables. Modifiers are written in front of the names of these elements, for example

`<Modifier> void withdraw(double amount).`

This section takes a brief look at the various modifiers. Most of the modifiers have been, or will be, dealt with in more detail elsewhere. This section is more concerned with giving the overall picture.

4.5.1 Access rights

You have probably already seen from the example of the Account classes (see Section 4.4.2) that it is useful to be able to limit access to classes, variables and methods. You can use the keywords *public*, *private* and *protected* to control the visibility and access protection available from other classes.

The following explanations apply to variables and methods.

Keyword private

Private members are the internal interface of the class. Only methods within the class itself can access these class components. They tend to be concerned with implementation details that other classes are not meant to see or manipulate. In the *UML* notation, private components are abbreviated by a "-" symbol in front of the name.

Keyword public

Public members are the public interface of the class. There is no access protection. These class components can be accessed from within any class. The UML abbreviation is "+".

Keyword protected

This access right is relevant to inheritance and is a combination of *private* and *public*. It allows access to the methods of a class and to the methods of all derived classes and any other classes within the package (see Section 4.10, note difference from C++). Access to protected methods and variables is prohibited from other program locations. The symbol in UML is the "#" character.

TAKE THAT!

Default

The default access right applies if no access modifier is specified at all. Access is then allowed for all methods of classes within the same package. Packages are dealt with in Section 4.10.

> **Tip** The private protected access right defined in JDK 1.0.1 (equivalent to protected in C++) is no longer supported in the current language standard.

```
public class Account  // publicly visible
{
  // Instance variables:
  private int number;         // only visible internally
                              // -> Access via get method
  protected double balance;   // visible internally and in
                                // sub-classes
                              // Constructors:
  public Account(){ [...] }   // publicly visible
  public Account(double newBalance) { [...] }
  public Account(int newNumber, double newBalance)
   { [...] }
  // Access methods:
  public int getNumber()      // publicly visible
   { [...] }
  public double getBalance() // publicly visible
   { [...] }
  public void setBalance(double amount) { [...] }
  // Additional methods:
   public void withdraw(double amount) { [...] }
   public void payin(double amount) { [...] }
  public void transfer(Account destinationAccount, double
amount)
     { [...] }
   private boolean checkTransfer(double amount)
     { [...] }
}
```

```
┌─────────────────────────────────────────────┐
│                  Account                       │
├─────────────────────────────────────────────┤
│- number : int                                 │
│#balance : double                              │
├─────────────────────────────────────────────┤
│<<Constructors>>                               │
│+Account()                                     │
│+Account(balance : double)                     │
│+Account(number : int, balance: double)        │
│                                               │
│<<Access methods>>                             │
│+getNumber() : int                             │
│+getBalance() : double                         │
│+setBalance(amount : double)                   │
│<<Additional Methods>>                         │
│+withdraw(amount : double)                     │
│+payin(amount: double)                         │
│+transfer(target Account: amount: double)      │
│-checkTransfer(amount : double) : boolean      │
└─────────────────────────────────────────────┘
```

Figure 4.3 *UML notation for the Account class*

The following example illustrates the use of the class *Account* in any other class with the `main` method:

```java
public static void main(String argv[])
{
    Account anAccount = new Account();
    [...]
    anAccount.payin(200);       // allowed because payin()
                                // is public
    anAccount.balance = 3000;   //not allowed, because
                                //balance is private
}
```

Access rights for classes and interfaces

Access rights are not restricted to variables and methods, but can also be applied in the same way to classes and interfaces. Logically, however, you are only allowed to use *public* and default protection so that the classes can actually be used.

> **Tip** Access rights and visibility are two different aspects. Each class that is meant to be accessed must be visible (e.g. by referencing the complete name or using import); the opposite is not true however, i.e. a method declared as private is visible in other classes of the package, but is not accessible.

4.5.2 static – class variables and methods

You can use the *static* modifier to assign methods and variables to the class as a whole instead of to the individual instances.

Class variables

In addition to the *instance variables* we have met so far, you can also create *class variables*. These do not belong to a specific object, but to the whole class. Memory space only needs to be reserved once for a class variable. It does not depend on the number of instances of the class that exist. The class variable can be addressed from every instance as though it were a variable of this instance, but any manipulation affects all instances.

Class variables can therefore be used for managing class-specific data, for instance for a counter recording the number of instances of this class that currently exist. They are subject to the same rules of access rights as instance variables.

Initialization

Class variables are globally valid. They should be initialized directly when declared. The constructor cannot be used for initialization because it can be called as often as required, or even not at all if no instance yet exists.

```
<Modifier> static <Type> variableName = <Initial value>;
```

Access

Static class variables can be accessed using the standard "." operator, but with the class name instead of a reference. Alternatively you can also access them using a current instance, for example you can write `anInstance.classVariable` instead of `AClass.classVariable`. However, this could give the impression that this is accessing an object-specific value. You should therefore aim to use the first option. Of course if no instances of a class have been created yet, then you can only access the variable via the class name.

We will use the *Account* class as an example again, with a counter for the number of objects that currently exist:

```java
public class Account
{
  private int number;
    public static int nextFreeAccountNumber = 1;
    public Account()      // Constructor
    {
      // Number assigned applies to this Account object:
      number = nextFreeAccountNumber;
```

```
      // New value applies to all Account objects:
      nextFreeAccountNumber++;
  }
  [...]
}
```

External access might use the following code:

```
int numberOfAccounts = Account.nextFreeAccountNumber - 1;
```

Class methods

Similarly you can also get class methods. In particular it makes sense to define access methods for (now private) class variables as *static*, since you may already want to access these methods before any instances exist:

```
private static int nextFreeAccountNumber = 1;
public static int getNextFreeAccountNumber()
{
    return nextFreeAccountNumber;
}
```

Once again you should call the method using the class name:

```
int NumberOfAccounts = Account.getNextFreeAccountNumber() - 1;
```

> **Tip** Class variables and methods are shown underlined in UML diagrams.

```
+--------------------------------------------------+
|                    Account                       |
+--------------------------------------------------+
| - number : int                                   |
| - NextFreeAccountNumber : int = 1                |
| #balance : double                                |
+--------------------------------------------------+
| <<Constructors>>                                 |
| +Account()                                       |
| +Account(balance : double)                       |
| +Account(number : int, balance : double)         |
|                                                  |
| <<Access methods>>                               |
| +getNumber() : int                               |
| +getNextFreeAccountNumber(): int                 |
+--------------------------------------------------+
```

Figure 4.4   *UML representation of static members*

The most important example of a *static* method is `main()`. This method is called before an application has instantiated any objects. It therefore has to be defined as static. An instance of the class itself can then be created within the `main()` method, resulting in the following construction that appears rather odd at first glance:

```
public class ExampleApplication {
   public static void main(String args[])
   {
      ExampleApplication runner =
         new ExampleApplication();
      runner.startProcessing();    // Call refers to
                                   // an instance.
   }
   public void startProcessing () { [...] }
}
```

> **Tip** When you call a static method such as `main()` there may be no instances at all of the class. This is why you cannot call any non-static methods or access instance variables from within it. If you do the compiler outputs the error
> `Can't make a static reference to nonstatic variable/method`
> It is a typical beginner's mistake to write the example above incorrectly as shown below:

```
public class ExampleApplication {
   public static void main(String args[])
   {
      startProcessing();  // Not allowed to call
         // a non-static method
   }
   public void startProcessing () { [...] }
}
```

4.5.3   final – prevention of inheritance, and constants

The *final* modifier states that implementation of a code element, or its assigned values, cannot be changed again at runtime. Specifically this means that the relevant class, variable or method cannot be overwritten when inherited. A final method is therefore fixed for all sub-classes, a final class cannot be inherited, and a final variable is constant after being initialized.

```java
public final class System{...}   // JDK system class
                                 // cannot be overrided
public class MySystem extends System{...} // Not allowed!
public class Object  // JDK system class
{
    /* Method getClass determines the current type,
       even for derived classes. */
    public final Class getClass(){[...]}
    /* Method toString outputs an instance
       of a string as a standard representation. */
    public String toString(){[...]}
    [...]
}
public class Account extends Object
{
    public final Class getClass(){[...]} // Not allowed!
            // "Account" must be returned as the class.
    /* toString on the other hand can or even should
       be overrided */
    public String toString(){[...]}
  [...]
}
```

Constants

A particularly important combination for variables is *static* and *final*. A constant class variable is initialized directly when declared and never changed again. This gives the compiler a good opportunity for optimization. *static final* is the de facto substitute for the *const* keyword that does not exist in Java.

```java
<Modifier> static final <Type> constantName = <value>;
```

One example is the number Pi, which can be called under Java using `Math.PI` and is defined as

```java
public static final double PI = 3.14159265897
```

Constants can also be declared in interfaces.

4.5.4 abstract – abstract classes

A class or method defined as *abstract* describes its appearance or programming interface, but does not implement it at all, or not in full. Abstract classes are therefore used as the basis for concrete classes that are meant to be derived from them. The declaration of an abstract class describes the common features of all sub-classes and specifies the minimum requirements for the sub-classes. You cannot create instances of abstract classes.

One example is the class *java.lang.Number*. This acts as a super class for the various numerical classes (e.g. *Integer, Double*). It ensures that all derived classes provide conversion methods for the elementary data types. Some are implemented directly (e.g. byteValue()); others are defined as purely abstract (e.g. doubleValue()), and so must be overridden and implemented every time by each derived class.

Abstract methods

Abstract methods describe just the signature, but do not contain any implementation instructions. An abstract method declaration is terminated with a semicolon instead of the implementation block. If a class contains an abstract method, the class itself must be defined as *abstract*.

```
public abstract class Number
{
    public abstract float  floatValue();
    public abstract double doubleValue();
    public abstract int intValue();
    public byte byteValue()
    {
        // This section would contain the common
        // implementation block for all sub-classes.
        // This method could actually be overrided
        // as it has not been declared as final
        [...]
    }
}
```

Interfaces

Interfaces represent an alternative concept to abstract classes (see Section 4.6). They are purely abstract interface descriptions and contain no code at all. You are not allowed to combine abstract and defined methods in interfaces, although multiple inheritance is permitted for the purpose. You should consider carefully for what purpose you are using interfaces or abstract classes. The two concepts are compared and explained in more detail in Part 3 of this book (Chapter 11 onwards).

4.5.5 synchronized and volatile – synchronization of threads

synchronized

In Java, multithreading is supported directly by the language. Threading means that more than one process can run in parallel. When several threads are used (mini-processes), there is of course the risk that different threads will manipulate the same objects or access the same resources. In order to avoid conflicts, undefined states and unexpected ("random") results, you can make a method run automatically by synchronizing it.

A synchronized method (modifier *synchronized*) is executed in full by the active thread, all other threads being suspended until the method has finished.

```java
public synchronized void criticalMethod()
{
    variableUsedBySeveralThreads += 5;
}

public synchronized void payin(double amount)
{
    balance += amount;
}
```

> **Tip** Note: Often you do not have to stop all threads until the whole method has been processed; instead you only need to protect just one or a few instructions. This is why you can also use synchronized blocks that only encompass the critical section (see Section 4.9.1).

volatile

A modifier that is rarely met is *volatile*. Using this modifier you can specify that a field, i.e. an instance variable or class variable, is used in a synchronized thread and so must be excluded from compiler optimizations. However, I do not know of a single compiler that generates erroneous code if you do not label such a field with *volatile*.

4.5.6 native – integration of non-Java code

The *native* modifier is used for integrating platform-specific binary code. Like abstract methods (Section 4.5.4), native methods for a class are only declared in the body of the class; the implementation is actually held in an external library, for instance in a DLL (Dynamic Link Library), which might be implemented in C, say.

```
public class NativeTest
{
  // load binary library
  static { System.loadLibrary("NativeTest"); }
    public static void main(String[] args)
  {
    NativeTest runner = new NativeTest();
    // Call to the C method
  float f = runner.nativeMethod(1, 2.0);
  }
  public native float nativeMethod(int i, double l);
}
```

Application

Native methods are not suitable for applets, first, because you never know in advance where these will run later, second, because they are also not normally allowed in applets for security reasons. But they are definitely a sensible choice for a server application with performance-critical routines or interfaces not supported by Java.

4.5.7   transient – non-persistent references

Serialization

Conversion of an object representation in memory into a byte stream is called *serialization*. This process is required if you want to save objects in a file or transport them over a network. When you serialize an object that references another object, then this other object also has to be serialized so that the original situation can be re-created in memory. If you continue the process recursively, you can end up with a whole network of really large numbers of objects from a single serialization call. This is also a reason why network protocols are often so slow at the object level, for instance the RMI protocols.

Those reference variables not required in a serialization should therefore be labeled with the *transient* modifier. Should serialization be performed, this indicates that the field is not a part of the persistent state of an object and so does not need to be transferred.

4.5.8   Summary and comments

Order

There is no prescribed order for modifiers, although the following sequence tends to be used:

`<Access>` **static abstract synchronized final native**

where `<Access>` stands for *private*, *protected, public,* or nothing at all (default protection).

Summary

Modifier	Class	Variable	Method
private	–	maximum access protection	
protected	–	access protection outside the package and sub-classes	
[default]		access protection outside the package	
public		no access protection	
static	–	class variable	class method
final	no sub-classes allowed	constant at object level	overriding not allowed
abstract	no instantia-tion possible	–	to be implemented by concrete classes
synchronized	–	–	critical method
volatile	–	critical variable	–
native	–	–	read from library
transient	–	not persistent for seri-alization	–

4.6 Interfaces

As explained in Section 3.2.3, you use interfaces for the abstract declaration of methods as a substitute for multiple inheritance.

An interface can contain method declarations and constants. Each concrete class that is meant to *implement* an interface, must define all the methods defined there. The interface itself contains no implementation at all. Interfaces are not derived from a base interface (analogous to *Object*, Section 6.1.1). They allow multiple inheritance.

Definition

An interface is defined in a similar way to a class:

```
[public] interface NameOfTheInterface
    [extends SuperInterface [, AnotherSuperInterface]*]]
    { <Method declarations and constants> }
```

A class that implements the interface is labeled with the keyword *implements*:

```
[public] class OneClass implements NameOfTheInterface
                    [, AnotherInterface]*]]
    {[...]}
```

In the same way as when deriving a concrete class from an abstract one, all the abstract methods in the interface must be implemented by the implementing class. Otherwise you get the compiler message:

```
class OneClass must be declared abstract. It does not
define void method() from interface NameOfTheInterface.
```

In order to add interest payments to different classes, such as a class for savings accounts and one for fixed-interest bearing securities, there should be a common interface *InterestBearing*.

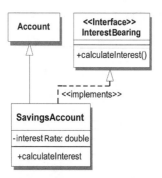

Figure 4.5 *UML representation of interfaces*

```
public interface InterestBearing
{
  public double calculateInterest();
}
public class SavingsAccount extends Account implements
InterestBearing
{
  private double interestRate;
  public double calculateInterest()
    {
        [...]
    }
}
```

Constants

In addition to methods, class variables can be defined in an interface (see Section 4.5.3).

```
interface NameOfTheInterface
{
    public static final int MINVALUE = 0;
}
```

Access is with the usual syntax NameOfTheInterface.MINVALUE.

```
public interface InterestBearing
{
  public final static int fixedInterest = 0;
  public final static int variable = 1;
  public final static int withPayout = 2;
  public final static int withCompoundInterest = 4;
  public double calculateInterest() {[...]}
}
int interestType = InterestBearing.variable +
  InterestBearing.withCompoundInterest;
```

Tip   An interface containing only constants and no method can be used in a similar way to the C++ enum construct not available in Java.

```
char c1 = 'F';
char newLine = '\n';
```

Unlike integer values, characters are not associated with a sign; they are pre-assigned the value '\u0000'.

4.8.3   Operators

The standard arithmetic and logic operations available in most programming languages are provided with the usual rules of precedence.

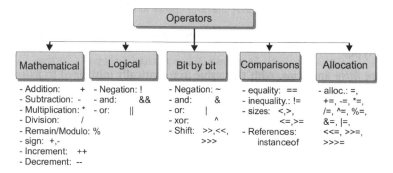

Figure 4.11   *Operators in Java*

Mathematical operators

The usual characters and rules found in almost all programming languages apply ("dot before dash" etc.). You can also use round brackets for bracketing.

The "%" operator (modulo) is provided for calculating the remainder in integer division. The "++" and "–" operators from C/C++ for increment and decrement have been adopted.

```
i = 0;
j = i++;                    // j = 0, i = 1
j = ++i;                    // j = 2, i = 2
```

With "++" as a prefix, the variable is incremented before the assignment; as a postfix (first line) it is only incremented afterwards.

Logical operators

The negation "!", AND operation "&&", and OR operation "||" are provided for boolean values.

Operation !a	a = true	a = false
!a	false	true

Operation (a && b)	a = true	a = false
b = true	true	false
b = false	false	false

Operation (a || b)	a = true	a = false
b = true	false	true
b = false	true	true

> **Tip** Boolean expressions are evaluated from left to right in Java. In fact if the result is already decided by the first value, then the second value is not evaluated. So expressions of the type
> `if ( (file != null) && (file.exists() )`
> are valid and are often used. If the second expression were evaluated even though the reference was equal to *null*, you would get an error.

Bitwise operators

The same action applies to bitwise operators as to logical operators, except that the bitwise operators are always performed in full and are usually applied to bit fields. The length is found from the type of the operator, e. g. *boolean*, *short*, *int* etc.

Operation (a | b)	a = 00	a = 01	a = 10	a = 11
b = 00	00	01	10	11
b = 01	01	01	11	11
b = 10	10	11	10	11
b = 11	11	11	11	11

The "^" operator designates the bitwise operator XOR. If you want to raise something to a power, use the method `Math.pow(base, exponent)`. (See Section 6.1.5.)

The shift operators move the bits to the left "<<" or to the right ">>".

TAKE THAT!

4

Operation (a << 1)	a = 00	a = 01	a = 10	a = 11
a << 1	00	10	00	10

The ">>" operator performs a bitwise shift to the right and fills the "new" bits on the left with the sign bit. If you want them filled with zeros though, then you can use the ">>>" operator in Java.

Variable assignment	Operator call	Result in decimal	Result in binary
i = 4	i	4	00000000000000000000000000000100
	i>>1	2	00000000000000000000000000000010
	i>>>1	2	00000000000000000000000000000010
	i<<1	8	00000000000000000000000000001000
i = -4	i	-4	11111111111111111111111111111100
	i>>1	-2	11111111111111111111111111111110
	i>>>1	2147483646	01111111111111111111111111111110
	i<<1	-8	11111111111111111111111111111000

Tip This is not a problem in the C language because it provides unsigned variables.

Comparisons

A double equals sign "==" is used for the equality, and the "!=" sign for the inequality. The usual size comparisons are also provided: "<, >, <=, >=". You can check references for a specific type using *instanceof*.

```
Account anAccount = new GiroAccount();
anAccount instanceof GiroAccount returns true,
anAccount instanceof Account returns true,
anAccount instanceof SavingsAccount returns false,
```

Assignments

As assignment is made using a single equals sign "=". In addition there are also some abbreviated assignments for the case when the modified value is meant to be assigned directly to the same variable again:

```
int   a = 5;    // Assignment
a += 2;         // Shorthand notation for a = a+2;
a -= 2;         // Shorthand notation for a = a-2;
a *= 2;         // Shorthand notation for a = a*2;
a /= 2;         // Shorthand notation for a = a/2;
a %= 2;         // Shorthand notation for a = a%2;
a ^= 2;         // Shorthand notation for a = a^2;  (XOR)
a &= 2;         // Shorthand notation for a = a&2;  (AND)
a |= 2;         // Shorthand notation for a = a|2;  (OR)
a <<= 2;        // Shorthand notation for a = a<<2;
a >>= 2;        // Shorthand notation for a = a>>2;
a >>>= 2;       // Shorthand notation for a = a>>>2;
```

Operators and precedence

The table below lists the operators in decreasing order of precedence. This means for instance that a + b / ++c is evaluated as a + (b / (++c)), because the increment is stronger than division, and this in turn is stronger than addition. Operators in the same table row have the same ranking and are evaluated from left to right.

Operator	Meaning	Example
( )	brackets	(a+b)/c
[]	field indexing	a[i]
.	object reference	a.setValue()
++, --	increment, decrement	a++, --b
+, -	sign	-a
!	logical negation	!(a & b)
~	bitwise negation	~a
*, /, %	multiplication, division, modulo	a*b/c
+, -	addition, subtraction	a+b
<<, >>, >>>	shift	a>>1
<, <=, >, >= instanceof	comparisons (greater than and smaller than) type comparisons	a <= b if (myDate instanceof Date) ...
==, !=	equality, inequality	if (a == b)
&	bitwise and / AND	a & b

Operator	Meaning	Example
^	bitwise XOR	a ^ b
|	bitwise or / OR	a | b
&&	logical and / AND	if (a && b)...
||	logical or / OR	if (a || b)...
=, +=, -=, *=,	assignments	a = b
/=, %=, ^=,		a /= 2, short for a = a/2
&=, |=,		
<<=, >>=,		
>>>=		

4.8.4 Reference types

References point to objects and are type-coded. You can assign a reference to an object of a compatible type at any time. References to classes and interfaces are dealt with under References.

The type of a reference must not necessarily agree with the class of the object. This is because an object of one class is also always an object of its super class, so the reference may have the type of a super class. The same applies to interfaces implemented by the class of an object.

```
Account anAccount = new SavingsAccount();      // Reference
                                    //type is super class
InterestBearing IntObj = new SavingsAccount(); // Reference
                                    //type is implemented class
InterestBearing intObj1 =
                (SavingsAccount)anAccount; // Only with
                                    //casting
```

> **Warning** The reference specifies the interface that the user can call. The last line in the example illustrates this. You cannot assign the object directly because the reference `anAccount` is of type *Account*, yet the *Account* class itself does not comply with the *InterestBearing* interface. Only the "actual" type of the object (*SavingsAccount*) implements this interface, which is why a type conversion (casting) is necessary (see also Section 4.8.2).

When passing reference types as parameters, only the reference but not the referenced object is copied (call by reference, see Section 4.8.7). This means that all the manipulations on the passed object are performed in the method on the original.

Null reference

Every reference, irrespective of its type, can be assigned the value *null*. This constant indicates that the reference is not pointing to any object at that moment. Instance and class variables that have not been explicitly initialized are also set to *null*.

You can set references explicitly to *null* in order to indicate to the runtime environment that the object behind this reference is no longer needed. If there is no other reference pointing to the object it is automatically removed.

```
Account k1 = null;      // null reference
k1 = new Account();     // k1 points to an object.
k1 = new GiroAccount(); // k1 points to a different object,
                        // the first can be removed.
k1 = null;              // null reference, the second
                        // object can also be removed.
```

In addition to the standard reference types there are two further types that provide extra functionality:

→ Strings
→ Arrays (matrices)

4.8.5   Strings

All *Strings* (character strings) in Java are derived as objects of the class *java.lang.String* (see Section 6.1.4). However strings have certain facilities not offered by other classes, for example the concatenation of strings and a simplified creation process.

> **Tip** All classes that begin with *java.lang* are imported automatically, so you can also write *String* for short instead of *java.lang.String*. More on this in Section 6.1.

Comparison with C++

In C and C++, strings are formed by null-terminated arrays of 8-bit characters. The string "hello" is therefore saved in the 6 sequential bytes "h", "e", "l", "l", "o", "\0". It is quite different in Java. Here strings are true objects and not terminated with null. Java uses 16-bit Unicode characters.

4.8.7 Differences in behavior between elementary and reference types

There are several important differences in the way elementary data types and reference types are treated. These are discussed below.

Definition of variables

If you define a variable of an elementary data type, memory is allocated automatically and the variable initialized. The *new* operator is not used. There are no constructors, and when the variables are defined they are initialized to the standard value or to the assigned value.

```
int i;  // Pre-assigned value = 0
long j = 123L;
```

If a reference is created then it is pre-assigned the null reference *null* by default. The *new* operator is required when explicitly initializing with (new) objects. The only exception are String literals for which there is a special shorthand notation:

```
Account acc; // Pre-assigned value = null
Account acc = new Account();
String name = "Kirsten";
```

Another difference is the action taken when parameters are passed.

Call by value

If an elementary data type is passed as the parameter of a method, the method is *called by value*. This means that a copy of the value is passed. Any manipulations performed on this copy do not change the value of the original in any way.

```
int x = 1;         // x=1
manipulateX(x);    // Call
[...]              // x=1
public void manipulateX(int rx)
{
  rx = 2;          // just changes a copy of x
}
```

Call by reference

In method calls containing reference types objects are passed *by reference*, which means that in the method the same object is used, just under a different name. Only the reference is copied, not the referenced object. This means that all the manipulations on the passed object are performed in the method on the original.

```
Account source        = new Account(3000.00);
Account destination   = new Account(0.0);
source.transfer(target, 500.0);   // Call
[...]                             // target.balance = 500
void transfer(Account targetAccount, double amount)
{
    withdraw(amount);     // changes the original object!
        targetAccount.payin(amount);
}
```

> **Tip** These types are handled differently for efficiency reasons. You get simpler handling for elementary types, which are small and used often, while for more complex and large objects you avoid frequent and unnecessary copying.
> Yet often you would like to adopt the behavior of reference types for elementary data types as well, in particular if you want to create collections (sets) of objects, for instance a vector of numbers. These collections are only defined for "real" objects.

Comparisons

When you compare two object references with the "==" operator, you only get the result *true* if both references are pointing to exactly the same object. Even if all attributes match for two different objects of the same class, the comparison results in *false*. The same happens if you use the equals() method, which behaves exactly like "==" in the standard case.

Often the equals() method is redefined so that the contents of the attributes are compared instead of purely comparing the references. One example of this is the *String* class (see section on Strings). Hence if we had redefined the equals method for the Account class in the same way, we would obtain the response illustrated in Figure 4.14. More on this in Section 6.1.1.

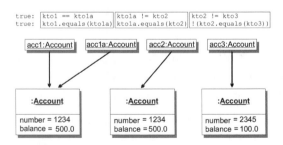

Figure 4.14 *Comparison of objects*

You can compare the type of a class using the instanceof operator, e.g.

```
if (anAccount instanceof Account)...
```

Wrapper classes

To enable call by reference, Java provides special *wrapper classes* (see Section 6.1.7) that package the elementary data types into classes. These are used when you need to pack elementary data types into unchangeable objects for instance, in order to incorporate them in a collection. Wrapper classes also provide conversion methods for converting from and to other data types, e.g. from a string into a number.

These classes start with a capital letter:

→ *Byte* instead of *byte*
→ *Short* instead of *short*
→ *Integer* instead of *int* (not Int!)
→ *Long* instead of *long*
→ *Character* instead of *char* (not Char!)
→ *Boolean* instead of *boolean*

Byte and *Short* did not appear until Java 1.1.

```
int i = 1;
Integer iAsObject = new Integer(i);
int j = iAsObject.intValue();
```

You cannot cast objects into elementary types. There are special conversion methods for this purpose, such as intValue().

4.9 Important language constructs

The control structures are practically identical to those of C/C++ and other programming languages. That is why I only give a brief summary here instead of going into detail.

4.9.1 Blocks

Blocks are enclosed in curly brackets "{}". Inside the brackets you can declare local variables that are only valid in this block. A block can also contain any statements or other blocks. Each statement is terminated by a semicolon ";".

Both classes and interfaces contain an implementation block, as do (non abstract) methods.

```
public class Account
```

```
{                        // Implementation block for the class
    private int      number;
    protected double balance;
    public void withdraw (double amount)
    {                     // Implementation block for the method
        if (balance > amount)
        {                 // Block for the series of statements
            int newBalance = balance - amount; //local variable
        balance = newBalance;
        }
    }
    [...]
}
```

> **Tip** You should work out a suitable formatting scheme for blocks. In this book each opening and closing bracket stands in its own line. The elements contained in these brackets are then indented by one level (tab).
> However you will often see the following scheme:
> ```
> public void withdraw(double amount) {
>     if (balance > amount) {
>         int newBalance = balance - amount;
>       balance = newBalance;
>     }
> }
> ```

Synchronized blocks

synchronized (<Object>) { <Statements> }

If you are working with several threads (see Section 6.1.10), i.e. you are getting different processes to run in parallel, there is the risk that different threads will manipulate the same objects or access the same resources. In order to avoid conflicts, undefined states and unexpected ("random") results, you can either make the whole method run atomically (see Section 4.5.5) or protect just certain objects in a synchronized block. Provided a thread is located in a synchronized block, only those other threads that also want to access the protected object have to wait until the block has finished.

```
synchronized (account)
{
account.withdraw(200.0);
```

}

4.9.2 Loops

In Java there are three types of loops: *while*, *do-while*, and *for*. They differ in the type of control for loop execution.

while loop

```
while ( <boolean expression> ) <Statement>
```

In the *while* loop a boolean expression (condition) is evaluated first. If this has a *true* result, the body (a block or a single statement) is executed. This is repeated until the condition, which is evaluated before each pass, returns *false*. Then execution resumes with the statement after the block.

```
while ( true ) anObject.doNothing();    // Endless loop
while ( enum.hasMoreElements() )
    { obj = enum.nextElement(); [...] }
```

Warning If you want to access the contents of components on a form you have produced yourself, e.g. an input field, you must do that before the form is removed from the memory, otherwise the data will be removed as well.

It is easy to forget to put inside the block brackets those statements that you want executed if the while condition is met. The compiler does not refer to the formatting but to the bracketing here. So take care.

```
while ( enum.hasMoreElements() )
   acc = enum.nextElement();  // without block brackets!
   acc.withdraw(100);            // misleading bracketing!
                        // only affects the
                        // last element!
```

do ... while loop

```
do <Statement> while ( <boolean expression> )
```

This is a version of the *while* loop where the body is worked through first before evaluating the condition. This means it is executed at least once.

```
do {anObject.doNothing();} while (true);// Endless loop
```

for loop

```
for (<Initialization>; <boolean expression>;
     <Increment>) <Statement>
```

The *for* loop provides more flexible control of loop execution. Initialization is performed in the header, where you might define a loop counter for instance. The expression `<boolean expression>` defines whether the next loop pass is executed. If true, the body is executed first and then the `<Increment>` statement. Normally, the loop counter is incremented here:

```
for (;;) { anObject.doNothing(); }  // Endless loop
// The following loop is executed 100 times:
for ( int i=0; i<100; i++ ) { anObject.doSomething(); }
// Iteration using the arguments of a main method:
for ( int j=0; j<argv.length; j++ )
   System.out.println(argv[j]);
```

You can also leave out the expressions and statements in the header completely, as shown in the first example.

Aborting loop execution: break

```
break <label>
```

Endless loops always raise the question of whether you can escape from them without a condition.

There are two statements for this purpose: *break* and *continue*. With *break* you escape the current block. You can also specify a label, so that you escape all blocks up to the block with the label (in place of *goto* in C):

```
aLabel:
for ( i=0 ; ; i++ )  // Loop labeled with a label
{
   while ( true )
   {
      if (i>100) break aLabel; // (1) escapes while and
                               // for loop
                //
```

protected

The same rule applies to the *protected* access right (not the same as C++ !). As we have already seen in this chapter (Access rights), sub-classes can also access these code elements.

4.10.5   Java archives

Java archives have nothing to do with programming, but are a means of supplying the code more simply. In a Java archive – a file with the ".jar" extension - Java bytecode files and resources are saved in compressed form.

The use of Java archives instead of separate class files speeds up transmission over a network. This is because only one large file is downloaded instead of lots of little ones, and this file is also compressed. This is why Java archives are particularly popular with applets.

A version of the ZIP format is used, so you can view the contents with a standard unzip program (e.g. WinZip). In addition to the individual classes and resources, the archive contains a *Manifest*, which contains metadata on the data saved in the archive, for instance the checksums of the compressed data. This Manifest is located under *meta-inf\Manifest.mf* and might for instance contain the following for an archive containing just one class:

```
Manifest Version: 1.0

Name: com/nittyGritty/java/banking/Account.class
Digest-Algorithms: SHA MD5
SHA-Digest: A8wxEo9x9zXae/deYR3iRaaMR3Y=
MD5-Digest: y9FGldOxNXYJR08uFwdqnw==
```

The Digest data represents the checksums. If the archive had also been digitally signed, there would be one or two extra signature files with the extension ".sf".

Creation

If you are working with the JDK (see Section 2.1), you can create Java archives using the *jar* utility. The syntax is similar to the Unix tool *tar* and reads:

```
jar -task [options] archiveName fileList
```

Task	Meaning
c	create new archive
u	update existing archive
t	list contents of archive
x	extract archive

Option	Meaning
f	specify archive name
v	display detailed messages (verbose)
0	no compression
M	do not create Manifest
m	import Manifest from external file
C <dir>	do not read files from the current directory, but from the <dir> directory

Create a new archive called *Banking.jar* containing all the classes in the current directory:

```
jar -cvf Banking.jar *.class
```

Update this archive with a new version of the class *Account*:

```
jar -uvf Banking.jar Account.class
```

> **Tip** Other development environments usually provide more convenient facilities for creating a Java archive. For instance in VisualAge you can select a complete project, find all the classes referenced from there, and save the result by exporting to a Java archive.

Usage

If you then want to use the *Account* class, the runtime environment obviously has no way of knowing that this class is located in the archive *Banking.jar*. However you can include the archive in the CLASSPATH. This works in exactly the same way as entering directories in the CLASSPATH (see Section 1.4), e.g.

```
set CLASSPATH=%CLASSPATH%;c:\Banking.jar
java AccountApp
```

or

```
java -classpath %CLASSPATH%;c:\Banking.jar AccountApp
```

With applets a Java archive is specified using a special tag in the HTML page (see Chapter 9).

```
<APPLET CODE="AccountApplet.class" ARCHIVE="Banking.jar"
WIDTH=300 HEIGHT=100>
```

Java 2 library

In the following chapters (5 to 10) I want to present the central packages of the Java class library. The aim of this chapter is not to refer to *all* classes. This section will give you an introduction to show you where to find certain functionalities, and will show you some particularly important concepts.

5.1 The most important packages – a short overview

Even the Standard Edition of the JDK contains what is, for the beginner, a vast quantity of final classes. Some of these will quickly become the daily companions of programmers; others will do their work in the background. According to the language standard, you will find these classes distributed over diverse packages. To give you a broad view of the most important of these classes, I would like to show you here the purpose and content of the individual JDK packages (see Figure 5.1) (those added in Java 2 are identified using (J2)) and to go into the most common classes in more detail.

java.applet	java.net	javax.swing.colorchooser (J2)
java.awt	java.rmi	javax.swing.event (J2)
java.awt.color (J2)	java.rmi.activation (J2)	javax.swing.filechooser (J2)
java.awt.datatransfer	java.rmi.dgc	javax.swing.plaf (J2)
java.awt.dnd (J2)	java.rmi.registry	javax.swing.plaf.basic (J2)
java.awt.dnd.peer (J2)	java.rmi.server	javax.swing.plaf.metal (J2)
java.awt.event	java.security	javax.swing.plaf.multi (J2)
java.awt.font (J2)	java.security.acl	javax.swing.table (J2)
java.awt.geom (J2)	java.security.cert (J2)	javax.swing.text (J2)
java.awt.im (J2)	java.security.interfaces	javax.swing.text.html (J2)
java.awt.image	java.security.spec (J2)	javax.swing.text.html.parser (J2)
java.awt.image.renderable (J2)	java.sql	javax.swing.text.rtf (J2)
java.awt.peer	java.text	javax.swing.tree (J2)
java.awt.print (J2)	java.text.resources	javax.swing.undo (J2)
java.beans	java.util	org.omg.CORBA (J2)
java.beans.beancontext (J2)	java.util.jar (J2)	org.omg.CORBA.DynAnyPackage (J2)
java.io	java.util.zip	org.omg.CORBA.ORBPackage (J2)
java.lang	javax.accessibility (J2)	org.omg.CORBA.portable (J2)
java.lang.ref (J2)	javax.swing (J2)	org.omg.CORBA.TypeCodePackage (J2)
java.lang.reflect	javax.swing.beaninfo (J2)	org.omg.CosNaming (J2)
java.math	javax.swing.border (J2)	org.omg.CosNaming.NamingContextPackage (J2)

Figure 5.1 *Packages in the Java standard class library*

> **Tip** In this short chapter, I want to give you a rough idea of which subject areas of which versions of Java are addressed. The description of the classes and interfaces contained within them will then be given in the following chapters.
>
> Unfortunately, it is impossible even just to explain all of the head words, as these would fill hundreds of pages. Java unites almost all areas of programming – one developer is more interested in 3D games, another more for host systems for secure transactions – and there is something for almost everyone in the sheer inexhaustible number of class libraries. So don't be frightened if you can't understand everything here; the attached reference section only deals with those classes that are important for everyone, but includes explanations and examples.

Since	SE	ME	EE
1.0	x	x	x

In the case of the classes under discussion, the above table shows from which Java language version they are contained and whether they are a component of the Standard Edition (SE, Section Java 2 Standard Edition), Micro Edition (ME, Java 2 Micro Edition) or Enterprise Edition (EE, Further Java class libraries).

5.2 Editions of the Java 2 platform

As already mentioned in the first chapter, Java has been available since version 2 in different editions depending on the field of application. I want to show their scopes in the following.

5.2.1   Java 2 Standard Edition

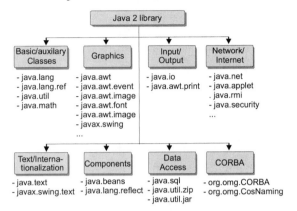

Figure 5.2 *Structure of the Java 2 Standard Edition*

Essential classes

On each platform, there is a set of fundamental classes available for creating Java applications. These include basic and help classes *(java.lang, java.util)*, classes for input/output *(java.io)*, classes for network communication, and libraries for the design of user interfaces.

Additional standard libraries in Java 1.1

The Standard Edition, intended for use in client computers, contains additional class libraries for accessing databases *(java.sql)*, for applets and other Internet applications *(java.applet, java.net)*. Up until Java 1.1, there was only the Abstract Windowing Toolkit *(java.awt)* for the design of user interfaces. Text processing and internationalization are addressed through the *java.text* package.

Java.beans and *java.lang.reflect* are used for component and tool-based development. Classes for the development of distributed applications *(java.rmi)* and for encryption and digital signatures *(java.security)* are also included in the Standard package.

5.2.2   Java 2 platform

With Java 2 (JDK 1.2), there has been a significant expansion of the APIs; however, these are not yet fully supported on many target platforms such as browsers and application servers. The most significant expansion is the Swing library *(javax.swing* with numerous subpackages) for the design of modern graphic user interfaces.

java.awt.color	javax.swing.filechooser
java.awt.dnd	javax.swing.plaf (32)
java.awt.dnd.peer	javax.swing.plaf.basic
java.awt.font	javax.swing.plaf.metal
java.awt.geom	javax.swing.plaf.multi
java.awt.im	javax.swing.table
java.awt.image.renderable	javax.swing.text
java.awt.print	javax.swing.text.html
java.beans.beancontext	javax.swing.text.html.parser
java.lang.ref	javax.swing.text.rtf
java.rmi.activation	javax.swing.tree
java.security.cert	javax.swing.undo
java.security.spec	org.omg.CORBA
java.util.jar	org.omg.CORBA.DynAnyPackage
javax.accessibility	org.omg.CORBA.ORBPackage
javax.swing	org.omg.CORBA.portable
javax.swing.beaninfo	org.omg.CORBA.TypeCodePackage
javax.swing.border	org.omg.CosNaming
javax.swing.colorchooser	org.omg.CosNaming.NamingContextPackage
javax.swing.event	

Figure 5.3 *Innovations in the Java 2 Standard Edition version 1.2*

Further features affect the graphics area (features in java.awt as well as diverse subpackages), *Drag&Drop* (*java.awt.dnd*), print (*java.awt.print*), formatted texts in HTML or RTF (*javax.swing.text*), *collection classes* (new classes in *java.util*), CORBA support (*org.omg.CORBA, org.omg.CosNaming*) and a new *security concept (java.security and subpackages)*.

Java 2 version 1.3

Version 1.3 does not offer much that is new in the libraries. However, it does include some libraries that were formerly available as extras, particularly in the area of client access to application servers. These include new CORBA and RMI classes, as well as libraries to address name servers. In addition, some packages are included that can be used as plug-in interfaces (SPI = Service Provider Interfaces) for future expansion by other companies.

Sound support has also been expanded.

java.awt.im.spi	javax.sound.midi
javax.naming	javax.sound.midi.spi
javax.naming.directory	javax.sound.sampled
javax.naming.event	javax.sound.sampled.spi
javax.naming.ldap	org.omg.CORBA_2_3
javax.naming.spi	org.omg.CORBA_2_3.portable
javax.rmi	org.omg.SendingContext
javax.rmi.CORBA	org.omg.stub.java.rmi

Figure 5.4 *Innovations in Java 2 Standard Edition version 1.3*

5.2.3   Java 2 Micro Edition

The *Micro Edition* is a slimmed-down version for devices with a low level of hardware equipment, such as palmtops/PDAs, mobile phones, on-board computers in automobiles, set-top boxes or kiosk systems. They are based on a mini version of the virtual machine, the KVM.

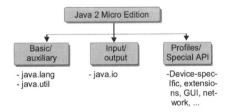

Figure 5.5   *Components of the Java 2 Micro Edition*

In addition to the fundamental class libraries, there are profiles for the device type, such as for palmtops with small graphic displays, for smart cards, telephones, etc., as well as device-specific feature APIs, as used in palmtops.

> **Tip** The Micro Edition is, however, still in its infancy, and is still in a state of flux.

5.2.4   Java 2 Enterprise Edition

The *Enterprise Edition* is an expansion of the Standard Edition for use in application servers. These servers should take over the control of business processors and the central processings of data in modern, distributed architectures. They should be able to integrate existing applications and data from backend systems such as databases, mainframes or complex business systems like SAP, support the widest range of clients' platforms, from WAP mobile phones, through web browsers, to complex swing applications.

The Enterprise Edition is not a product but just a collection of interfaces that an application server has to support. Manufacturers of application servers that cover all interfaces can have their compatibility checked against the Sun reference implementation and are given a logo. This process should ensure that manufacturers such as IBM, BEA, or Inprise produce servers that are compatible with each other and that the developer can also write applications and components that are independent of the platform and manufacturer on the server side.

javax.activation	javax.naming.spi
javax.ejb	javax.rmi
javax.jms	javax.rmi.CORBA
javax.mail	javax.servlet
javax.mail.event	javax.servlet.http
javax.mail.internet	javax.servlet.jsp
javax.mail.search	javax.servlet.jsp.tagext
javax.naming	javax.sql
javax.naming.directory	javax.transaction
javax.naming.event	javax.transaction.xa
javax.naming.ldap	

Figure 5.6 *Additional packages in the Java 2 Enterprise Edition*

The Enterprise Edition is broken down into the following fields: Servlets and Java Server Pages (*javax.servlet.**) to support HTML clients, Enterprise JavaBeans (*javax.ejb*) as a component model that offers services such as naming (*javax.naming*), transaction security (*javax.transaction*) and persistency (*java.sql, javax.sql*). In addition, you can access a mailservice using *javax.mail.**. There is an optional messaging service for the asynchronous transmission of messages (*javax.jms*), such as the broadcasting of a message to registered users.

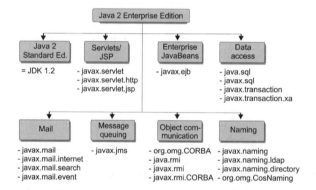

Figure 5.7 *Structure of the Java 2 Enterprise Edition*

5.2.5   Further Java class libraries

In addition, there are further Java classes that are not part of a complete edition but which are available as extensions to the Java API for special purposes. Sun calls these optional libraries *Java Extensions*. Many individual components of the Enterprise Edition are available as extensions, such as *Enterprise JavaBeans*, a transaction service (*JTS = Java Transaction Service*), an interface to different naming services (*JNDI = Java Name and Directory Interface*), servlets, the mail API, and much more.

This does not just address the server area. For clients, there is a 3D API and Jini for connecting different types of devices such as household electrical equipment and printers. The table show a few examples:

Extension	Description
Java 3D	API for three-dimensional graphics
Java Advanced Imaging	Image processing
Java Media Framework	Videos (MPEG, AVI etc.)
	Audio (MP3, Wav etc.)
Java Speech	API for voice recognition
Jini	Networking technology for devices
JavaHelp	HTML-based help systems
Java Cryptographic Extensions	Encryption classes
Secure Socket Extensions	SSL encryption for diverse Internet protocols

Other manufacturers

In addition to these standard libraries and programming interfaces that are maintained by Sun Microsystems, there are many others from different manufacturers. Some of these are programming interfaces, creating bridges to existing software products, or complete collections of independent software modules, such as Lotus eSuite or the JClass products from Sitraka (formerly the KLGroup).

There are facilities to obtain catalogues, place orders and download information from the Internet. Try JARS (www.jars.com), Gamelan (www.gamelan.com) or Component Source (www.componentsource.com/java).

TAKE THAT!

Basic and system classes

6

In the following section, you will get to know the basic classes of the *java.lang* package. The majority of them exist in every virtual machine (no matter what version, and even in the Micro Edition). The *java.math* package (see Section 6.2) supplements the library with a mathematical functionality.

6.1 Data types and system classes – java.lang

The *java.lang* package is the most important of all of the packages. Because of its elementary importance, the compiler automatically imports the *java.lang* package into each class before translating the source code. You can, therefore, when writing a class feel free to leave out the line import java.lang.*.

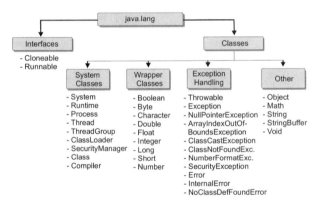

Figure 6.1   *Classes in the java.lang package*

6.1.1   The Object class

since	SE	ME	EE
1.0	×	×	×

In order to define a class hierarchy or library, you first need a base or root that defines the fundamental behavior of all classes. In Java, this root is provided in the form of the *Object* class. All Java classes form a hierarchy with *java.lang.Object* as its common basic class.

> **Tip** How does this work with classes that are not declared as subclasses? If a class does not contain the key word *extends* in the declaration, then the compiler will automatically add `extends java.lang.Object`, so that this class is actually seen as the "original class".

Methods

Because of this behavior as a root class, you can take advantage of the basic functionality that provides the *Object* in its methods for that object in any class. These are shown in Figure 6.2.

> **Tip** The schematic representation shows the class in UML. The "#" character stands for the *protected* access right, and "+" for *public*.

```
              Object

+ equals(obj : Object)
# finalize()
+ toString()
+ getClass()
# clone()
+ wait()
+ notify()
...
```

Figure 6.2 *Object class*

→ `boolean equals( Object obj )` for comparatives
→ `Object clone()` for the duplication of objects
→ `void finalize()` for clearing up before the deletion of an object
→ `String toString()` for the issuing of object descriptions
→ `void wait()` and `notify()` for the notification mechanism
→ `Class getClass()` for run-time type information

Comparing and copying

In strings (see Section 4.8.5), you have probably already got to know the `equals()` method, which compares two objects with each other. When the object has this method, two objects of any type can be compared.

This method is defined as standard so that it compares references just like the operator "==". This means that it gives *true* if both object references indicate exactly the same object. Even if two objects of the same class have allocated attributes that are completely the same, they are still different objects.

However, sometimes it makes sense to rewrite this method in a suitable way for subclasses. One example is the class *String*, in which the method gives *true* if the same character chain is in the content of both objects.

There are two variants:

1 plain comparison of attributes

2 recursive content comparison.

In the first case, `equals()` would be rewritten, for example, as follows:

```
public boolean equals(Object obj)
{
    // same type?
    if ( !(obj instanceof Account) ) return false;
    Account ofObj = (Account)obj; // type conversion
    return ((number  == ofObj.getNumber()) &&
            (balance == ofObj.getBalance()) &&
            (holder  == ofObj.getHolder()));
}
```

This results in a comparison of fields on a referential basis. In Figure 6.3, you can see three instances of the *Account* class with identical data. A comparison of the `acc1==acc2` or `acc2==acc3` type would give false , as it is a matter of different objects. It is different when applying the `equals` method. The comparison `acc1.equals(acc2)` would give *false* as a result, although both objects of the *Person* class have the same value assigned. `acc2.equals(acc3)` gives *true*, because here both references indicate the same instance of the *Person* class.

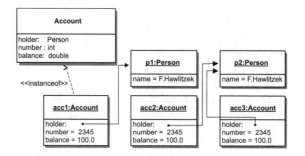

Figure 6.3 *Comparison of instances*

Conversely, if you want to carry out the comparison in a recursive manner, i.e. to extend the comparison of the content to both *Person* objects, you must rewrite the equals() method as follows:

```
public boolean equals(Object obj)
{
    // same type?
    if ( !(obj instanceof Account) ) return false;
    Account ofObj = (Account)obj; // Type conversion
    if (number != ofObj.getNumber() ||
        balance != ofObj.getBalance()) return false;
    return (holder.equals(ofObj.getHolder()));
}
```

The *Person* class must also offer a content comparison here, which is conversely based on the equals method of the *String* class:

```
class Person
{
    private String name;
    public boolean equals(Object obj)
    {
        if ( !(obj instanceof Person) ) return false;
        return (name.equals(((Person)obj).getName()));
    }
}
```

It is similar for clone(). As standard, this method copies an object with its references (shallow copy), but not the referenced objects (deep copy). clone() and equals() should always be changed together in order to guarantee consistent behavior. In order to ensure that the developer has given thought to the behavior of clone() before using the method, this method is declared in *Object protected* and creates a *CloneNotSupportedException*, as long as the *Cloneable* interface is not implemented (see Section entitled "The cloneable interface").

Variant 1: Shallow Copy - copy indicates the same owner object

```
public class Account implements Cloneable
{
    [...]
    // clone method inherited from java.lang.Object
    // -> shallow copy
    public Object clone()
    {
        super.clone();
    }
}
```

Variant 2: Deep Copy - copy indicates copy of holder object

```
public class Account implements Cloneable
{
    [...]
    public Object clone()
    {
        // rewritten clone method
        Account copy = zero;
        try
        {
            copy = (Account)super.clone();
            // deep copy (class Person is cloneable)
            clone.setHolder((Person)this.holder.clone());
        }
        catch (CloneNotSupportedException e) { [...] }
        return clone;
    }
}
```

> **Tip** In the Micro Edition, the `clone()` method of the *Object* class is missing as well as the *Cloneable* interface.

Object deletion

We have already met the `finalize()` method in Section 4.4.3, which is called up by the Garbage Collector before objects are destroyed. You should carry out tidying work using this method, such as decrementing instance counters or releasing non-critical resources. However, you should not rely too much on calling up this method, for on the one hand the call-up time through the different Garbage Collectors is uncertain and, on the other hand, the methods may not be executed at all through an unplanned program abort. Therefore, time-critical or important releases such as those from the database connections or the writing out of a buffer to a file do not have to look for anything (`flush`) in `finalize()`.

```
protected void finalize()
{
    openFile.close(); // Example of resource release
}
```

Object output

Using the `toString()` method, each object can be output as a text string. In the case of standard classes, an overview of the most important data is output with this, for example `java.awt.Color[20, 150, 255]` for an object of the *Color* class with the color proportions of 20 for red, 150 for green and 255 for blue. In the case of your own classes, the class name is output as standard with an object-identifying suffix, for example `com.ars.test.Date@562e` or `com.nittyGritty. java.banking.Account@da9`. You should therefore rewrite the `toString()` method in a suitable way, so that `com.nittyGritty. java.banking.Account[0436577800: 18663.0, Florian Hawlitzek]` is output:

```
public String toString()
{
    return getClass().getName() + "[" + number
            + ": " + balance + ", " + holder.getName() + "]";
}
```

We will find out what the calling up of `getClass()` is supposed to mean, in looking at the *Class* class (see Section 6.1.3).

Tip `Wait()`, `notify()` and `notifyAll()` are methods that you cannot rewrite. They are mainly used for internal Java thread synchronization. An object blocked using `wait()` can be revived by calling up one of the `notify` methods.

6.1.2   The Cloneable interface

since	SE	ME	EE
1.0	x	-	x

Each class inherits a clone() method from an *object*. However, this is only defined as *protected* so that it can be rewritten as the public method that calls up super.clone(). The duplication (cloning) is, however, only authorized if a class explicitly implements the (empty) *Cloneable* interface. This ensures that the programmer has considered the type of cloning (deep/shallow copy) (see Section 6.1.1).

> **Tip** Empty interfaces only used to ensure certain facts are also called marking interfaces.

6.1.3   The Class class

since	SE	ME	EE
1.0	x	x	x

This class is a type of metaclass. This means that an object in this class describes the name and structure of another class. This is carried out in just the same way as SQL databases, in which system tables of the same design document the structure of a table, for example the number and data types of the columns. The *Class* class is particularly important in association with self-documented components, *JavaBeans*, which we will look at in Section 10.4.

Methods

Figure 6.4 shows the most important methods of *Class* in the form of a UML class diagram. Class methods and class variables – i.e. static defined elements – are shown underlined in UML. The most important methods are:

→ String getName() and toString() to output the class name
→ Package getPackage() and Class getSuperclass() to classify the class
→ Class forName(String) to dynamically load the classes
→ Object newInstance(), Field[] getFields(), Method[] get-Methods(), Constructor[] getConstructors(), boolean isArray(), boolean isInterface() and so on, for the analysis and generic use of unknown classes.

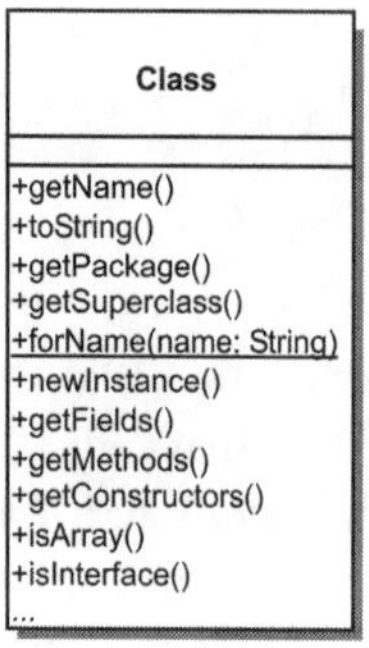

```
                 Class

+getName()
+toString()
+getPackage()
+getSuperclass()
+forName(name: String)
+newInstance()
+getFields()
+getMethods()
+getConstructors()
+isArray()
+isInterface()
...
```

Figure 6.4 *The Class class*

Comparisons

If you want to find out if two objects belong to the same class, you can make a comparison using

```
if ( (obj1.getClass()).equals(obj2.getClass()) )
```

However, this comparison does not take any inheritance into account. If you are not concerned about the actual class affiliation, you should use the key word *instanceof*, as shown in the following example. The application in the second case is also simpler and the execution quicker.

```
Object anAccount = new CurrentAccount(2000.0);
  // The object is intentionally allocated here
  // to a reference of a
  // general type. In practice, you often only get
  // object references back from collections
  // and first have to find out
  // the actual type.


// provides false:
boolean b1 = anAccount.getClass().equals(
   Class.forName("com.nittyGritty.java.banking.Account") );
// provides true:
boolean b2 = (anAccount instanceof Account);
```

Output of a class name

Using the `getName()` method, you can obtain the fully qualified name of the class as a string, i.e. including the package name. Alternatively, you can also call `toString()`, then the type of the "class" is additionally prefixed: class or interface (see Section 4.6).

Classification in the class hierarchy

In the same way, `getPackage()` supplies back the package (see Section 4.10) to which the class of the transferred object belongs (since Java 1.2). However, this is not done as a string, but as the object of the class package. If you are only interested in the name, you can call up `obj.getPackage().toString()`. You can get the superclass using the method `getSuperclass()`, though as the object of the *Class* class.

Loading and analyzing classes

In the above comparison, the class method `Class.forName(String class name)` was also used. In this context, it is used to generate and supply back a *Class* object for a named class. Using `newInstance()`, you can then instantiate an object of this class. However, the `forName()` method also has an additional effect: if the stated class has not yet been used, i.e. has not been statically referenced in one of the .class files, then the class is dynamically searched for in CLASSPATH or on the original server of the applet at the runtime of the application and loaded in the runtime environment.

6

TAKE THAT!

Tip Dynamic loading and linking of classes "on demand" is a Java specialty. You can write applications that only load the essential classes at the start and thus start up very quickly and occupy small amounts of memory. On using additional functionalities, they only load up the classes necessary for this and so the application is optimized to the behavior of the user.
It is even possible to create a completely new class at the runtime and to use it immediately. A more detailed explanation of this capability would, however, exceed the scope of this short Java introduction.

Class has a whole range of additional methods that are used mainly to describe the interface of a class and to categorize the class hierarchy. This abstract and dynamic documentation of classes is called *Reflection* (see Section 10.3). In this, *class* contributes methods for identifying the superclass (`getSuperclass()`), the methods (`getMethods()`), constructors (`getConstructors()`) and variables (`getFields()`) of a class. In addition, you can enquire whether it is a class or an interface (`isInterface()`).

Tip In the Micro Edition, there are almost no analysis methods.

6.1.4   The String class

since	SE	ME	EE
1.0	x	x	x

The string classes *String* (see Section 4.8.5) and *StringBuffer* are additional important data structures of this package. The chaining of strings using "+" and other *string* operations is relatively slow. This is due to Java creating a new *string* object for the outcome (and interim outcomes) each time. Objects of the *String* class are **constant** after their creation, i.e. you cannot change or replace any character. Better suited to *String* manipulation is the *StringBuffer* class, which can carry out most operations "on site". It also provides methods for inserting and appending additional characters.

```
┌─────────────────────────┐   ┌─────────────────────────────┐
│         String          │   │        StringBuffer         │
├─────────────────────────┤   ├─────────────────────────────┤
│+length()                │   │+length()                    │
│+trim()                  │   │+setLength(len : int)        │
│+concat(s : String)      │   │+toString()                  │
│+charAt(index : int)     │   │+append(o : ...)             │
│+compareTo(s : String)   │   │+insert(index : int, o : ...)│
│+equals(obj : Object)    │   │+charAt(index : int)         │
│+getBytes()              │   │+setCharAt(index : int, ch : char)│
│+indexOf(char : int)     │   │+capacity()                  │
│+indexOf(substring : String)│ │+reverse()                   │
│+valueOf(n : ...)        │   │...                          │
│+substring(from : int, to : int)│└─────────────────────────┘
│+toUpperCase()           │
│+toLowerCase()           │
│+replace(old : char, new : char)│
│...                      │
└─────────────────────────┘
```

Figure 6.5 *The String and StringBuffer classes*

Creation

Strings can be created in several ways:

→ by allocating a literal: `s = "This is a string"`
→ from a string buffer: `s = new String(buf)`
→ from an primitive datatype: `s = String.valueOf(number)`
→ from an array of characters or bytes: `s = new String(chars)`

If you convert a byte field into a *String*, you have the option of stating the encoding. Java uses internal Unicodes; other encoding such as ISO8859-1, UTF-8, EBCDIC, etc. can also be read using suitable converters.

StringBuffer: You can create objects from a *string* or blank, stating the maximum possible character length (capacity).

Methods

`length()` in the case of both classes gives the length of the strings (number of characters). Using `charAt(index)`, you can interrogate a character in an index position, and in the case of *StringBuffer* objects you can re-occupy it using `setCharAt(index, character)`.

You can chain *string* objects using the "+" character or the `concat()` method; in the case of string buffer objects there are also `append` and `insert` methods for different data types.

In addition to `equals()`, you can also use the `compareTo()` method for comparisons, which carries out an alphabetic comparison. In addition, there are different index and search functions for characters and character chains in a string.

You can create variants to a string using the following methods:

→ `trim()` gives the string, but without the leading and trailing blank characters
→ using `substring(from, to)` you get a part of the character chain
→ `toUpperCase()` or `toLowerCase()` give text completely in upper or lower case.

6.1.5 The Math class

since	SE	ME	EE
1.0	x	(x)	x

The *Math* class contains all conventional mathematical functions as class methods as well as constants such as Euler's figure e (`Math.E`) and pi (`Math.PI`). In the Micro Edition, however, it is restricted to the amount and the minimum and maximum calculation.

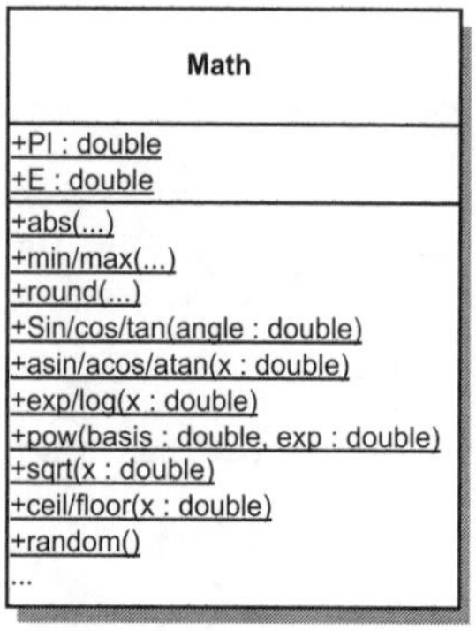

```
                 Math

+PI : double
+E : double
+abs(...)
+min/max(...)
+round(...)
+Sin/cos/tan(angle : double)
+asin/acos/atan(x : double)
+exp/log(x : double)
+pow(basis : double, exp : double)
+sqrt(x : double)
+ceil/floor(x : double)
+random()
...
```

Figure 6.6 *The Math class*

Methods

No instances are created by *Math*, but instead class methods are called up, e.g. `root = Math.sqrt(5.0)`. The methods are defined respectively for different elementary number datatypes. `abs()` calculates the (absolute) amount, `min/max()` the minimum or maximum of two figures, `round()` rounds a number, `ceil/floor()` give the next whole number for *double* values. `pow(a, exp)` calculates a^{exp} and `sqrt()` the root. Using `random()`, you can create a random number between 0.0 and 1.0.

> **Tip** In addition to these mathematical functions based on whole and floating point numbers, there are a number of classes for long and fixed point numbers in the *java.math* package (see Section 6.2). These are particularly important if you want to avoid rounding errors or have accurate specifications on the number of places to be calculated behind the point or if rounding has to take place according to these specifications.

6.1.6 The StrictMath class

since	SE	ME	EE
1.3	x	-	-

The *StrictMath* class newly included in JDK 1.3 contains the same functionality as *Math*, but the results correspond to numerical methods up to bit-standardized algorithms.

6.1.7 The Number class and Wrapper classes

since	SE	ME	EE
1.0/1.1	x	(x)	x

The abstract class *Number* forms a basic structure for the encapsulation of elementary datatypes of *byte, short, int, long, float,* and *double*. It demands conversion methods from the classes derived from Number in all numerical elementary datatypes.

In data conversions, the Wrapper classes of (*Boolean, Character, Byte, Short, Integer, Long, Float* and *Double*) are often used. They can be used as number types packaged in object form:

```
double d = 354.42;
Double dAsObject = new Double(d);
```

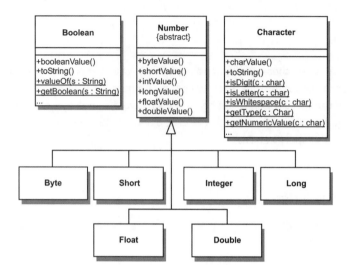

Figure 6.7 *Wrapper classes*

However, you frequently do not create an object but only use the class methods:

```
// Conversion String -> prim. datatype:
int i = Integer.parseInt(aNumberAsString);
// Conversion prim. datatype -> String:
String s = Double.toString(d);
```

If you want to convert a *String* into a numerical elementary datatype, use the class method `parse<Type>()` of corresponding number types (e.g. `parseInt()`); if, on the other hand, you want a Wrapper class object, use the respective constructor or the method `valueOf()`. `<Type>Value()` (e.g. `intValue()`) converts the object back into a primitive datatype, `toString()` into a normal character chain.

The *Character* class offers some useful methods to determine the type of a character, such as letter, number or blank/space character. Using `getNumericValue(character)`, you can determine the Unicode number of a character.

Tip Although not in the *java.lang* package, in *java.math* the two classes *BigInteger* and *BigDecimal*, subclasses of Number, are used to depict large numbers that do not fit in the stated value ranges of the primitive datatypes and their wrappers. Objects of the *BigDecimal* type are fixed point numbers, in which you can state almost any level of accuracy and the rounding scheme in the case of calculation operations (see Section 6.2). The Micro Edition simply contains restricted variants of *Boolean*, *Byte*, *Short*, *Integer,* and *Long*.

6.1.8 The System class

since	SE	ME	EE
1.0	x	x	x

Even the *System* class is located here in this package. It consists solely of class variables and methods and cannot be instantiated. It constitutes the connection to the subordinate operating system and allows access to the standard input/output, for example. Additional tasks of *System* are the loading of libraries and the locating of system information, such as system time or the name and version of the operating system.

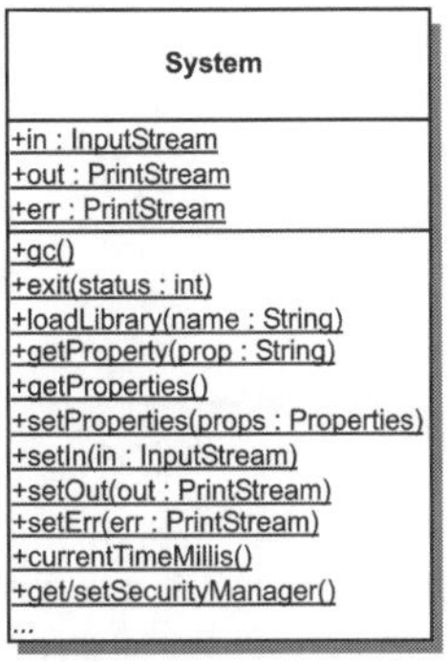

System

+in : InputStream
+out : PrintStream
+err : PrintStream

+gc()
+exit(status : int)
+loadLibrary(name : String)
+getProperty(prop : String)
+getProperties()
+setProperties(props : Properties)
+setIn(in : InputStream)
+setOut(out : PrintStream)
+setErr(err : PrintStream)
+currentTimeMillis()
+get/setSecurityManager()
...

Figure 6.8 *The System class*

The class variables `in`, `out`, and `err` provide the standard input, standard output, and error output. You have already used these variables for text output on the console, for example (`System.out.println(aString);`).

```
System.gc();     // calls the Garbage Collector manually
System.exit(0);  // ends the virtual machine
                 // currently being used
System.getProperty("java.version"); // interrogates system
                                     // variables
System.getProperty("user.dir");      // interrogates system
                                     // variables
System.loadLibrary("testlib");       // loads a DLL,
                                     // e.g. testlib.dll
                                     // under Windows
System.currentTimeMillis();          // gives the
                                     // current time
```

Here are a few standard properties, of which some properties cannot be accessed in unsigned applets, for security reasons:

Property	Meaning	Not in applets
java.version	JRE Version	
java.home	JRE directory	x
java.class.path	current CLASSPATH	x
os.name	Name of the operating system	
os.version	Version of the operating system	
file.separator	Path separators (e.g. "/" or "\")	
line.separator	Line separators (e.g. "\n")	
user.name	User name	x
user.home	Home directory of the user	x
user.dir	Current work directory	x

6.1.9   The Runtime and Process classes

since	SE	ME	EE
1.0	x	-	x

To call up programs, you use the classes *Runtime* and *Process*. *Process* is a reference to an external program. It is executed by calling the method `exec()` of the *Runtime* class.

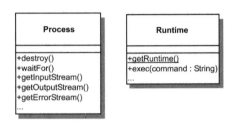

Figure 6.9 *The Runtime and Process classes*

```
Runtime.getRuntime().exec("notepad");
```

As the result of an `exec` call, you will get a *Process* object back. You can use it to build streams on the input/output of the process, wait for the end of the process (`waitFor()`) or end it using `destroy()`.

6.1.10 Thread classes

since	SE	ME	EE
1.0	x	x	x

Threads are a type of mini-process that runs almost parallel in the same address space. The same code can thus be carried out several times "at the same time" or individual tasks of an application can run "simultaneously" in their own threads. Java has supported multithreading using the *Thread* and *ThreadGroup* classes, the interface *Runnable* as well as *ThreadLocal* since 1.2.

Here are just a few tips on multithreading.

Creation

You can derive new threads either as classes of *Thread* or – if this does not work due to another inheritance hierarchy – implement the *Runnable* interface and transfer this object to the thread constructor. Then start up the thread using `start()`.

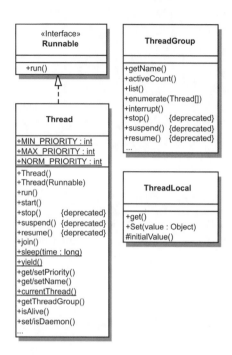

Figure 6.10 *Thread classes*

Methods

The *Thread* class contains many methods of flow control; some, however, are "deprecated" (should no longer be used), as they could lead to states of deadlock in the program or to abnormal terminations without release of resources. If you have created many threads that you want to control together, then you can use the *ThreadGroup* class.

All threads run in a common address space. Problems are therefore easily caused if several threads try to manipulate the same resources or variables at the same time. Using the *synchronized* modifier (see Section 4.5.5) and *synchronized* blocks (see Section 4.9.1), you can guarantee exclusive access to a thread. If, on the other hand, you want to create one variable per thread, you can do this from JDK 1.2 onwards using the *ThreadLocal* class.

> **Tip** *ThreadGroup* and *ThreadLocal* are missing in the Micro Edition.

6.1.11   Exceptions and errors

since	SE	ME	EE
1.0	x	x	x

In the framework of the section on fault handling (Chapter 11), we will get to know the *Throwable* class as the basic class for all *Exceptions* and *Errors* (fatal errors). You have possibly already met the exceptions *NullPointerException, ArrayIndexOutOfBoundsException, SecurityException, IOException* or the error *NoClassDefFoundError* .

Methods

All errors and exceptions are derived from the *Throwable* class. To output, it provides three methods:

→ `toString()` gives name and description of the exception
→ `getMessage()` only displays the message (if present)
→ `printStackTrace()` prints the exception with its life history on the standard error output `System.err`.

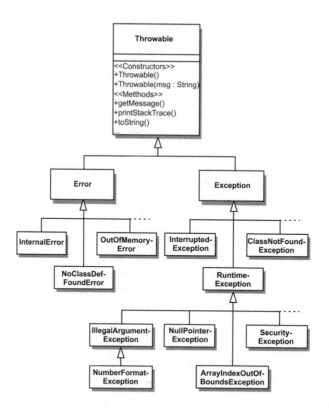

Figure 6.11 *Exceptions and errors in java.lang*

Derived classes

Errors and exception classes are derived from the standard classes. Generally, particular exception classes contain no more than two constructors (with and without message string), but only the name and the internally stored stacktrace say very much about the cause of the fault (see Section 11.3.3).

Errors are fatal faults that can occur at any time and that you cannot usefully catch. *Exceptions* should generally be dealt with. With the exception of exceptions derived from *RuntimeException*, the compiler forces the developer to deal with the fault.

6.1.12   Additional classes

The other classes of the *java.lang* package are important for the internal workings of the virtual machine, but are seldom used directly by the developer.

The *ClassLoader* is responsible for the loading of classes in the runtime environment; depending on the type, it also determines the access rights to system resources. In turn, these are controlled by the *SecurityManager*.

6.2   Mathematical classes – java.math

since	SE	ME	EE
1.1	x	-	x

Both of the classes *BigInteger* and *BigDecimal* are subclasses of *java.lang. Number* for representing large numbers, which do not fit in the stated value range of the primitive datatypes and their wrappers. These are particularly important if you want to avoid rounding errors or have exact standards of how many places after the point to calculate or standards under which rounding should take place.

Objects of the *BigInteger* type are long whole numbers and *BigDecimal* are fixed point numbers. The classes provide conventional mathematical operations (see Sections 6.1.5 to 6.1.7). In addition, in the case of *BigDecimal* objects, you can state an accuracy (places after the point) and the rounding scheme in the case of calculation operations. This is particularly useful if you are dealing with sums of money, as, for example, to convert from Euros there are fixed six-figure standards and a rounding mode that differ from the display (two places after the point).

TAKE THAT!

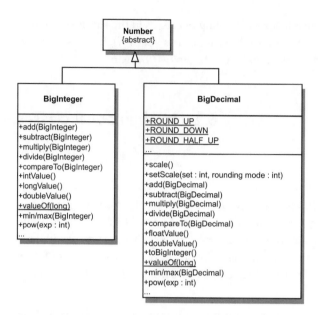

Figure 6.12 *The BigInteger and BigDecimal classes*

Data storage and communication

Data is output or edited in almost every application. Yet this data must first have been loaded from some source, and it should be possible to save it again after making any changes. Java provides wide-ranging support in this area for files (Section 7.1), databases (7.3), as well as TCP/IP and Internet (7.2), and even covers distributed object communication via RMI, CORBA, and Enterprise Java-Beans.

7.1 Input/output – java.io

The *java.io* package contains classes for input and output. The most important of these are *File, DataInputStream* (binary input), *FileInputStream* (reading from a file), similarly *DataOutputStream* and *FileOutputStream* and finally *PrintStream* for character-based text output. These classes let the programmer import from storage media data required for program execution, and to save processed data during program execution. We have already used the print() and println() methods of the *PrintStream* class many times in the standard output System.out.

Figure 7.1 lists the huge number of other classes in this package, which we categorize as shown.

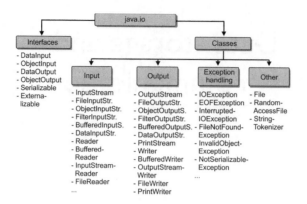

Figure 7.1 *Classes in the java.io package*

7.1.1 Streams

Streams are a key concept for input/output. To help understand them, it helps to think of streams as pipes in which a fluid – in this case data – is flowing. Not without reason we also talk of "data flow". Streams are usually unidirectional, which means that the data can only flow in one direction (see Figure 7.2).

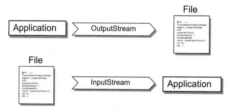

Figure 7.2 *Streams between an application and a file*

Data sources

Streams in Java always have a well-defined source. When you first create a stream you must specify from where you intend to get the data. These data sources can be very different. By using the appropriate streams you can for instance read from files or URLs (*Uniform Resource Locators*, or `file:///c:/NGJavaBook/streams.txt`) or even exchange data with other computers via socket connections.

In addition you can also chain together suitable streams, for instance to implement buffers or filters (see Figure 7.3). In the diagram the streams are represented by arrows indicating the direction of the data flow.

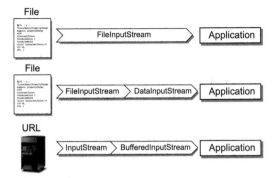

Figure 7.3 *Chaining streams*

Types of streams

Sections 7.1.3 to 7.1.10 explain the different types of streams. The comparison in Section 7.1.11 shows you which type is best suited to what task.

7.1.2   The File class

from	SE	ME	EE
1.0	x	-	x

Java's platform independence would obviously soon reach its limits if it involved a file system for a specific platform. For instance in the Unix world the path for a text file might be given by:

`/home/username/NGJavaBook/streams.txt`

whereas under Windows the same file would be localized as:

`z:\NGJavaBook\streams.txt`

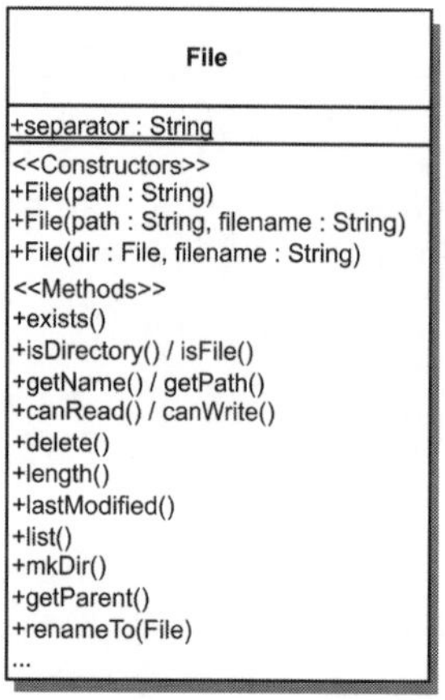

```
┌─────────────────────────────────────┐
│                 File                 │
├─────────────────────────────────────┤
│ +separator : String                  │
├─────────────────────────────────────┤
│ <<Constructors>>                     │
│ +File(path : String)                 │
│ +File(path : String, filename : String) │
│ +File(dir : File, filename : String) │
│ <<Methods>>                          │
│ +exists()                            │
│ +isDirectory() / isFile()            │
│ +getName() / getPath()               │
│ +canRead() / canWrite()              │
│ +delete()                            │
│ +length()                            │
│ +lastModified()                      │
│ +list()                              │
│ +mkDir()                             │
│ +getParent()                         │
│ +renameTo(File)                      │
│ ...                                  │
└─────────────────────────────────────┘
```

Figure 7.4   *The File class*

Methods

Java provides the *File* class to get round this platform independence. This is a platform-independent interface for functions that depend on specific operating systems. It includes methods such as `exists()` for ascertaining that a file exists, plus `canRead()`, `canWrite()`, `length()` and `lastModified()`, which you can use to determine the relevant attribute. The name of the methods `renameTo()` and `delete()` also speak for themselves.

```
// Check before reading from a file
if ( (file != null) && (file.exists()) && (file.canRead()) )
[...] // Safe reading from a file
```

Directories

A *File* object can represent a *file* in the usual sense, as well as a *directory*. The methods `isDirectory()` and `isFile()` can be used to distinguish between the two. If the object is a directory, the `list()` method returns a String array containing the names of all the files included in the directory. Calling the `mkdir()` method creates a sub-directory with the directory name that represents the object. For example you can quickly write a simple application to output the contents of the current directory, like the `dir` command under Windows.

A short program to output the directory contents:

```java
import java.io.*;
public class Dir
{
    public static void main (String[] args)
    {
        String filesList[];
        // Determine current directory:
        File directory = new File(
            System.getProperty("user.dir"));
        // Files and directories contained in it:
        filesList = directory.list();
        for (int i=0; i < filesList.length; i++)
        {
    File curFile = new File (directory,
                                    filesList[i]);

            // formatted time stamp,
            // here as Quick and Dirty solution:
            String timestamp =
              (new java.util.Date(
                curFile.lastModified())).toLocaleString();

    if (curFile.isDirectory())
                System.out.println(timestamp +
                    "\t <DIR> \t\t" + filesList[i]);
            else
                System.out.println(timestamp + "\t\t" +
                    curFile.length() + "\t"
                                + filesList[i]);
        }
    }
}
```

The program generates an object of type *File*. `System.getProperty("user.dir")` returns the path of the current directory. The `< DIR>` prefix is applied in the *for* loop to directories so that you can see the difference between directories and "normal" files. The output might read:

```
d:\java> java Dir
24.04.2000 12:19:29       <DIR>               NGJavaBook
20.06.1999 14:29:54       <DIR>               VAJBook
20.08.1998 11:34:04                 379781    vajtips.zip
22.02.1999 09:57:18       <DIR>               websphere
26.04.1999 13:12:22                 752       Counter1.class
26.04.1999 13:07:04                 424       Counter1.java
```

Tip There are two reasons why the time-stamp formatting is a quick and dirty implementation.
→ It is not guaranteed that the return value from `lastModified()` of type `long` has the format required by the constructor of the Date class on every platform, although this is the case under Windows, for example.
→ The `toLocaleString()` method of the Date class is *deprecated*, which means that it should not be used any more, because there is a better alternative. In this case the alternative would be the *java.text.DateFormat* class. The formulation of this small example would have been slightly less clear with this option.

Paths

As already mentioned, paths are represented differently in different operating systems, particularly when it comes to the delimiters. In order to represent a path in a platform-independent format, you can use the `File.separator` constant, for instance `path + File.separator + fileName` instead of `path + "/" + fileName` (Unix) or `path + "\\" + fileName` (Windows).

The `getPath()` method returns the complete path, which includes the file name for files. `getParent()` gives just the path for files, and for directories just the top-level directory.

```
File aFile = new File("z:\\NGJavaBook\\streams.txt");
String path1 = aFile.getPath();
                // returns "z:\\NGJavaBook\\streams.txt"
String path2 = aFile.getParent();
                // returns "z:\\NGJavaBook\\"
File aDir = new File("z:\\demo");
String path3 = aDir.getParent();
                // returns "z:\\"
```

7.1.3   Reading from files - FileInputStream

from	SE	ME	EE
1.0	x	-	x

The *File* class does not provide a facility for reading from the referenced file or writing to it. But even this task does not represent a great obstacle in Java. The *FileInputStream* is available for reading from files (see Figure 7.5).

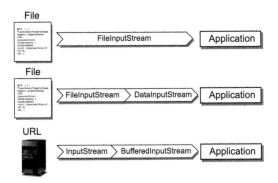

Figure 7.5   *The FileInputStream class*

Generation

An instance of *FileInputStream* is normally generated with an object of type *File* as argument. A constructor call for this might read:

```
File aFile;
...                 // assign a valid object to "aFile"
FileInputStream fiStream = new FileInputStream(aFile);
```

Alternatively the constructor of type *FileInputStream* could also be called with a *String* object containing the data name.

Warning This extract will not work reliably because the constructor might generate a *FileNot-FoundException* forcing handling with a *throws* statement (see Section 11.3.4). We will look at *IOException* and the classes derived from it in Section 7.1.13. The correct syntax – this time for the other constructor – reads:

```
try
{
    FileInputStream fiStream =
        new FileInputStream("streams.txt");
}
catch (FileNotFoundException e)
{
    System.out.println("The file \"streams.txt\" was" +
                    + " not found in the current" +
                    + " directory!");
}
```

In applets – or possibly also in applications in Java 2 – a *SecurityException* may also occur if there is at least no read authority.

Methods

Using the read() method you can then read individual bytes or groups of bytes from this file into an array. The return value –1 symbolizes the end of file. If the end of the file has not been reached, but no bytes are available temporarily, the method blocks, which means it waits until it can continue data input - this can take an infinitely long time. This is why the available() method is provided for determining the number of bytes that can be read without blocking. You can use skip(n) to skip n bytes and close() to close the stream. You should never forget to close the file, otherwise the file stays open until the virtual machine terminates or the stream is deleted by the Garbage Collector.

FilterStreams

The *FileInputStream* class provides access to the individual bytes in a file, but can be combined with any *FilterStreams*. A FilterStream is attached to another stream, adding extra functionality. FilterStreams are for example *represented* by the classes *BufferedInputStream* (with read buffer), *DataInputStream* (line-based and data-type-oriented reading) and *LineNumberInputStream* (notes the line numbers). Their constructors are called with the InputStream on which they are based. The following nesting of streams is possible for instance for reading a file line-by-line while displaying the line numbers.

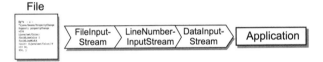

Figure 7.6 *FilterStreams*

```
FileInputStream fiStream;
LineNumberInputStream lniStream;
DataInputStream diStream;
fiStream = new FileInputStream("streams.txt");
lniStream = new LineNumberInputStream(fiStream);
diStream = new DataInputStream (lniStream);

String line;
while ( (line = diStream.readLine()) != null )
{
    int ln = lniStream.getLineNumber();
    System.out.println(""+ ln + ": " + line);
}
fiStream.close();
lniStream.close();
diStream.close();
```

7.1.4   The Reader and BufferedReader classes

from	SE	ME	EE
1.1	x	(x)	x

Unicode characters

It used to be the case that streams read data from files in bytes. For example, there are lots of old files in ASCII format that use a byte for each character. However, Java and modern operating systems use Unicode for representing (international) characters, with two bytes per character. For many of the classes described there are also Unicode versions designated *Readers* (e.g. *FileReader, FilterReader, LineNumberReader, BufferedReader,* etc.). If the data retrieved from an InputStream needs to be interpreted as Unicode characters of type *char* for instance, then you should use an object of type *InputStreamReader*. The constructor call of *InputStreamReader* has a reference to *InputStream* as argument from which the data is obtained:

```
InputStreamReader diStream =
    new DataInputStream (lniStream);
```

```
┌─────────────────────────────────────┐
│              Reader                  │
│            {abstract}                │
├─────────────────────────────────────┤
│+read()                               │
│+read(buffer : char[])                │
│+read(buffer: byte[], offset: int, length: int)│
│+close()                              │
│+ready()                              │
│+skip(anz : long)                     │
│+mark(int)                            │
│+reset()                              │
│...                                   │
└─────────────────────────────────────┘
```

Figure 7.7 *The Reader class*

Read buffer

If the data flow still needs to be buffered because the data originates from a slow data source or from a source supplying data at an erratic rate such as a file or network, it is a good idea to also use a *BufferedReader*. This is based on a Reader, and so must be generated with a Reader as the constructor argument.

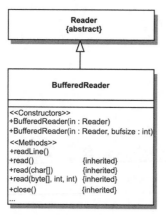

Figure 7.8 *The BufferedReader class*

The following program outputs the contents of a text file on the standard console (similar to the `type` command in DOS):

```java
import java.io.*;
public class Type
{
    public static void main(String[] args)
    {
        File aFile;
```

```
   String line;
FileInputStream fiStream;
  InputStreamReader isReader;
  BufferedReader bufReader;
  if (args.length > 0) aFile = new File(args[0]);
  else
  {
     System.out.println("Usage: Type <textfile>");
     return;
  }
  try
  {
     fiStream = new FileInputStream(file);
     isReader = new InputStreamReader(fiStream);
     bufReader = new BufferedReader(isReader);
     line= bufReader.readLine();
     while (line != null)
     {
        System.out.println(line);
       line= bufReader.readLine();
     }
  }
  catch (FileNotFoundException e)
  {
     System.out.println("The file " +
        afile.toString() + " could " +
        "not be found!");
  }
  catch (IOException e)
  {
     System.out.println("IOException!");
  }
  }
}
```

Tip The Micro Edition only includes the *Reader* class and the *InputStreamReader* derived from it.

7.1.5 Serialization ObjectInput/OutputStream

So far we have only read characters or character strings. However, with Java you can also write and read Java objects with all their attributes. If another object is referenced in an instance variable, this is also saved. The *Serializable* interface must be implemented to save objects (*Serialization*).

The Serializable interface

from	SE	ME	EE
1.1	x	-	x

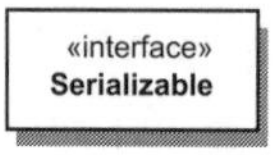

```
«interface»
Serializable
```

Figure 7.9   *The Serializable interface*

Serializable objects can be saved in files or transferred over networks. It must be possible to convert them into a byte format for the purpose. The marking interface *Serializable* identifies a class as serializable. Like *Cloneable* (see Section 6.1.2), no methods need to be implemented for this, but all referenced classes must be serializable, otherwise a *NotSerializableException* is generated. If you do not want to use the standard serialization mechanism, you can override the `writeObject()` and `readObject()` methods.

The ObjectInputStream class

from	SE	ME	EE
1.1	x	-	x

ObjectInputStream has an *InputStream* as constructor parameter. A serialized object is read using the `readObject()` method and then converted to a suitable type by casting. The class also provides methods for reading primitive data types.

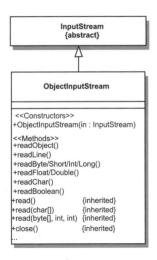

Figure 7.10 *The ObjectInputStream class*

The following extract of code first reads the number of date objects of class *Date* from a file, and then reads them out in series.

```
FileInputStream fiStream = new FileInputStream(aFile);
ObjectInputStream oinStream =
   new ObjectInputStream(fiStream);
if (oinStream != null)    // File found
{
   // Read number of objects and create array:
   int num = oinStream.readInt();
   Date[] date = new Date[num];
   for (int i=0; i<num; i++)
   {
      date[i] = (Date) oinStream.readObject();
   }
}
oinStream.close();
fiStream.close();
```

> **Warning** Exception handling has been omitted for the sake of simplicity (see Chapter 11). There are yet more exceptions that can arise when reading objects, for instance a *ClassNotFoundException* is generated if an object is read with a type whose class definition cannot be found.

The ObjectOutputStream class

from	SE	ME	EE
1.1	x	-	x

Data and objects that can be read must once have been saved. There are a set of *OutputStream* classes for the purpose that correspond to the *InputStream* classes. Use the *ObjectOutputStream* to write objects.

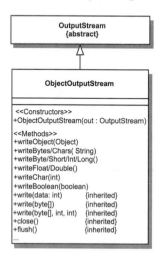

Figure 7.11   *The ObjectOutputStream class*

Methods

This stream is based on a different *OutputStream* depending on the purpose. After instantiation you can output different (serializable) data types using different `write` methods. You can output strings with `writeBytes()` or `writeChars()`, depending on what display format you want. The `writeObject()` method takes any serializable object, converts it to a byte format and outputs it in the *OutputStream*. It is important after writing the data to call the `flush()` method, which clears the write buffer. You should also call `close()` once you have finished all write operations.

Here is the central code section for saving the data imported in the earlier example in the same format.

```
ObjectOutputStream ooutStream =
    new ObjectOutputStream(aFileOutStream);
[...]
ooutStream.writeInt(date.length);
for (int i = 0; i < date.length; i++)
{
    ooutStream.writeObject(date[i]);
}
ooutStream.flush();
ooutStream.close();
```

> **Warning** *ObjectInput/OutputStreams* are based on whatever *Input/OutputStreams* you like. They can even be used for transferring serialized objects over networks. In this case you replace the *FileInput/OutputStreams* with *SocketStreams* (see Section 7.2.2).
> → I would urge caution when serializing objects. Firstly you should make sure that the existence of objects stays consistent, i.e. several copies of the same object should not exist at a critical time. Secondly, you should consider what will happen to objects that are referenced by an object for serialization. Normally these objects would also be serialized.
> → You can attach the transient modifier to attributes that you do not want serialized with an object.
> If the object behavior is meant to be implemented differently in serialization, then the following two methods should be created:
> ```
>     private void writeObject(ObjectOutputStream out)
>         throws IOException
>     private void readObject(ObjectInputStream in)
>         throws IOException, ClassNotFoundException
> ```

7.1.6   Writing to files – FileOutputStream

from	SE	ME	EE
1.0	x	-	x

Although it is quite possible to output complex data types using a high-level class, this must still be based on a low-level stream that allows byte-wise writing to a particular destination, for instance to a file or via a pipe to another computer. The *FileOutputStream* class is used for creating files and providing write access.

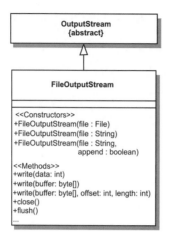

Figure 7.12 *The FileOutputStream class*

Warning The destination file is specified as a file name or File object for the constructor. If this file does not yet exist, then it is created when first accessed. If the file already exists, then its contents are deleted at the first access and the file overwritten. So you must exercise extreme caution when working with *FileOutputStream*!

There are two options for preventing the file contents being overwritten.

→ If you want to add the new data to the end of an existing file, you can use a constructor that specifies the *append* mode as a boolean flag.

→ If you just want to check whether the file already exists, first create an object of the *File* class (see Section 7.1.2) and then ask after the file using `exists()`. You can then use the *FileOutputStream* constructor that has the *File* object for a parameter.

In the earlier example we used an *ObjectOuputStream* for writing. However this on its own will not work because it is only based on another *OutputStream*. If you need to write to a file then this is typically a *FileOuputStream*:

```
File newFile = new File("data.dat");
if (newFile.exists())
    System.out.println("The file already exists.");
else
{
    FileOutputStream aFileOutStream =
        new FileOutputStream(newFile);
```

```
ObjectOutputStream ooutStream =
    new ObjectOutputStream(aFileOutStream);
...  // Writing the data as in the example above
aFileOutStream.close();
}
```

Closing streams

FileInputStream objects can be deleted without a problem by the Garbage Collector when leaving the area of validity in which they were defined. With *OutputStream* objects however (particularly in buffered outputs), you need to ensure that these are closed in a valid way by including a flush statement for clearing the buffer. The method for this purpose is close(), which contains an implicit flush() call. Any data still in the stream chain might otherwise be lost if the object were deleted.

7.1.7   The OutputStream and PrintStream classes

from	SE	ME	EE
1.0	x	x	x

With *FileOutputStream* objects you are only working at the byte level. However, like the *InputStream* objects, there are also high-level classes such as the *ObjectOutputStream* already dealt with in Section 7.1.5, the *BufferedOutputStream* or the *DataOutputStream*, which supports elementary data types and strings (see Figure 7.13). All OutputStreams are based on the common abstract *OutputStream* base class, which provides operations for writing individual bytes, for clearing the buffer (flush()) and closing the stream.

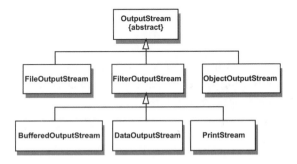

Figure 7.13 *OutputStream hierarchy*

The PrintStream class

Although the classes dealt with so far provide the facility to write various data types, you have yet to meet a polymorphous class with a method to which you can pass an object of any data type whatever.

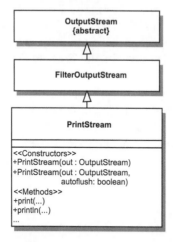

Methods

The *PrintStream* class fulfills this requirement with the `print()` and `println()` methods, which are defined both for elementary data types and references. When you pass any object, this method calls the `toString` method for the object (see Section 6.1.1) and outputs this String representation. `println()` performs a new-line command after the output. By using the `auto-flush` parameter in one of the constructors you can force automatic flushing after every method call.

System.out

The `print()` and `println()` methods are obviously familiar because we have used them many times already for writing to the standard output. In fact the `out` class variable of the *System* class is of type *PrintStream*.

Warning The *PrintStream* class should not be used in your own programs, however, as Sun has declared this class and its constructors as deprecated since JDK 1.1. You should instead use the *PrintWriter* class which has an identical functionality.

7.1.8 Writing with Writer classes

from	SE	ME	EE
1.1	x	x	x

If you want to output 16-bit coded Unicode character data, then you use a reference of type *Writer* or one of the classes derived from it. The *Writer* class works in the same way as the *Reader* class, but in the reverse sense. A *Writer* object is based on an *OutputStream* object that as always must be specified when creating the instance.

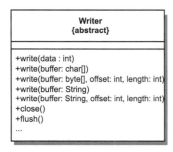

Writer
{abstract}

+write(data : int)
+write(buffer: char[])
+write(buffer: byte[], offset: int, length: int)
+write(buffer: String)
+write(buffer: String, offset: int, length: int)
+close()
+flush()
...

Figure 7.15 *The Writer class*

Like the *OutputStream* classes, there is a series of high-level classes derived from the *Writer* class (see Figure 7.1.6).

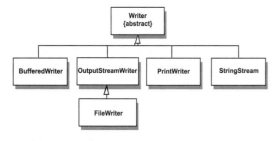

Figure 7.16 *Writer hierarchy*

7.1.9 The DataInput and DataOutput interfaces

from	SE	ME	EE
1.0	x	x	x

The *DataInput* interface provides methods for reading elementary data types (see Section 4.8.2), while *DataOutput* provides similar methods for writing. You can look up the individual methods in Section 7.1.5 under the *ObjectInput-*

Stream and *ObjectOutputStream* classes that implement these interfaces. Another implementing class pair is *DataInput/OutputStream*, although these only have use of a subset of the ObjectStream functions. These are therefore only worth using when the ObjectStream functions are not available in the current runtime environment (e.g. in the Micro Edition).

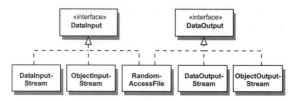

Figure 7.17 *The DataInput and DataOutput interfaces*

Tip The *RandomAccessFile* class combines read/write and file operations in one class, and therefore includes some overloading. It is discussed in more detail in Section 7.1.12.

7.1.10   The FileReader and FileWriter classes

from	SE	ME	EE
1.1	x	x	x

FileReader and *FileWriter* are the equivalent classes to *FileInputStream* (see Section 7.1.3) and *FileOutputStream* (see Section 7.1.6), but like all *Reader/Writer* classes process 16-bit Unicode characters.

The FileReader class

The *FileReader* class does not provide any extra functionality compared with its byte-oriented counterpart *FileInputStream*. Unlike the other *Reader* classes, however, this need not be based on another *Reader* class. It is therefore better suited as a low-level stream for Unicode streams (see Section 7.1.11).

The FileWriter class

The same applies to the *FileWriter* class, but unlike the *OutputStreams* you can use it to write strings directly to a file (in addition to characters of type *char*), which saves you the bother of nesting streams (see Section 7.1.11).

7.1.11   Nesting and summary

Low-level and high-level

We have now learnt about numerous classes that themselves are normally nested inside each other at runtime. In order to understand how they interact it helps to think of access as a two-stage process. A low-level stream is selected for byte-wise or character-wise reading from a specific source or for writing to a specific destination. For example this might be a file or even a TCP/IP socket (see Section 7.2.2). On top of this sits a high-level stream that can handle Java data types and, for instance, can read lines as strings or even read complex serialized Java objects. If you then want to change a program to allow network access, for example, instead of accessing the local hard disk, there is no need for you to change the application logic. All you need to change is the low-level stream. If the source or destination is not reliable or not fast enough, you can also insert a buffer in the stream.

Summary

Task	Type	Input	Output
Accessing files	Low level	*FileInputStream/FileReader*	*FileOutputStream/File-Writer*
Accessing pipes/threads	Low level	*PipedInputStream/Reader*	*PipedOutputStream/Writer*
Reading/writing data of elementary data type	High level	*DataInputStream*	*DataOutputStream*
Reading/writing objects	High level	*ObjectInputStream*	*ObjectOutputStream*
Writing any types to text output	High level	–	*PrintStream*
Buffering streams	Filter	*BufferedInputStream/BufferedReader*	*BufferedOutputStream/BufferedWriter*
Noting line numbers	Filter	*LineNumberInputStream/LineNumberReader*	–
Read-ahead (reading in advance with push-back)	Filter	*PushbackInputStream/PushbackReader*	–

Tip Whether you should use the Reader/Writer or Input/OutputStream version for a particular case depends on whether you want to read or write Unicode characters or bytes.

TAKE THAT!

Stream classes in other packages

In addition to these classes in the *java.io* package there are also other stream classes sorted into other packages according to subject.

Task	Type	Input	Output
Accessing TCP sockets	Low level	java.net.SocketInputStream	java.net.SocketOutput-Stream
Calculating checksum	Filter	java.util.zip.CheckedInput-Stream	java.util.zip.Checked-OutputStream
Data compression	Filter	java.util.zip.ZipInputStream	java.util.zip.ZipOutput-Stream
Reading/writing Java archives	Filter	java.util.jar.JarInputStream	java.util.jar.JarOutput-Stream
Writing HTML	High level	(via parser)	javax.swing.text.html.HTMLWriter
Reading/writing audio data	High level	javax.sound.sampled.spi.AudioFileReader, javax.sound.sampled.AudioInputStream, javax.sound.midi.spi.MidiFileReader	javax.sound.sampled.spi.AudioFileWriter, javax.sound.midi.spi.MidiFileWriter

7.1.12   Parsing with RandomAccessFile and StreamTokenizer

The following classes can be used to read and write to structured files. With a *Tokenizer* you can split a file back down into its syntactic components. For instance HTML or XML files are structured in this way, as well as C and Java sources.

The RandomAccessFile class

from	SE	ME	EE
1.0	x	-	x

C programmers will probably miss direct access to specific positions in files. The solution for this in Java is provided by the *RandomAccessFile* class. This class implements both the *DataInput* interface and the *DataOutput* interface (see Section 7.1.9) with its own methods.

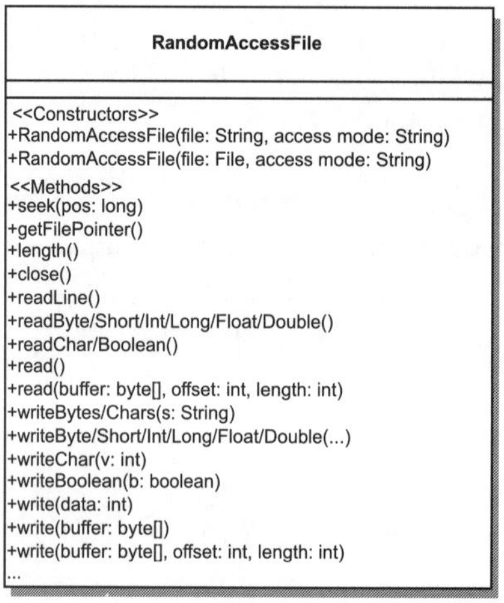

```
┌─────────────────────────────────────────────────┐
│              RandomAccessFile                     │
├─────────────────────────────────────────────────┤
│ <<Constructors>>                                  │
│ +RandomAccessFile(file: String, access mode: String)
│ +RandomAccessFile(file: File, access mode: String)
│                                                   │
│ <<Methods>>                                       │
│ +seek(pos: long)                                  │
│ +getFilePointer()                                 │
│ +length()                                         │
│ +close()                                          │
│ +readLine()                                       │
│ +readByte/Short/Int/Long/Float/Double()           │
│ +readChar/Boolean()                               │
│ +read()                                           │
│ +read(buffer: byte[], offset: int, length: int)   │
│ +writeBytes/Chars(s: String)                      │
│ +writeByte/Short/Int/Long/Float/Double(...)       │
│ +writeChar(v: int)                                │
│ +writeBoolean(b: boolean)                         │
│ +write(data: int)                                 │
│ +write(buffer: byte[])                            │
│ +write(buffer: byte[], offset: int, length: int)  │
│ ...                                               │
└─────────────────────────────────────────────────┘
```

Figure 7.18   *The RandomAccessFile class*

Methods

The *RandomAccessFile* class is instantiated either with the constructor

`RandomAccessFile (String aFile, String accessMode),`

or with

`RandomAccessFile (File aFile, String accessMode),`

The second parameter defines the type of file access. If the second parameter has the value "r" then the file is only opened for reading, while "rw" stands for read/write access. The `seek(long)` method sets the *FilePointer* – a kind of read/write offset – to the specified position. Reading or writing is performed from this position onwards when one of the `read()` or `write()` methods is called (or any of their variants). `getFilePointer()` returns the current position of the *FilePointer*.

The StreamTokenizer class

from	SE	ME	EE
1.0	x	-	x

The *StreamTokenizer* class is also suitable for parsing structured files. A *StreamTokenizer* object is based on an *InputStream* object or a *Reader* object, and provides the programmer with a facility for reading the imported data in separate parts, called *Tokens*. A set of specific *char* values are interpreted as delimiters when reading the stream.

Delimiters

```
┌─────────────────────────────────────┐
│           StreamTokenizer            │
├─────────────────────────────────────┤
│ +sval : String                      │
│ +nval : double                      │
├─────────────────────────────────────┤
│ <<Constructors>>                    │
│ +StreamTokenizer(in: InputStream)   │
│ +StreamTokenizer(in: Reader)        │
│ <<Methods>>                         │
│ +nextToken()                        │
│ +toString()                         │
│ +lineno()                           │
│ +pushBack()                         │
│ +ordinaryChar(ch: int)              │
│ +ordinaryChars(low: int, hi: int)   │
│ +whitespaceChars(low: int, hi: int) │
│ +commentChar(ch: int)               │
│ +quoteChar(ch: int)                 │
│ +wordChars(low: int, hi: int)       │
│ +lowerCaseMode(b: boolean)          │
│ ...                                 │
└─────────────────────────────────────┘
```

Figure 7.19 *The StreamTokenizer class*

The `whitespaceChars(int, int)` method lets you define delimiters. All characters lying between two delimiters are taken to be tokens.

Token

The `nextToken()` method returns an *int* value. This value indicates among other things whether the token that has been read can be interpreted as a numerical value. The value of the token that has been read is obtained from accessing the `sval` or `nval` fields declared as public. Which field is accessed depends on whether you want to read a string or a numerical value respectively. Using `pushBack()` you can place the token that has been read back in the stream.

Additional methods

The *StreamTokenizer* class provides far greater functionality than has been described here. For instance you can also specify comment characters, string delimiters or characters to be ignored.

> **Tip** Further classes for parsing structured files are included in other packages. *java.text* and *javax.swing.text* are suitable for structured and formatted texts, *javax.swing.text.html* for the HTML format (Hypertext Markup Language), and *javax.swing.text.rtf* for RTF (Rich Text Format).

7.1.13   IOExceptions

Many operations during input/output can lead to error situations. As an example, consider a program that has write access to a network drive. If the computer on which the drive is physically located is disconnected from the network during operation, then the write process must be terminated with an error message. The general class for exceptions in *java.io* is called *IOException* and is inherited by a series of more specialized classes (see Figure 7.20).

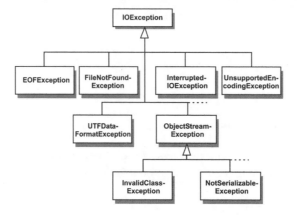

Figure 7.20   *Exceptions in the java.io package*

Often you catch the *IOException* globally (see Chapter 11) and do not classify it into separate errors. However there are situations where more detailed handling makes sense.

Accessing files

If you are reading from files, the specified file may not be found, which results in a *FileNotFoundException*. If you try to read beyond the end of the file, you receive an *EOFException*.

Serialization

Serializable objects are saved in files or transferred over networks. It must be possible to convert them into a byte format for the purpose. If one of the referenced classes does not implement the *Serializable* interface, then a *NotSerializableException* is thrown. If you try to read an object of a specific type although the stream contains an object of a different type, this results in an *InvalidClassException* or *ClassNotFoundException*. Another reason for an *InvalidClassException* may be that the class version that has been read is not compatible with that for writing.

7.1.14 Input/output and security

File access is subject to various protection mechanisms. For instance the underlying operating system may have assigned the permissions to the user that block read or write access. In addition there are also the security policies of Java (see Section 10.5).

In the sandbox model of Java 1.0 and 1.1, all file accesses from unsigned applets are prohibited (see Section 9.3). This is also the default setting since Java 1.2. Unauthorized access attempts result in *SecurityExceptions*.

You can use the `canRead()` and `canWrite()` methods of the *File* class to test whether access is allowed.

The FilePermission class

from	SE	ME	EE
1.2	x	-	x

Java 1.2 introduced a fine structure to this access protection, with every type of resource having a permission that can be set in the user settings. For files this is the *FilePermission* class.

The class recognizes the following permission types (*actions*):

→ *read*
→ *write*
→ *execute*
→ *delete*

> **Tip** The default definitions for these permissions are held in the file
> `<JRE PATH>\LIB\SECURITY\JAVA.POLICY`, and can be edited with the *policytool* tool.

7.1.15 Notes on input/output

In our overview of the *java.io* package we have learnt about many aspects of input and output. There are, however, even more packages related to this topic.

Network and RMI

Network programming with sockets is based on streams, while *RMI* (Remote Method Invocation) uses serialization for object transfer. We look at these topics more closely in Section 7.2.

FileDialog class

The *java.awt* package (see Section 8.2), which mainly contains graphics control elements, includes a *FileDialog* class (see Section 8.2.11) that enables files and paths to be displayed and selected according to the type of runtime platform. This class also implements the *java.io.FilenameFilter* interface, which can be used to define specific name restrictions, for example selecting all files that end in ".html".

7.2 TCP/IP programming – java.net

The *java.net* package contains classes for programming TCP/IP network accesses. This (Internet) protocol forms the basis for all Java network accesses. Higher-level network protocols are based on this, such as RMI for remote method calls and distributed applications, and Enterprise JavaBeans for distributed objects.

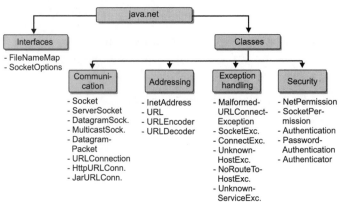

Figure 7.21 *Classes in the java.net package*

7.2.1 TCP/IP communication links

Communication between two computers using the TCP/IP network protocol can be handled via a *socket connection*. TCP/IP, the standard protocol for the Internet and many local area networks (LANs), uses a device ID called the IP address to identify all devices connected to the network. This ID consists of four bytes in string format separated by full stops. Each computer with an installed TCP/IP has (at least) one IP address which might, for instance, read:

```
122.153.2.102
```

Different devices cannot have the same IP address. IP addresses work like a zip code to find the message recipient. Often you can also use symbolic names of the type `webserver.nitty-gritty.uk.co`, which can be mapped onto the IP addresses.

For different programs (web browser, file transfer by ftp etc.) to be able to exchange data simultaneously on a computer with one IP address, each of these program uses its own channel for communication called a *port*. This port can have practically any number between 1 and 65,535.

> **Warning** Note when using ports that all numbers less than 1000 are either assigned to specific program types or are reserved, e.g. 80 for HTTP. It makes no difference to the application how high the port number is, but more than one program must never use the same port.

Two computers can either have a fixed connection (telephone principle) or send messages asynchronously (letter principle). The asynchronous messages are called datagrams in the Internet Protocol (IP).

7.2.2   The Socket and ServerSocket classes

from	SE	ME	EE
1.0	x	-	x

Sockets

A *socket* is the end-point of a communications link to a computer, and is identified by the IP address of the computer and a port number. You can use an object of the *Socket* class to transfer objects referenced as *InputStream* or *OutputStream* via TCP or protocols based on TCP.

Client/Server communication

If you need to set up a connection between two sockets (*socket connection*), then one computer must act as a server, which in this context can be referred to as the service provider. There must be at least one instance of a *ServerSocket* on this computer. The *ServerSocket* object is assigned a port number in its constructor, and waits – if required to do so – for requests to this server. Requests addressed to this computer but with a different port number, are ignored, because it is assumed that these are intended for a different program. The *ServerSocket* is only used for establishing a socket connection. The client computer or computers register with the server using a *Socket* instantiated on their side, whose port number must match that of the server program. If the server accepts the connection, then it will create an instance of *Socket* on its side.

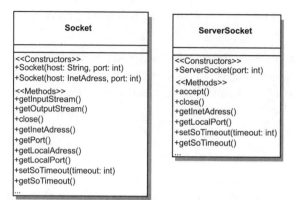

Figure 7.22 *The Socket and ServerSocket classes*

Communication sequence

On the client side you create an object of type *Socket*, specifying the server address and agreed port number. If you want to receive data from the server you get a reference of type `InputStream` for a read connection to the server by calling *getInputStream*; for sending data you do the same but with `getOutput-Stream()`. You can set up further streams on top of this stream depending on the type of data, for example *ObjectInput/OutputStreams* (see Section 7.1.5) or *DataInput/OutputStreams* (see Section 7.1.11).

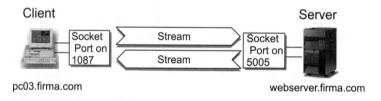

Figure 7.23 *Socket connection via streams*

```
Socket linkToServer = new Socket(serverHostname, 5005);
ObjectInputStream fromServer =
    new ObjectInputStream(linkToServer.getInputStream());
DataOutputStream toServer =
    new DataOutputStream(linkToServer.getOutputStream());
// Send object to server:
toServer.writeChars("getDate\n");

// Receive object from server:
Date d = (Date) fromServer.readObject();

fromServer.close();
toServer.close();
linkToServer.close();
```

> **Tip** The `getInputStream()` method is declared in such a way that you get a reference of the abstractly defined type *InputStream*. The actual type of the object remains hidden. This is typical of Java class libraries, because it is irrelevant to the user which low-level stream class the object belongs to. Any high-level or filter streams you want can be added to this to suit your requirements.
>
> The same applies to the *OutputStream*. In practice the *SocketInput / OutputStream* classes are used which in turn are packed in *BufferedInput/OutputStreams*.

Server

The server instantiates first of all a *ServerSocket* with the same port number that the client will later access. The constructor need not be given any server address, because a *ServerSocket* object can only ever be created for the actual computer it is on. Calling the `accept()` method places the server in the wait state until a client accesses this server and thereby establishes a socket connection. The connection is set up automatically, as soon as a client instantiates a *Socket* object. The `accept` call returns in this case a reference to an object of the *Socket* class, which is used for communication between client and server.

TAKE THAT!

```
ServerSocket server = new ServerSocket(portNumber);
Socket linkToClient = server.accept();
// Link to client established;
BufferedReader fromClient = new BufferedReader(
  new InputStreamReader(linkToClient.getInputStream()));
ObjectOutputStream toClient =
  new ObjectOutputStream(linkToClient.getOutputStream());
// Read client request
String req = fromClient.readLine();
if (req.equals("getDate"))
{
   Date d = new Date();
   // Send object to client:
   toClient.writeObject(d);
}
fromClient.close();
toClient.close();
linkToClient.close();
```

Exceptions

Exception handling has been omitted in this example (see Chapter 11). In a real application the following exceptions might arise requiring appropriate handling:

1 *UnknownHostException*, if no computer can be reached under the host name.

2 *SocketException* is the super class for a range of exceptions (*BindException, ConnectionException, NoRouteToHostException*) that indicate a connection cannot be established between the ports of the two computers because of network problems. For example, the required client port might already be occupied by another application, or the server does not respond on the specified port (`SocketException: Connection refused`).

3 *IOExceptions* can also occur, because network communication is based on the *java.io* classes.

Warning Unsigned applets have the restriction that network connections can only be established with the server that downloaded the applet. This means that you can communicate with this server on all ports (allowed by the firewall), but if you try to establish a connection to other computers you would get a *SecurityException*.

TAKE THAT!

Drawbacks

Socket connections are rooted way down in the TCP/IP protocol stack, and so constitute a primitive, but also very fast type of communication. The developer, however, must personally tackle numerous problems of network programming:

→ Interruption and restoration of communication
→ Loss of data
→ Data format problems and serialization
→ Conversion of object-oriented calls into channels that only transport bytes
→ Encoding of a communication link.

All these drawbacks mean higher protocols are normally used, such as RMI, CORBA, or Enterprise JavaBeans, which provide solutions to these problems and so make the programmer's job easier. For instance with RMI we could send our `getDate` directly to the server as a method call, and would then get the *Date* object back as a result, without having to tackle streams.

The following design is worth adopting if you want to write a server application that serves more than one client:

→ Place the server in an endless loop that stays in the `accept` state of a *ServerSocket* with a port number known to all clients, until a new client registers itself.
→ A new client receives from the server over this channel a new, exclusive port number for communication with the server.
→ The server generates a separate thread for a new client and waits for the client in this thread using the `accept()` of a new *ServerSocket*.
→ The client constructs another socket connection – this time a dedicated socket connection – to the server on the port it was given by the server.

7.2.3   Datagrams

So far we have discussed *Sockets* for synchronous, connection-based communication (socket connection) in Java; but Java also provides support for the connectionless datagram service. You can think of datagrams as letters that are sent to an addressee. The sender posts off the message, but does not know when or even if it arrives.

TAKE THAT!

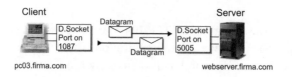

Figure 7.24 *Datagrams*

Tip Like the TCP protocol, the UDP datagram protocol is also based on the IP Internet protocol, and uses its services for addressing and data transfer.

The DatagramSocket and DatagramPacket classes

from	SE	ME	EE
1.0	x	-	x

An object of the *DatagramSocket* class can send data packets, or rather *datagrams*, using `send()`, and receive them with `receive()`. The datagrams themselves are objects of type *DatagramPacket*, which contain data in byte format.

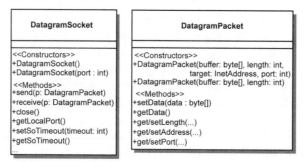

Figure 7.25 *The DatagramSocket and DatagramPacket classes*

Server:

```
//Create data packet:
byte[] buffer = (new String("TestData")).getBytes();
DatagramPacket data =
   new DatagramPacket(buffer, buffer.length,
                      destAddress, destPort);
// Create sender:
DatagramSocket sender = new DatagramSocket();
sender.send(data); // Send data
sender.close();
```

Client:

```
//Create empty data packet:
byte[] buffer = new byte[256];
DatagramPacket data =
   new DatagramPacket(buffer, buffer.length);
// Create recipient:
DatagramSocket recipient = new DatagramSocket(portNo);
recipient.receive(data); // wait for incoming data
buffer = data.getData();  // Extract data
String read = new String(buffer);
recipient.close();
```

Tip Error handling has not been included in the example. The same errors can occur as for sockets (see Section 7.2.2).

Tip It is easy to test network applications locally: "localhost" serves as a symbolic name for the given computer, and the loop-back address for packets not meant to leave the computer is 127.0.0.1.

The MulticastSocket class

from	SE	ME	EE
1.1	x	-	x

You can use the *MulticastSocket* class to send datagrams to groups of computers as well.

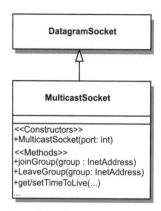

```
┌─────────────────────────────────┐
│       DatagramSocket            │
└─────────────────────────────────┘
                △
                │
┌─────────────────────────────────┐
│       MulticastSocket           │
├─────────────────────────────────┤
│ <<Constructors>>                │
│ +MulticastSocket(port: int)     │
│ <<Methods>>                     │
│ +joinGroup(group : InetAddress) │
│ +LeaveGroup(group: InetAddress) │
│ +get/setTimeToLive(...)         │
│ ...                             │
└─────────────────────────────────┘
```

Figure 7.26   *The MulticastSocket class*

Methods

This class is derived from the conventional *DatagramSocket* class, and sends packets to an IP address in the specially reserved address space between 224.0.0.1 and 239.255.255.255 inclusive. A computer can join or leave a group identified by an address in this range using the methods `joinGroup()` and `leaveGroup()` respectively. If you then send a datagram to this group, all members of the group will receive it.

Tip The *MulticastSocket* class is similar to a publish and subscribe system. Registered users receive the information, others not, and the sender need not bother about anything after sending it. This service is very primitive, however, and cannot be compared with a professional message queuing system. For instance, you can only send bytes, not objects with datagrams; also there are no security mechanisms or other quality-of-service definitions for distribution. However, there is an optional messaging service in the Java 2 Enterprise Edition, whose interface is defined in the *javax.jms* package.

Datagrams in the Micro Edition

from	SE	ME	EE
Beta	-	x	-

The Java 2 Micro Edition does not actually include the *java.net* package, although it does contain a simplified version called *javax.microedition.io*. The *Datagram* interface included in this version combines the *DatagramSocket* and *DatagramPacket* classes.

```
            «Interface»
            Datagram

+setData(buffer: byte[],
   offset:int, length: int)
+getData()
+get/setLength(...)
+get/setAddress(...)
...
```

Figure 7.27 *The Datagram interface*

> **Tip** In this case *InetAddress* objects are not used for addressing, just simple strings.

7.2.4 Addresses, resources, and URLs

The InetAddress class

from	SE	ME	EE
1.0	x	-	x

Up to now we have used IP addresses or the symbolic host name for identifying computers. While host names are represented in Java by simple String objects, you use objects of the *InetAddress* class to specify IP addresses. This measure ensures that you can only create syntactically correct address objects.

```
         InetAddress

+getLocalHost()
+getByName(host: String)
+getHostAdress()
+getHostName()
+getAdress()
+toString()
+equals()
```

Figure 7.28 *The InetAddress class*

Methods

The *InetAddress* class has no (public) constructor. An object of this class tends to be generated by calling the static methods `getLocalHost()` or `getByName(hostname)`. The latter method tries to resolve the symbolic name into the address format, e.g. to convert the software IP name `pc02.firma.com` into 192.145.32.5. Using `getHostAddress()` and `getHostName()`, respectively, you can obtain both formats as strings.

The URL class

from	SE	ME	EE
1.0	x	-	x

In the WWW, resources are identified using URLs (*Universal Resource Locators*). A URL starts with a protocol name, for example `http` (HTML), `file` (local files), `ftp` (file transfer), `rmi` (Remote Method Invocation), `iiop` (Internet Inter ORB Protocol) or `jdbc` (Java Database Connectivity). After the protocol comes a colon followed by two forward slashes and, optionally, a host name or a host address and port number. If the computer is not specified, the current computer (local host) is used; known default port numbers are used when no port number is given. Finally the resource name is specified, typically with a path.

```
http://www.nitty-gritty.co.uk/java/index.html
file:///c:/jdk12/docs/index.html
ftp://125.65.3.107/public/download/updates
jdbc:db2://dbserver:8008/sampledb
```

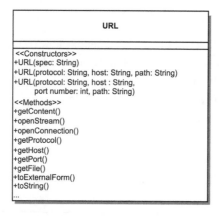

Figure 7.29 *The URL class*

Methods

Since the URLs must conform to a fixed structure, a Java class called *URL* is provided for the purpose. The constructor lets you generate the object as a string or from the name components. You should include here exception handling for the *MalformedURLException*, which displays invalid URLs. This is also defined in the *java.net* package. The separate parts of the URL can be retrieved using `get` methods (`getProtocol()`, `getHost()`, `getPort()`, `getFile()`). Finally, `toString()` calls `toExternalForm()` and returns the whole URL as a character string.

You can access the contents of the resource behind the URL using the `getContent()`, `openConnection()`, or `openStream()` methods, depending on the type of resource.

`getContent()` is a convenient means of downloading objects behind the URL. The download process identifies the type from the extension (".txt", ".gif" etc.) and returns an object of a sub-class for accessing the file, e.g. *PlainTextInputStream* for a text file or *URLImageSource* for a picture.

`openConnection()` returns a suitable connection depending on the protocol for downloading an object, e.g. *FileURLConnection* for reading from local files or *HttpURLConnection* for access using the HTTP protocol. `openStream()` does the same, opening an *InputStream* immediately in this new connection, and returning this.

URLs and applets

URLs are also used in web browsers for identifying websites and resources. An applet can use the `getDocumentBase()` method to retrieve a *URL* object from the page from which it was downloaded.

By using URLs in an applet running in a browser, you can also reference another document and display it in the browser. To do this you need a reference to the browser and you can then display the page in the browser using `showDocument(WebSiteURL)`. The following example shows an applet having a URL as a parameter, which when run in the web browser immediately displays the page specified with this URL in the current browser window.

TAKE THAT!

```
public class RedirectorApplet extends java.applet.Applet
{
    // Method start, all other methods can
    // remain unchanged
    public void start()
    {
        // the destination address is held in the URL
        // parameter
        // in the applet tag for the HTML page
        String destination = getParameter("URL");
        try
        {
            URL destURL = new URL(destination);
            getAppletContext().showDocument(destURL);
        }
        catch (java.net.MalformedURLException e)
        {
            System.out.println("URL " + destination +
                            " is invalid ");
        }
    }
}
```

Tip There is an even more versatile version of the showDocument(URL document, string frame) method. Here the second parameter can specify the name of the frame in which the document should be displayed. The constant "_self" specifies the frame of the applet, "_top" the main frame, while "_blank" can be used to display the document in a new browser window.

The URLConnection class and derived classes

from	SE	ME	EE
1.0	x	-	x

You can set up a *URLConnection* by calling the openConnection() method of a URL object. This object lets you read the contents of the resource as well as providing information on the type of the object. The abstract *URLConnection* is implemented by different concrete classes depending on the type of the object and the protocol, for example *HttpURLConnection, AppletResourceConnection, FileURLConnection, FtpURLConnection* or *MailToURLConnection*.

You normally access a *URLConnection* or one of its sub-classes via the open-Connection() call of a *URL* object. If you only want to read the contents as an object or as a stream, then the getContent() or openStream() methods of *URL* suffice, which themselves lead through method calls in URLConnection (see Figure 7.30).

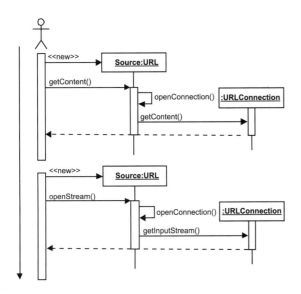

URLConnection also provides a facility for retrieving information about the resource, such as its length, date etc. The *ContentType* is particularly important here, which identifies the type of resource and how it is handled as an object. It is specified as an MIME type (standard for Internet mail extension). Examples are text/plain, text/html, image/gif or application/zip.

Later Java versions contain more specific implementations for connections to resources. The *HttpURLConnection* (from Java 1.1 onwards, see Figure 7.31: the URLConnection class) adds a few methods for the HTTP protocol, for example get/setRequestMethod() to define the type of the request (PUT, GET etc.), or getResponseCode/Message() for processing return values. For instance the number 404 stands for a page that was not found. Constants have also been defined for the values to improve readability, e.g. HTTP_NOT_FOUND.

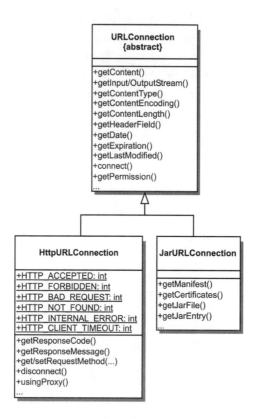

Figure 7.31 *The URLConnection class*

The *JarURLConnection* has been included since Java 1.2. This can be used to query the contents of a Java archive (see Section 4.10.5) and to retrieve information such as the manifest or certificates that it contains.

ContentConnections in the Micro Edition

from	SE	ME	EE
Beta	-	x	-

The Java 2 Micro Edition does not actually include the *java.net* package, although it does contain a simplified version called *javax.microedition.io*. This includes a *Connector* class that contains several class methods for creating *Connections*. *ContentConnection* is a special *Connection* that is a "light version" of *java.net.URLConnection*. You can use its methods to create Input/Output-Streams, and to query the length, type and encoding of the resource.

7.2.5 Network exceptions

Numerous problems can arise, even with network access. For instance a port might already be reserved by another application, or it might not be possible to access a computer. All exceptions in the *java.net* package are derived from the *IOException* in *java.io* (see Figure 7.32).

Often you catch the *IOException* globally (see Chapter 11) and do not classify it into separate errors. However there are situations where more detailed handling makes sense.

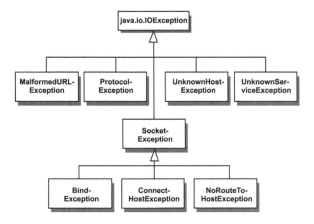

Figure 7.32 *Exceptions in the java.net package*

Accessing resources

If you are working with URLs then the compiler forces you to handle the *MalformedURLException* that arises if a URL does not have the correct structure, for instance it might be missing a component. An *UnknownHostException* occurs if the specified IP name cannot be resolved into an IP address.

Communication

Problems in the underlying TCP/IP protocol are signaled with exceptions of type *ProtocolException* or *SocketException*. A *BindException* normally arises if the local port that you want to access is already in use. The other sub-classes of the *SocketException* tend to indicate that something is wrong in the remote destination system or in the route to it.

7.2.6 Network access and security

Access procedures and network resources are subject to various protection mechanisms. One method is to prompt for manual authentication (e.g. user ID and password), another is to define specific IP addresses and ports in Java's security policies (see Section 10.5). Firewalls provide a further mechanism for restricting network traffic.

In the sandbox model of Java 1.0 and 1.1, any network accesses from unsigned applets (see Section 9.3) are only permitted if they are to the server from which the applet was downloaded. Unauthorized access attempts result in *SecurityExceptions*.

The SocketPermission class

from	SE	ME	EE
1.2	x	-	x

Java 1.2 introduced a fine structure to access protection, with every type of resource having a permission that can be configured in the user settings. For sockets this is the *SocketPermission* class.

This class recognizes the following permission types (*actions*):

→ *connect*: sets up connection
→ *resolve*: resolves address
→ *accept*: accepts incoming connections
→ *listen*: waits for incoming connections

```
SocketPermission("localhost:1024-8000",
                 "accept,connect,listen");
```

The NetPermission class and authentication

from	SE	ME	EE
1.2	x	-	x

In addition there is also a more general permission called *NetPermission*. It does not have its own permission types (*actions*), but does include a method for setting an *authenticator*.

The abstract *Authenticator* class and its *PasswordAuthenticator* sub-class are used for checking an access attempt to a resource. Usually the check involves entering a user ID and password. However you can use a different mechanism by deriving a class from the *Authenticator* class and overriding the method `getPasswordAuthentication()`.

> **Tip** The default definitions for these permissions are held in the file `<JRE PATH>\LIB\SECURITY\JAVA.POLICY`, and can be edited with the *policytool* tool.

7.3 Accessing databases – java.sql

The *java.sql* package contains all the classes and interfaces required for accessing relational databases. A large number of classes have been added in Java 2, but many databases still only support the old interfaces. The Enterprise Edition includes the *javax.sql* package for server applications with a large incidence of queries and where several data sources need to be managed.

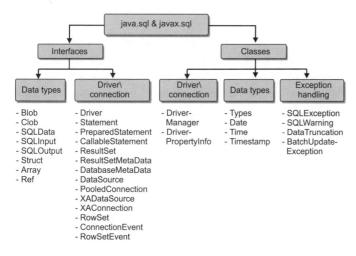

Figure 7.33 *Classes in the java.sql package*

7.3.1 JDBC

JDBC (Java DataBase Connectivity) is a defined interface to relational databases. It is based on the database language SQL (Structured Query Language). An intermediate layer screens the developer from the actual implementation of database accesses. This means that it makes no difference to the developer whether IBM's Universal Database/DB2 is used as the database server, or whether Oracle, Sybase, or Microsoft SQL is used – the programming interface is always the same. A database driver takes on the task of converting from JDBC to the relevant native interface of the database. Initially (JDBC 1.0) access was limited to the most important SQL data types. The JDBC 2.0 version introduced with Java 2 now also supports structured types and can provide simplified management of larger data sets.

This library only contains very rudimentary commands for managing database access, for instance establishing and releasing a connection, access protocols etc. *java.sql* consists largely of abstract interfaces specifying the API, but does not actually implement these itself.

JDBC drivers

The *java.sql* package contains mainly interfaces specifying access to the database. This is adequate for developing a database application, and JDBC's main advantage is that it does not depend on actual database implementations. The programs that are developed require a JDBC driver at runtime to implement the interfaces for the database used. These drivers tend to be included with the relevant database server or developer package, or must be obtained from a third-part supplier.

There are now JDBC drivers for practically every relational database, although there are still only a few that support Java 2.0. You can even have different drivers for the same database, for instance a driver for thin clients, which does not require a locally installed database client, and a slimmer version for computers that do have a database client.

JDBC-ODBC bridge

The PC platform has a database interface called ODBC (Open DataBase Connectivity) that is similar to JDBC. If there is no JDBC driver for your database, you can also work with a JDBC-ODBC bridge. This converts every JDBC command into an ODBC command, then passes it to the ODBC driver which in turn converts the command into a database command. These numerous conversions are very time consuming, however, so you cannot get good performance with this technique. You are always best off using a database with JDBC drivers.

7.3.2   Database access sequence

1   First a specific database driver that implements the *driver* interface is loaded via the *DriverManager*.

2   This allows a database connection (type *Connection*) to be set up.

3   In the next step an SQL command is packed in an object of type *Statement* and then executed.

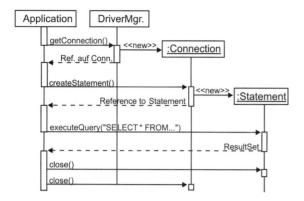

Figure 7.34 *With java.sql*

4   The result is usually an array of data records contained in a *ResultSet* object, which you can run through using iterators called *cursors*.

5   Finally the *Statement* and the *Connection* must be closed.

Drawbacks

Difficulties arise because the data in relational databases is not object oriented, but is based on tables, which means that it needs to be converted. In addition, the SQL data types are not the same as the Java types, so that conversion is also necessary here. This process is called *mapping*. There are a range of commercial tools and development environments available for the purpose, making database programming far simpler.

7.3.3   The DriverManager class

from	SE	ME	EE
1.0	x	-	x

This class serves as an interface between the abstract programming interfaces of *java.sql* and the actual database drivers.

First of all you must make known the drivers available on the computer. You can either specify the driver classes in the *jdbc.drivers* environment variable or load them explicitly using `Class.forName()`:

```
jdbc:drivers=sun.jdbc.odbc.JdbcOdbcDriver
```

or

```
Class.forName("COM.ibm.db2.jdbc.app.DB2Driver");
```

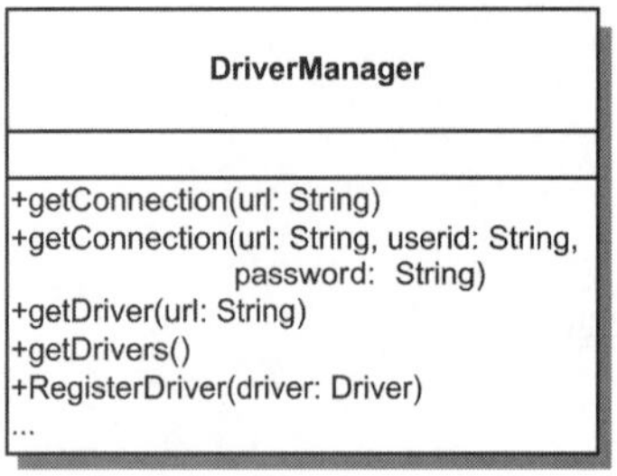

```
┌─────────────────────────────────────┐
│          DriverManager              │
├─────────────────────────────────────┤
│                                      │
├─────────────────────────────────────┤
│ +getConnection(url: String)         │
│ +getConnection(url: String, userid: String,│
│              password:  String)     │
│ +getDriver(url: String)             │
│ +getDrivers()                       │
│ +RegisterDriver(driver: Driver)     │
│ ...                                  │
└─────────────────────────────────────┘
```

Figure 7.35 *The DriverManager class*

Methods

If one or more drivers are available, you can set up a connection using `getConnection()`, with the destination database specified as a URL in this call. This string must have the following construction:

```
jdbc:<Subprotocol>:<localDBName>
jdbc:<Subprotocol>://<destinationComputer>:<port>/<destinationDBName>
```

The Subprotocol refers to the database driver used. This is followed by the name of a locally catalogued database or the address and optionally the port of a database on a server.

```
jdbc:odbc:AccountDatabase
jdbc:db2://dbserver:4567/AccountDatabase
```

The remaining methods are used for managing drivers.

7.3.4   The Connection interface

from	SE	ME	EE
1.0	x	-	x

This interface is the core interface for managing a database connection. You can use it to create database queries and to define and retrieve their attributes.

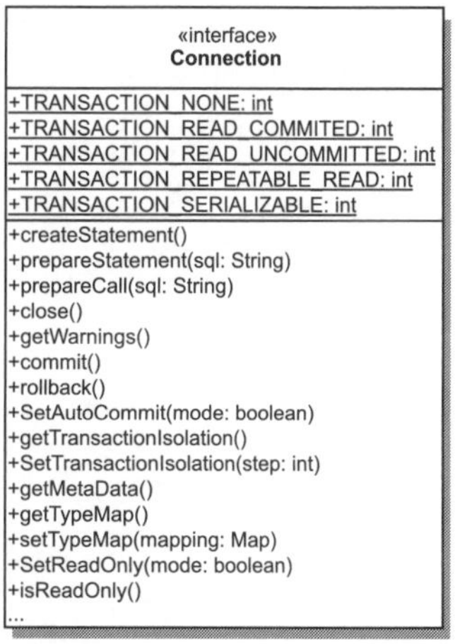

```
              «interface»
              Connection
+TRANSACTION_NONE: int
+TRANSACTION_READ_COMMITED: int
+TRANSACTION_READ_UNCOMMITTED: int
+TRANSACTION_REPEATABLE_READ: int
+TRANSACTION_SERIALIZABLE: int
+createStatement()
+prepareStatement(sql: String)
+prepareCall(sql: String)
+close()
+getWarnings()
+commit()
+rollback()
+SetAutoCommit(mode: boolean)
+getTransactionIsolation()
+SetTransactionIsolation(step: int)
+getMetaData()
+getTypeMap()
+setTypeMap(mapping: Map)
+SetReadOnly(mode: boolean)
+isReadOnly()
...
```

Figure 7.36 *The Connection interface*

Methods

The most important methods are those that create statements (for queries, changes etc., see Section 7.3.5). Once you no longer need the database connection, you must not forget to close it with close(). You can use getWarnings() to retrieve warning messages from the database. Errors can occur as *SQLExecptions* in most methods, and must be caught.

In addition there is a whole series of methods and constants for controlling transactions, in other words for protected execution of statements. A discussion of transaction control lies outside the scope of this book however.

```
Connection con =
DriverManager.getConnection("jdbc:odbc:AccountDatabase",
                        userID, password);
Statement stmt = con.createStatement();
```

7.3.5   Statement interfaces

from	SE	ME	EE
1.0	x	-	x

Statements contain SQL statements for the database, for example for retrieving, changing, inserting and deleting data records. You can save frequently used statements as *PreparedStatements*, and just assign the appropriate parameters as required. You can use *CallableStatements* to open stored procedures in the database.

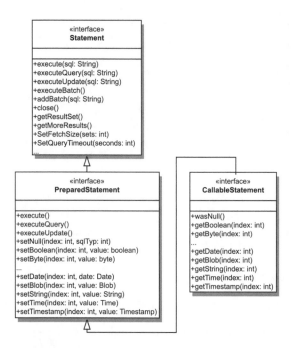

Figure 7.37 *Statement interfaces*

Methods

For read accesses (queries) you would normally use the executeQuery(sql) method, which returns a *ResultSet* object (a series of data records). For write accesses, i.e. the SQL commands INSERT, UPDATE and DELETE, you would use executeUpdate(sql). Statements must also be closed with close().

PreparedStatements are ideal for frequently recurring queries that only differ in the parameters of the SQL query. These are specified as question marks ("?") in the SQL statement. Before the query is executed you can assign the parameters using different set statements, for instance setByte(index, value), where the index is the number of the parameter being assigned.

Parameters are assigned in the same way in *CallableStatements*. However these do not normally return a *ResultSet*, but possess a series of output parameters that you can retrieve using get statements. wasNull() indicates whether there was no parameter assigned.

```
Statement stmt = con.createStatement();
String query = "SELECT * FROM ACCOUNT";
ResultSet rs = stmt.executeQuery(query);

PreparedStatement pStmt =
```

```
con.prepareStatement("SELECT * FROM ACCOUNT WHERE NR = ?");
pStmt.setInt(1, 643425600);
ResultSet pRs = pStmt.executeQuery();
```

7.3.6   ResultSet interfaces

from	SE	ME	EE
1.0	x	-	x

ResultSets contain the results of a database query. Generally they consist of several data records that you can run through using a cursor. The interface has been improved significantly by additions in JDBC 2.0 (see Figure 7.38).

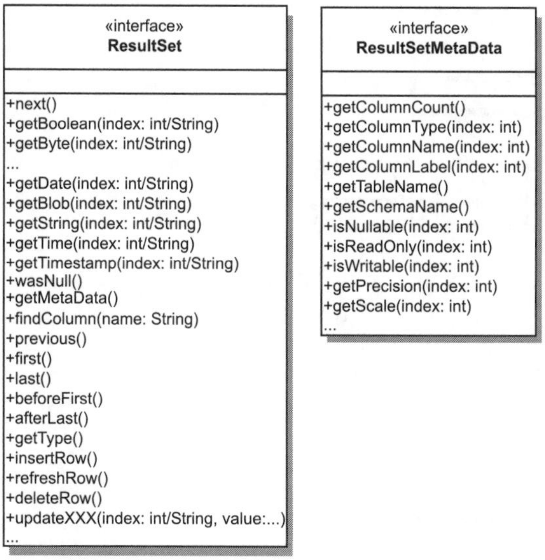

```
«interface»
ResultSet

+next()
+getBoolean(index: int/String)
+getByte(index: int/String)
...
+getDate(index: int/String)
+getBlob(index: int/String)
+getString(index: int/String)
+getTime(index: int/String)
+getTimestamp(index: int/String)
+wasNull()
+getMetaData()
+findColumn(name: String)
+previous()
+first()
+last()
+beforeFirst()
+afterLast()
+getType()
+insertRow()
+refreshRow()
+deleteRow()
+updateXXX(index: int/String, value:...)
...
```

```
«interface»
ResultSetMetaData

+getColumnCount()
+getColumnType(index: int)
+getColumnName(index: int)
+getColumnLabel(index: int)
+getTableName()
+getSchemaName()
+isNullable(index: int)
+isReadOnly(index: int)
+isWritable(index: int)
+getPrecision(index: int)
+getScale(index: int)
...
```

Figure 7.38   *The ResultSet interface*

Methods

Initially you access the first data record. Each next () method then moves the cursor one record further on so long as next () returns *true*. You can retrieve the individual values of a data record using various get statements, for example getByte(index) where the index represents either the number or name of the result column. wasNull () indicates whether there was a value assigned in the last column queried in the current database. If you need further information on a column, such as its name or SQL types (see Section 7.3.7), you can obtain this information as *ResultSetMetaData* using getMetaData ().

A navigable cursor has been added to *ResultSet* in JDBC 2.0. You can now use `first()`, `last()`, `previous()` and other methods to move freely about the result set. It is also possible now to change individual data records and save them back in the database.

7.3.7   SQL data types

SQL has a range of standard data types that do not match those in Java one to one. For example it has the VARCHAR type that designates a variable character area with a maximum number of characters, or CHAR, a character area of fixed length. The *Types* class contains constants for the SQL types. In addition there are the *Date*, *Time* and *Timestamp* classes for time values. In JDBC 2.0 there are even more classes for structured and generic types.

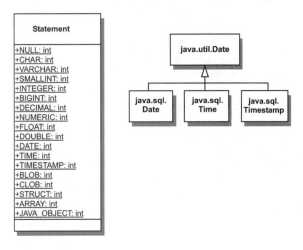

Figure 7.39 *SQL types under JDBC 1.0*

You can use the `getColumnType` method of an object of type *ResultSetMeta-Data* to retrieve the data types in a number format. However the number "12" does not exactly suggest the data type intuitively, so it is actually better to use the constants from *Types*, in this case `Types.VARCHAR` (see Figure 7.39).

The classes for the SQL time and date types are small wrappers around the *java.util.Date* standard class (see Section 10.1.2).

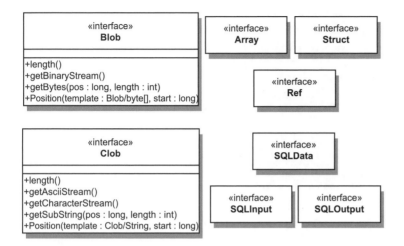

Figure 7.40 *New SQL types under JDBC 2.0*

JDBC 2.0 (see Figure 7.40) introduced support for some more up-to-date SQL types. *BLOBs* (*Binary Large OBjects*) and *CLOBs* (*Character Large OBjects*) are meant for large data sets. For instance a BLOB might contain a graphic, and a CLOB an HTML or XML document.

Array and *Struct* stand for structured types and *Ref* for persistent references to these, but you rarely meet these types in practice.

SQLData, *SQLInput* and *SQLOutput* are generic interfaces for converting the "user-defined types" of the database into Java data types. Normally you would not use these yourself.

7.4 Servlets – javax.servlet

from	SE	ME	EE
1.0	-	-	x

Servlets are a server-side architecture (see comparison in Chapter 13) that allow simple communication between simple clients (usually web browsers) and a web (application) server. Servlets tend to be used in conjunction with the HTTP protocol for generating dynamic HTML pages. Similar to Enterprise JavaBeans, Servlets require a special infrastructure on the web server on which they are active. In this case it is called the *servlet engine* (see Figure 7.41).

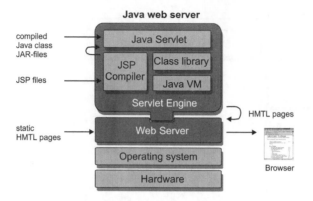

Figure 7.41 *Structure of a Java web server*

The *javax.servlet* and *javax.servlet.http* libraries required for servlets are included in the Java 2 Enterprise Edition (see Section 5.2.4), but can also be provided as extensions in the form of servlet engine products in the web application server.

The *Java Server Pages* (*JSPs*) are an extension (*javax.servlet.jsp*), and allow the use of Java as a server-side script language for web servers. The Java commands embedded in the HTML pages are converted into servlets at runtime.

Tip If you want to get deeper into the topic of server architecture then I would recommend you read the Sun documentation (http://java.sun.com/products/servlets), or refer to a specialist book on the subject.

Programming user interfaces

8

There are two alternatives for graphical user interfaces in Java. The *Abstract Windowing Toolkit (AWT)* has been included since the start of Java as a collection of simple control elements and primitive graphical functions (see Figure 8.1). Since Java 2, there has been a larger collection with *Swing*, which also provides modern control elements such as tables or tree views (see Figure 8.2).

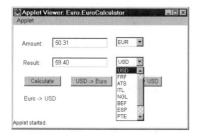

Figure 8.1 *A simple AWT user interface*

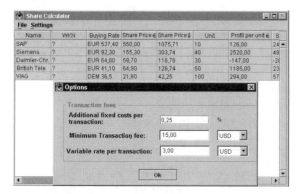

Figure 8.2 *A Swing application*

8.1 Overview

The following overview (Figure 8.3) shows the task areas of the individual packages, in order to give you a clue where you will have to keep a lookout for special classes and interfaces, because it's not possible to present all classes in this area in this book (there are more than 1100).

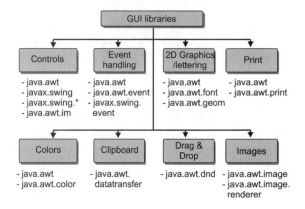

Figure 8.3 *Overview of the GUI packages*

Packages

The graphical classes are distributed over several packages:

→ *java.awt* contains the most important classes for creating graphical user interfaces such as windows, colors, fonts, 2D-graphics, and for printing.

→ *java.awt.event* contains classes for event handling.

→ *java.awt.font* (since Java 2). You will only need this if you want to analyze or transform fonts.

→ *java.awt.geom* (since Java 2) expands the 2D-graphic functionality of java.awt by adding shapes and surfaces.

→ *java.awt.print* (since Java 2) simplifies the setting of print options for multi-page documents (compared to *java.awt.PrintJob*).

→ *java.awt.color* (since Java 2) supports additional color models in addition to RGB and HSB in *java.awt.Color* class.

→ *java.awt.datatransfer* is for the use of the clipboard.

→ *java.awt.dnd* (since Java 2) helps you in setting up user interfaces, which support Drag&Drop.

→ *java.awt.image* provides classes for depicting bitmaps.

→ *java.awt.im* (since Java 2) is used for entering text using Asiatic characters

→ *javax.swing* (since Java 2) contains modern control elements; some of the necessary classes are found in additional subpackages (e.g. *javax.swing.border* for borders, *javax.swing.text* for formatted documents, *javax.swing.table* for tables, *javax.swing.tree* for tree views, etc.)

8.1.1   Comparison of AWT and Swing

There are many common features between AWT and Swing. How are the two related, and which library is better suited for which purpose?

Swing is based on the windows and graphics classes of AWT and uses its event handling.

The main difference is that in the depiction of control elements (buttons, checkboxes, lists), AWT is based on the windows system of the underlying operating system and uses its graphics libraries (*heavy-weight components*). Swing, on the other hand, draws all of its control elements itself (*light-weight components*). One result of this is that AWT can only depict the smallest common denominators of all operating system control elements; Swing, on the other hand, can depict practically all conventional ones.

AWT user interfaces are quick to depict, relatively quick to implement and are supported by almost all browsers. Depending on the operating system, however, there are small differences in depiction, so that we recommend testing an application on at least one Windows and one Unix system.

As *Swing* has only been contained as standard since Java 2, this library is not yet directly supported by many browsers (see tip on p.206). Swing is particularly suitable for complex user interfaces, in which tree views, tables or notebook control elements are used, for example, for the structured representation of structured data. Through a clean separation of the presentation and the data keeping, even complex user interfaces are manageable and maintainable. As the concrete form of representation (e.g. Windows Look & Feel) is drawn on all platforms by Swing itself, each user interface looks the same on all operating systems. However, Swing user interfaces have a high memory requirement and are really slow on older hardware.

	AWT	*Swing*
Advantages	simple design	maximum flexibility
	quick output to runtime	several display variants for one data model
		easy interchangeability of models, views and renderers

	AWT	Swing
		"Look & Feel" independent of platform, as no native code is contained
		any transparent representation (round buttons) and more complex control elements (tables, tree representations)
Disadvantages	restricted display facilities due to non-transparent, rectangular system components	complex programming
	dual administration of data in data and user interface objects	slow output to runtime

As a rule of thumb, you could say: if you don't need Swing functionality, use AWT because of its quicker display. This applies in particular for applets, as Swing is still hardly ever supported in browsers. In practice, however, you can reach the boundaries of AWT even in relatively simple applications.

Tip Browsers such as Netscape Communicator 4.x or Internet Explorer 4/5 still contain Java 1.1 and thus no Swing support. Indeed, you can provide the necessary Swing classes on the web server, but even in a packed form, this will be about 2 megabytes that have to be taken via the network. We therefore recommend using the Java plug-in (see Section 1.3), available in the JRE scope of delivery (from Version 1.2 onwards). This clicks into specially marked HTML pages and ensures that embedded applets are executed in the virtual machine of the JRE instead of that of the browser. In this way, the applet can also use Java 2 packages such as Swing without a download. Netscape Communicator 6 already contains a current virtual machine and, if required, can be set directly on an installed JRE, so that no plug-in is needed for this browser.

8.2 Simple user interfaces – java.awt

Almost all programs with graphical user prompting import the *AWT (Abstract Windowing Toolkit)*, which contains the classes for windows and control elements, for event handling (see Section 8.4), as well as for graphics and for printing (see Section 8.5).

The *java.awt* package contains the most important classes and interfaces for the Java beginner, such as windows, graphical control elements, as well as graphic primitives and the drawing of lines and surfaces (see Section 8.2.2). As a supplement, you will use the *java.awt.event* classes and Listener interfaces for handling events and *java.awt.datatransfer* for using the clipboard.

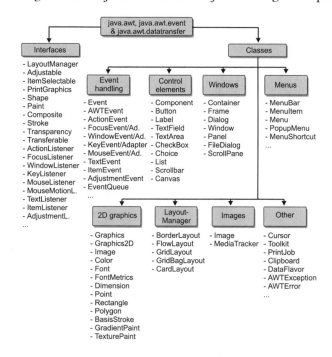

Figure 8.4 *The classes of the AWT package*

Tip Programming graphical user interfaces without accessories requires a good imagination. In addition, due to the volume and the routine activities, programming is susceptible to errors and the code produced is hard to maintain. We therefore recommend the use of GUI editors, which can be found in many integrated development environments.

8.2.1 The AWT basic class component

since	SE	ME	EE
1.0	x	-	x

All control elements are derived from a common abstract basic class, which provides the functionality for the appearance, the positioning, the output and the runtime behavior (focus, cursor, visibility). Concrete classes such as *Frame* (see Section 8.6.14) or *Button* (see Section 8.2.3) are derived from this class.

```
┌─────────────────────────────────────────────┐
│              Component                        │
│              {abstract}                       │
├─────────────────────────────────────────────┤
│                                               │
├─────────────────────────────────────────────┤
│ +get/setName(name: String)                    │
│ +getParent()                                  │
│ +contains(x: int, y: int)                     │
│ +SetVisible(visibility: boolean)              │
│ +isVisible()                                  │
│ +SetEnabled(active: boolean)                  │
│ +isEnabled()                                  │
│ +isShowing()                                  │
│ +get/setForeground(c: Color)                  │
│ +get/setBackground(c: Color)                  │
│ +Get/setFont(font: Font)                      │
│ +get/setBounds(x: int, y: int, width: int, hight: int) │
│ +getWidth/Height()                            │
│ +getX/Y()                                     │
│ +get/setSize(...)                             │
│ +get/setMinimum/MaximumSize(...)              │
│ +get/setLocation(...)                         │
│ +Get/setCursor(curser: Cursor)                │
│ +paint(target: Graphics)                      │
│ +repaint()                                    │
│ +paintAll(target: Graphics)                   │
│ +Update(target: Graphics)                     │
│ +Print(target: Graphics)                      │
│ +PrintAll(target: Graphics)                   │
│ +hasFocus()                                   │
│ +requestFocus()                               │
│ +transferFocus()                              │
│ +addFocusListener(l: FocusListener)           │
│ +addKeyListener(l: KeyListener)               │
│ +addMouseListener(l: MouseListener)           │
│ +Get/setLocale(locale: Locale)                │
│ +Add(menu: PopupMenu)                         │
│ ...                                           │
└─────────────────────────────────────────────┘
```

Figure 8.5 *The Component class*

Methods

All components should be named using `setName()`, in order to facilitate easy identification (e.g. in the case of debugging). Components are generally nested in each other. So, for example, a window (*Frame* class) could contain a number of layout regions (*Panel*), which surround one or more buttons (*Button*). Components that contain other control elements are called *Containers*. For each control element, you can determine its explicit surrounding Container using the `getParent()` method.

By means of `setVisible(true)`, you can make visible an invisible control element; using `setEnabled(true)` you can switch on its operating functionality. Using `isVisible()` or `isEnabled()`, you can interrogate its current status. The majority of control elements are visible and active as standard but windows, for example, are initially invisible and must be identified by the programmer. In the case of menus, checkboxes and buttons, an inactive status can be visually displayed.

Additional functions can be used to set the foreground or background colors or the font, if this is sensible for this type of control element and is supported by the operating system. Under Windows, for example, all buttons are gray (*background*) with black lettering (*foreground*). There is a whole range of self-explanatory methods used to determine and to set the size and position.

Using `setCursor()`, you can select the type of cursor that is displayed when it is over the control element. These include the pointer form (Cursor.`DEFAULT_CURSOR`), a text input line (Cursor.`TEXT_CURSOR`), a wait symbol (Cursor.`WAIT_CURSOR`) and cross-hairs (Cursor.`CROSSHAIR_CURSOR`). If the value is not set, then the cursor of the parent container is used. The Cursor class is discussed in Section 8.5.6.

`paint()` outputs the control element on the screen, `print()` outputs it to other devices. Both variants are identical as standard. The methods `paintAll()` and `printAll()` also do this for all subcomponents. The `paint` methods are not, however, normally called up by the developer but by the Java runtime system. `repaint()`, on the other hand, forces a redrawing from the code and update `()` deletes the surface and calls up `paint()`.

Using `hasFocus()`, you can determine whether the current control element has the input focus. If not, you can obtain this using `requestFocus()`. `transferFocus()` switches it to the next control element.

In addition, there are a number of Listener functions, through which you can switch on the event handling (see Section 8.4) for focus, keyboard, or mouse events.

Finally, you can even select your own locale or language per control element (setLocale()) or add a popup menu (add()).

8.2.2 Overview of the AWT control elements

The following table is an overview of the most important functions of AWT control elements, which, together with the standard functionality of all *components* (see Section 8.2.1), are presumed to cover 90% of all application cases.

> **Tip** The numbers in brackets refer to explanations that can be found following the overview.

I AWT beans

Name	Description	Special Properties	Methods	Events
Button	Button, Action button	label actionCommand enabled		action-Performed
Check box	Option	label state checkboxGroup(1)		
Check box-Group	for grouping existing checkboxes as option switches	this (1) selectedCheckbox		
Label	static text	text alignment (LEFT/RIGHT/ CENTER)	setText(String)	
TextField	single line text input	text selectedText selectionStart/End columns echoChar (2) editable	setText(String) selectAll() select(int, in)	textValue-Changed keyTyped keyPressed keyReleased

Name	Description	Special Properties	Methods	Events
TextArea	multi-line text input	text selectedText selectionStart/End columns/rows editable	setText(String) selectAll() select(int, int) append(String) insert(String, int)	textValue- Changed key Typed keyPressed keyReleased
List	List of Strings	items itemCount selectedItem[s] selectedIndex[es] multipleMode (3) rows	add/add- Item(String) add/add- Item(String, int) getItem(int) remove(...) removeAll() select/isSe- lected(int)	itemState- Changed
Choice	Drop-down list	selectedItem selectedIndex	add/add- Item(String) remove(...) removeAll() select(...)	itemState- Changed
Scrollbar	Scrollbar (horizontal and vertical)	value minimum/maxi mum block-/unitIncre ment orientation (VERTICAL/ HORIZONTAL) visibleAmount	setValue(int) setValues(int, int, int, int)	adjustment- Value- Changed
Panel	Panel, window area for layout	layout	add(Component) getCompo- nent[At](...) getComponents() getComponent- Count() remove(...) removeAll()	component- Added component- Removed
ScrollPane	ScrollPane	scrollBarDisplay- Policy scrollPosition		

Name	Description	Special Properties	Methods	Events
Frame	Application window	title layout resizable size iconImage menuBar	setVisible (boolean) dispose() repaint() add/remove(...) getFocusOwner()	window- Opened window- Closing window- Activated window- Deactivated
Dialog	Dialog window, Message window	title layout resizable size modal	setVisible (boolean) show() dispose() repaint() add/remove(...) getFocusOwner()	window- Opened window- Closing window- Activated window- Deactivated
FileDia- log	File selection	directory file mode (LOAD/SAVE) fileNameFilter title modal	setVisible (boolean) dispose()	
MenuBar	Menu bar	menuCount helpMenu	add/remove(...) shortcuts() getShortcut Menu-Item (MenuShortcut)	
Popup- Menu	Context menu	label actionCommand shortcut itemCount	add/insert/ remove(...) getItem(int) show(Compo nent, int, int) add/insert Separator()	action- Performed

Name	Description	Special Properties	Methods	Events
Menu	Menu in a MenuBar or as a submenu	label actionCommand shortcut itemCount	add/insert/ remove(...) getItem(int) add/insert Separator()	action- Performed
Menu- Item	Menu item	label actionCommand shortcut		action- Performed
Check box- Menu Item	Menu item	label actionCommand shortcut state		action- Performed itemState- Changed

Notes

1 In order to collect several checkboxes into one group, in which only one option box can be selected respectively (*Radiobuttons*), you must allocate a reference of the *CheckboxGroup* type to the checkboxGroup-attribute of each checkbox. The appearance of the checkboxes then changes at the runtime (round buttons instead of square).

2 By setting the properties echoChar to a character (e.g. "*"), a *TextField* can be used for inputting passwords. Instead of the character entered, the echoChar is used; neither can the password be copied to the clipboard.
Caution: the definition of an echoChar can no longer be undone, which means that if the field is not to be used as a password field, it must be replaced completely.

3 Switching on the multipleMode allows the selection of several list items.

8.2.3   The Button class

since	SE	ME	EE
1.0	x	-	x

An AWT Button |

Figure 8.6 *Displaying a button*

Buttons, frequently also called *switches* or pushbuttons, are rectangular buttons that trigger an action when the user clicks on them.

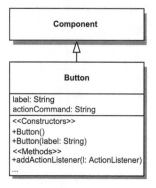

Figure 8.7 *The Button class*

Methods and attributes

The most important attributes are the `Label`, i.e. the lettering, and `actionCommand`, a string that characterizes the button in the *ActionEvent* (sent with the event object, see Section 8.4). The event is triggered using the associated `action Performed()` method when the button is pressed. If `actionCommand` is not occupied, then it is given the value of `Label`; however, in the case of multi-language user interfaces it can be sensible if the two values differ. Both attributes are read or changed – like all AWT control elements – by means of `get` or `set` methods.

As described in the section on event handling, all classes that are to be notified when the button is pressed must register a *Listener* using `addActionListener()`.

Warning Of course, in addition, all of the general methods defined in the superclass *java.awt.Component* are available (see Section 8.2.1).

```
Button okButton = new Button("OK");
okButton.setActionCommand("OK");
okButton.addActionListener(eventHandler);
```

8.2.4   The Checkbox class

since	SE	ME	EE
1.0	x	-	x

☑ An AWT checkbox

◉ An AWT checkbox as radio button

Figure 8.8 *Display of checkboxes*

The *Checkbox* represents an option that can be selected or deselected by clicking on a box. A tick symbolizes a selected checkbox.

Methods and attributes

Like the *Button*, the *Checkbox* has a `Label` property, and in addition the `State` status (on or off) is also important. A change in the status is signaled by an *ItemEvent* (`itemStateChanged()`). However, you often do not react immediately to a change, but instead only interrogate the status of an option on starting up an action.

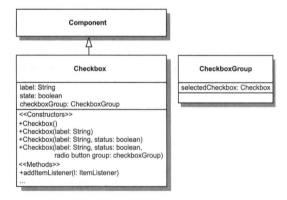

Figure 8.9 *The Checkbox and CheckboxGroup classes*

The CheckboxGroup class

Checkboxes can also be used as radio buttons, i.e. for a number of mutually exclusive options. The property `CheckboxGroup` in each checkbox is used for the allocation of checkboxes to such a group. The display of the control elements (see Section 8.2.4.) then changes at the runtime. Using the *CheckboxGroup*, the currently selected option can be interrogated.

```
CheckboxGroup options = new CheckboxGroup();
Checkbox option1 = new Checkbox("screen output",
                                true, options);
Checkbox option2 = new Checkbox("print output",
                                false, options);
[...]
boolean print = option2.getState();
Checkbox selected = options.getSelectedCheckbox();
```

8.2.5   The Label class

since	SE	ME	EE
1.0	x	-	x

An AWT-Label

Labelling

Figure 8.10   *Display of labels*

A *label* is a static text used for lettering inside windows.

Methods and attributes

The text presented is in the Text attribute and can be modified using the set-Text() method. The justification can be selected as left justified (presetting, Label.LEFT), right justified (Label.RIGHT) or centered (Label.CENTER).

```
Label lettering = new Label("a Label");
lettering.setAlignment(Label.CENTER);
```

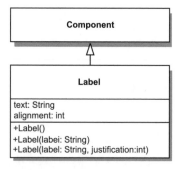

Figure 8.11   *The Label class*

8.2.6   The TextField and TextArea classes

since	SE	ME	EE
1.0	x	-	x

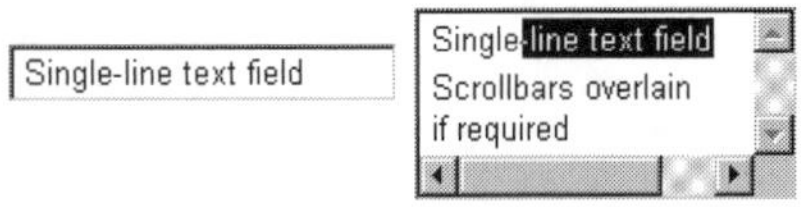

Figure 8.12   *Display of a TextField and a TextArea*

A *TextField* is a single-line input field, and a *TextArea* is a multi-line input field. Both are derived from the common *TextComponent* basic class, which provides functionalities such as selection or editing. A *TextField* can also be used for masked fields, for instance for the entry of passwords. However, you cannot define masks (e.g. numbers only) and you cannot determine a fixed input length.

Methods and attributes

As with *Label*, there is a `Text` attribute. In the case of input fields, this text is generally able to be edited, and you can switch off this function using `setEditable(false)`. Using different `Select` methods, you can mark a text area or interrogate the marking. The `caretPosition` gives the position of the input cursor. In the case of *TextComponents*, the *TextEvent* (`textValueChanged()`) is important, as it is used for checking the input, for example whether the characters entered are numerical or whether a stated maximum length has been reached.

In the case of *TextFields*, there is an additional attribute of `echoChar`, used to ascertain whether the text entered should be visible or whether it is a password, for example, where each entered character is to be replaced with a replacement character such as "*".

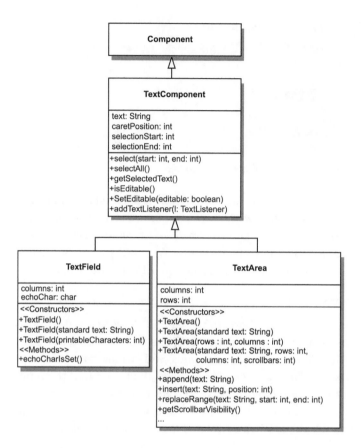

Figure 8.13 *The TextField and TextArea classes*

Columns and rows state how large the field has to be dimensioned in the case of dynamic layouts (see Section 8.3), so that there is room for the stated number of characters in the set font.

Warning Neither values have any influence on how many characters can actually be entered.

The multi-line *TextArea* allows the text to be changed using `append()`, in-`sert()` and `replaceRange()`. In addition, scrollbars can be added if required, as soon as the text exceeds the stated horizontal or vertical dimensions.

> **Tip** Whether scrollbars that are not required are to be displayed depends on the implementation of the virtual machine and – unlike in Swing – this can be influenced by the programmer. However, the scrollbars can also be switched off in whole or in part in constructor
>
> (`TextArea`.SCROLLBARS_NONE, `TextArea`. SCROLLBARS_VERTICAL_ONLY, `TextArea`.SCROLLBARS_ HORIZONTAL_ONLY).

```
TextField passwordField = new TextField();
passwordField.setEchoChar("*");

TextArea editor = new TextArea();
editor.setText("a multi-line text window.");
editor.append("\nScrollbar are added if \n" +
              "required");
editor.select(4, 29);
```

8.2.7   The Scrollbar class

since	SE	ME	EE
1.0	x	-	x

Figure 8.14 *Scrollbar display*

The *scrollbar* is an elevator (also scrollbar) for graphical selection of numerical values. For all classes that represent an integer value that can lie between a minimum and a maximum, there is an *Adjustable* interface, which also implements the *Scrollbar* class.

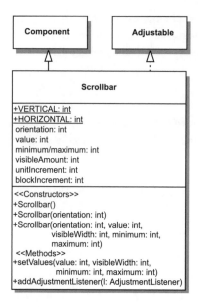

Figure 8.15 *The Scrollbar class*

Methods and attributes

Scrollbars have either a horizontal (`Scrollbar.HORIZONTAL`) or vertical orientation (`Scrollbar.VERTICAL`). `Value` is the value currently set, `visibleAmount` is the area embodied by the gray part of the scrollbar (see "Attributes of a scrollbar"). If, for example, 60% of a text is visible, then this value should be set to (`get-Maximum() – getMinimum()) *0.6`. `Minimum` and `maximum` can also be negative values. `UnitIncrement` is the step distance taken when you click on the arrow keys (1 is standard), `blockIncrement` is that of a mouse click on the white background of the scrollbar (10 is standard).

Using `addAdjustmentListener()`, the Listener is registered for an event that occurs when scrolling and also contains the information on how the user has changed the set value.

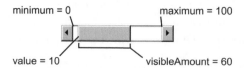

Figure 8.16 *Attributes of a scrollbar*

```
Scrollbar controller = new Scrollbar(Scrollbar.HORIZONTAL);
controller.setValues(10, 60, 0, 100);
controller.setBlockIncrement(5);
```

8.2.8   The List and Choice classes

since	SE	ME	EE
1.0	x	-	x

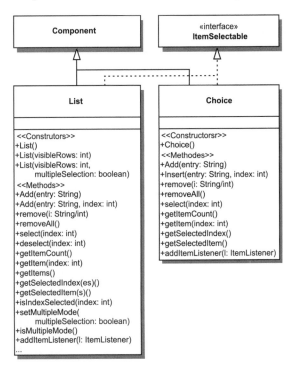

Figure8.17 *Display of List and Choice*

To select fixed elements, there are the two control elements *Choice* and *List*. The *List* class is a list that as an option can also allow the selection of several entries, whilst in the case of *Choice* just one is selected and the selection list is only dropped down (drop-down). However, it is not a Combobox, because the user cannot put in his own values. Both classes implement the *ItemSelectable* interface.

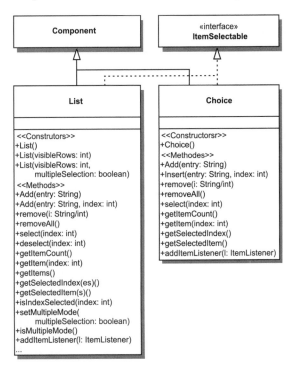

Figure8.18 *The List and Choice classes*

Methods and attributes

Both classes have the `add()` method for adding new elements as well as `remove/ removeAll()` for deleting. Using `select()`, you can select elements and using `getSelectedItem/Index()` you can interrogate them. Some methods are duplicated, once with the index position and once with the entry as a parameter. `getItemCount()` gives the number of elements and `getItem(i)` the i entry.

In the case of an object of the *List* class, you can determine using `setMulti- pleMode()` whether one or several values can be marked at the same time. In this case, additional methods are available for numbers of entries, such as `getSelectedItems/Indexes()`.

If there should be a reaction in selecting or deselecting a list element, the *Item-Event* in the `itemStateChanged()` method of a registered listener can be used (see Section 8.4).

```
List list = new List();
list.setMultipleMode(true);
list.add("List entry 1");
list.add("List entry 2");
list.add("List entry 3");
list.select(0);
list.select(list.getItemCount()-1);
```

8.2.9 The Container class

since	SE	ME	EE
1.0	x	-	x

Containers are windows or window areas in which other control elements can be placed. Many support LayoutManager, using which the platform-independent display and placing of the control elements contained in them can be controlled (see Section 8.3).

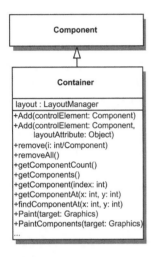

Figure 8.19 *The Container class*

Methods and attributes

Using add() you can add control elements to a container; using remove/removeAll() you can then remove them. getComponentCount() gives the number of control elements contained; getComponents() gives an array with their references. getComponent-At(x, y) gives the control element contained at the stated position, findComponentAt(x, y), on the other hand, works recursively and gives the uppermost one.

8.2.10   The Frame and Dialog classes

since	SE	ME	EE
1.0	x	-	x

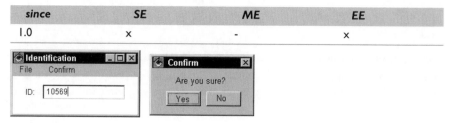

Figure 8.20   *Display of Frame and Dialog*

Window is a class that depicts a rectangular window. The class is seldom used independently, but rather as a common superclass of *Frame*, a main window, and *Dialog*, a dependent dialog box. A *Frame* object can have a menu bar and a symbol, which appears when the window is minimized. A *Dialog* object does not have these properties; however, it can be modal with reference to its main window, which means that it is always in front of this window, to which you cannot return until the dialog box is closed.

Methods and attributes

The most important method is the method inherited from *Component* `setVisible(true)` (or `show()`), as windows are not visible as standard. `dispose()` not only makes the window invisible but also releases all associated resources. This is important, as the lifecycle of a window is controlled by the operating system, which does not recognize any automatic Garbage Collection. The *WindowEvents* and their methods `windowOpened()` *and* `window-Closing()` are also frequently used, in which an initialization or purge can be carried out.

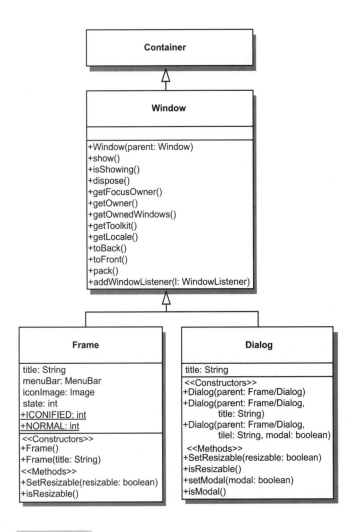

Figure 8.21 *The Frame and Dialog classes*

Tip If you want to end an application on closing the window (e.g. by clicking on the "X" button or (Alt)(F4)), you will have to call `windowClosing() System.exit(0)` for WindowEvent methods.

Written in short with an inner class (see Section 8.4):

```
window.addWindowListener(new WindowAdapter()
    {
public void windowClosing(WindowEvent e)
        {System.exit(0);}
    });
```

Warning In addition, there are of course all of the common methods defined in the superclasses of *Component* (see Section 8.2.1) and *Container* (see Section 8.2.9). In the case of Container objects, LayoutManagers are often used (see Section 8.3).

Frame

A *Frame* is a full-value window, as generally used for applications. It has a frame with a title bar (`Title` attribute) and can have a *menu bar* (`MenuBar` attribute). `Resizable` states whether the user can change the size of the window and `iconImage` is used to determine a symbol, if the window assumes the status (state) `Frame.ICONIFIED`.

Dialog

A rather restricted variant of a window is *Dialog*. Each dialog object has a clear *owner*, which in general is the creating *Frame* or *Dialog* object. Unlike *Frame*, there is no icon and neither can a *menubar* be allocated. An additional feature of the dialog is `Modal`, which states whether the dialog window has to be closed before the user can then access the parent window, or whether both windows can be used simultaneously.

> **Tip** In Java, there is no system modality, as exists in Windows. There can thus be no Java window that blocks all other windows on the screen.

```
import java.awt.*;
import java.awt.event.*;
public class WinDemo extends Frame
{
    public static void main(String[] args)
    {
        WinDemo win = new WinDemo();
        win.setTitle("Identification");
        // even distribution of the control elements:
        win.setLayout(new FlowLayout());
        win.add(new Label("ID: "));
        win.add(new TextField(6));
        // End of application on closing the window:
        win.addWindowListener(new WindowAdapter()
        {
        public void windowClosing(WindowEvent e)
            {System.exit(0);}
        });
        // Position and display window:
        win.setBounds(100, 100, 200, 80);
        win.setVisible(true);
    }
}
```

8.2.11 The FileDialog class

since	SE	ME	EE
1.0	x	-	x

The *FileDialog* class, derived from *Dialog*, provides a ready-made dialog window for accessing files. This opens the file dialog of the respective host operating system.

Figure 8.22 *Display of the FileDialog under Windows*

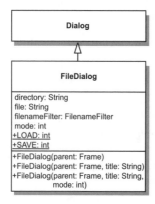

Figure 8.23 *The FileDialog class*

Methods and attributes

`Directory` is the preset path with which *FileDialog* is opened, and gives the derived path according to the selection of the user. The same applies for the `File` attribute for file names. Using `filenameFilter`, you can set up a filter for files, which allows or forbids the selection of certain files. For this, a class has to be implemented that fulfils the interface *java.io.FilenameFilter* using the method `accept()`. Mode is the mode of the *FileDialog*, `FileDialog.LOAD` is for opening files, and `FileDialog.SAVE` for saving them.

```
FileDialog fileSelection =
  new FileDialog(win, "open document", FileDialog.LOAD);
fileSelection.setVisible(true);
// FileDialog is modal, so wait for the result:
String path = fileSelection.getDirectory();
String filename = fileSelection.getFile();
```

8.2.12 The Panel class

since	SE	ME	EE
1.0	x	-	x

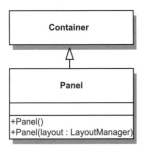

Figure 8.24 *Displaying a panel*

A *panel* is a window area in which other control elements can be placed (*container*). The main task is the design and subdivision of user interfaces in Window systems.

```
┌─────────────────────────┐
│        Container         │
└─────────────────────────┘
            △
┌─────────────────────────┐
│          Panel           │
├─────────────────────────┤
│ +Panel()                 │
│ +Panel(layout : LayoutManager) │
└─────────────────────────┘
```

Figure 8.25 *The Panel class*

A LayoutManager can be allocated through the inherited `layout` attribute. Frequently, several panels are nested in each other using different LayoutManagers (see Section 8.3).

> **Tip** The Applet class (see Chapter 9) is also derived from *Panel*.

8.2.13 Menu classes

since	SE	ME	EE
1.0	x	-	x

Menus are used in the selection of functions and options in applications. Menus can occur either in the form of *MenuBars* on the top side of windows or as pop-up menus in any position. Menus are often nested.

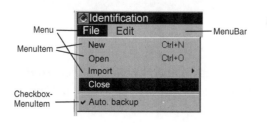

Figure 8.26 *Displaying different menu objects*

A menu is either embedded in a menu bar of a *Frame* object (*MenuBar* class) or appears as a context menu (*PopupMenu* class) when called. They contain either submenus (*Menu* class) or menu items (*MenuItem* class). In Java, the inheritance hierarchy is shown in the AWT menu classes.

Tip Menu elements that in turn contain other menu components (such as *Menu*, *MenuBar*, or *PopupMenu*), implement the *MenuContainer* interface.

Methods and attributes

Each *Menu* object has a `label` and an `actionCommand`, a String, which characterizes the menu in the *ActionEvent*, and is triggered when you click on the entry. For menus, you can state *shortcuts*, i.e. key shortcuts.

A *MenuItem* is an item in a menu, which changes an option on selection (*CheckboxMenuItem*) or deletes a command. A *MenuItem* object is added to a *Menu* object in exactly the same way using `add` methods as a *menu* is added to a *MenuBar*. The latter is allocated to a *Frame* object using the method `setMenuBar()`.

Tip A *PopupMenu* object is positioned relative to the stated components. It is therefore wrong to state the cursor position for x and y of the show methods.

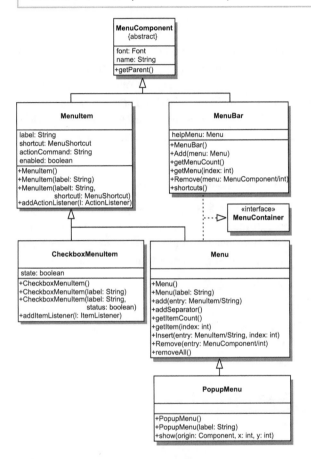

Figure 8.27 *The AWT menu classes*

```
MenuBar menuBar = new MenuBar();
Menu fileMenu = new Menu("File");
menuBar.add(fileMenu);
win.setMenuBar(menuBar);
MenuItem new = new MenuItem("New",
   new MenuShortcut(KeyEvent.VK_N));
new.addActionListener(eventHandler);
fileMenu.add(new);
MenuItem open = new MenuItem("Open",
```

```
new MenuShortcut(KeyEvent.VK_O));
open.addActionListener(eventHandler);
fileMenu.add(open);
```

8.3 LayoutManager

Java must be defined independent of an absolute size in the position, window, and control elements. Using a *LayoutManager*, you can logically define a user interface; the dimensions and positions of the control elements in a window are then calculated at the runtime independent of the size of the window. There are five standard LayoutManagers in JDK 1.1 and, in addition, the *BoxLayout* from Java 2, which is shown in types of LayoutManager. In addition, you can also write your own LayoutManager, by implementing the *LayoutManager* interface.

Changing dimensions and control elements of variable sizes

If the dimensions of a container – i.e. a window, applet, or panel containing control elements – changes, then an automatic adaptation of the dimensions and position will take place using certain marginal conditions (*constraints*). These conditions can be very different, depending on the type of the LayoutManager.

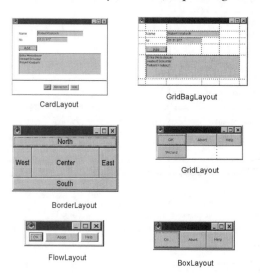

Figure 8.28   *Types of LayoutManagers*

LayoutManagers also take into consideration the differences in the display of control elements on different operating systems and in different languages. Thus one font can be defined differently or a foreign language message can be longer than an English one. Without LayoutManagers, the texts would only be shown in part under certain circumstances.

8.3.1   The BorderLayout class

since	SE	ME	EE
1.0	x	-	x

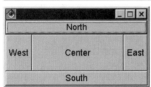

Figure 8.29   *Display of a BorderLayout application*

The *BorderLayout* arranges the inserted components at the edges of a container. These are identified by the points of the compass or CENTER . A maximum of five control elements can be inserted.

Figure 8.30   *The BorderLayout class*

Control elements	Description	Possible values
of the container	LayoutManager settings:	
	hgap/vgap: distance between the control elements	>= 0
control elements contained	Position	CENTER, NORTH, SOUTH, WEST, EAST
calculating dimensions	using preferredSize, minimum and maximum of the contained constrains	

Use

The *BorderLayout* is applied in particular when using toolbars and state bars placed in the north, west, or south areas.

```
Frame win = new Frame("BorderLayout");
win.setLayout(new BorderLayout());
win.add(new Button("Center"), BorderLayout.CENTER);
win.add(new Button("North"), BorderLayout.NORTH);
win.add(new Button("South"), BorderLayout.SOUTH);
win.add(new Button("West"), BorderLayout.WEST);
win.add(new Button("East"), BorderLayout.EAST);
win.setBounds(100, 100, 200, 150);
win.setVisible(true);
```

8.3.2   The FlowLayout class

since	SE	ME	EE
1.0	x	-	x

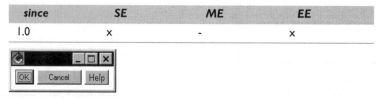

Figure 8.31   *Displaying a dialog using FlowLayout*

The *FlowLayout* arranges all components one after another in a sequence until the edge of the container is reached. Additional components are added on a new line. You can influence the appearance of the final result by determining the properties alignment, hgap, and vgap.

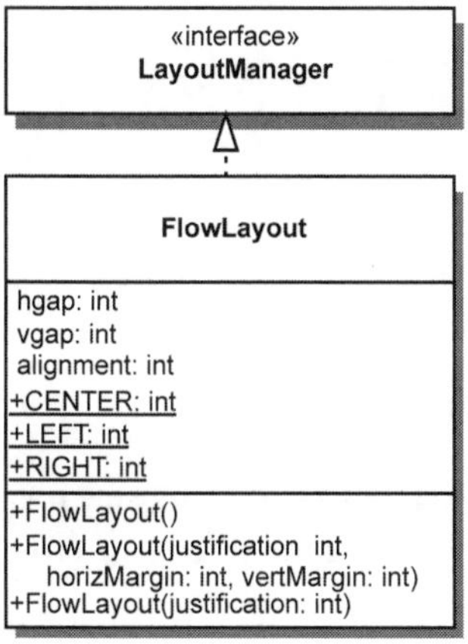

```
            «interface»
            LayoutManager
```

```
            FlowLayout
```

```
hgap: int
vgap: int
alignment: int
+CENTER: int
+LEFT: int
+RIGHT: int
```

```
+FlowLayout()
+FlowLayout(justification  int,
    horizMargin: int, vertMargin: int)
+FlowLayout(justification: int)
```

Figure 8.32 *The FlowLayout class*

Control elements	Description	Possible values
of the container	LayoutManager settings:	
	alignment: Orientation of the control elements	CENTER, LEFT, RIGHT
	hgap/vgap: Distance between the control elements	>= 0
control elements contained	-	<none>
dimension calculation	using preferredSize, minimum and maximum of the contained control elements	

Use

A typical application of the *FlowLayout* is in the grouping of the same types of control element, for example a row of buttons: "OK", "Cancel", "Help".

```
Dialog win = new Dialog(parentFrame);
win.setLayout(new FlowLayout(FlowLayout.CENTER, 5, 5));
win.add(new Button("OK"));
win.add(new Button("Cancel"));
win.add(new Button("Help"));
win.setBounds(100, 100, 200, 100);
win.setVisible(true);
```

8.3.3   The BoxLayout class

since	SE	ME	EE
1.2	x	-	x

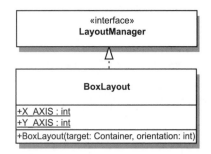

Figure 8.33 *Displaying a dialog using BoxLayout*

The first *javax.swing.BoxLayout* contained in the Swing package is closely related to the *FlowLayout* and the *GridLayout*. It arranges the components in a row or a column, but does not break these up.

```
               «interface»
             LayoutManager


                  △
                  ¦

               BoxLayout

+X_AXIS : int
+Y_AXIS : int
+BoxLayout(target: Container, orientation: int)
```

Figure 8.34 *The BoxLayout class*

Control elements	Description	Possible values
of the container	LayoutManager settings: `axis`: Orientation of the control elements	`X_AXIS`, `Y_AXIS`
control elements contained	-	`<none>`
dimension calculation	using `preferredSize`, `minimum` and `maximum` of the contained control elements	

Use

The *BoxLayout* is often used with a group of the same type of control elements and a number of nested containers as a replacement for the complex *GridBagLayout*.

Use

Use is recommended in all user interfaces, in which more information can be presented to a user with a higher screen resolution. This is particularly the case with windows containing lists, tables, or tree diagrams.

```
Frame win = new Frame();
win.setLayout(new GridBagLayout());
// Basic element with common attributes:
GridBagConstraints basic = new GridBagConstraints();
basic.insets = new Insets(5, 10, 5, 10);
basic.anchor = GridBagConstraints.WEST;
GridBagConstraints labelAttr =
   (GridBagConstraints) basic.clone();
labelAttr.gridx = 0; labelAttr.gridy = 0;    // left top
win.add(new Label("Search for:"), labelAttr);
GridBagConstraints enterAttr =
   (GridBagConstraints) basic.clone();
enterAttr.gridx = 1; enterAttr.gridy = 0;  // beside it
win.add(new TextField(10), enterAttr);
GridBagConstraints listAttr =
   (GridBagConstraints) basic.clone();
listAttr.gridx = 0; listAttr.gridy = 1;        // underneath
listAttr.gridwidth = 2;                 // two cells wide
// fill available remaining space:
listAttr.fill = GridBagConstraints.BOTH;
listAttr.weightx = 0.1; listAttr.weighty = 0.1;
win.add(new List(), listAttr);
win.setBounds(100, 100, 300, 150);
win.setVisible(true);
```

Tip As you can see, the code to be programmed is long and hard to read. It is particularly difficult if you want to insert a new control element between the rows at a later date, as the cell numbering is absolute.

We recommend first drawing the desired result on paper and entering the grid lines. If possible, use a development environment which graphically supports the use of *GridBagLayouts* (e.g. IBM VisualAge), or instead nest *Panels* in each other using the vertical and horizontal *BoxLayouts*.

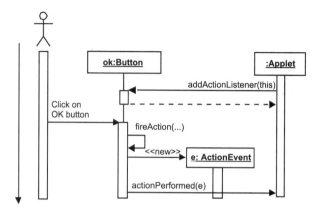

Figure 8.43 *Example run of an action event*

In the following table you can find some examples of event classes and listeners from the *java.beans* and *java.awt* packages. However, it is also possible to create new event and listener pairs (*Event Sets*) yourself.

Event	Event type	Listener	Listener method
Change of property	Property Change Event	PropertyChange Listener	propertyChanged()
Button clicked or menu item selected	Action Event	ActionListener	actionPerformed()
Focus got or lost	FocusEvent	FocusListener	focusGained() focusLost()
List entry (de)selected	ItemEvent	ItemListener	itemStateChanged()
Mouse events	MouseEvent	MouseListener	mouseClicked() mouseEntered() mouseExited() mousePressed() mouseReleased() mouseMoved()
	Mouse Motion Event	MouseMotion Listener	mouseDragged()
Key entry	KeyEvent	KeyListener	keyTyped() keyPressed() keyReleased()

Event	Event type	Listener	Listener method

Window events	`WindowEvent`	`WindowListener`	`windowOpened()`
			`windowClosing()`
			`windowClosed()`
			`windowActivated()`
			`windowDeactivted()`
			`windowIconified()`
			`windowDeiconified()`

Text change	`TextEvent`	`TextListener`	`textValueChanged()`
Controller changed	`Adjustment Event`	`Adjustment Listener`	`adjustmentValue Changed()`

In addition, it is possible to use additional Swing Event classes and Listeners in the *javax.swing.event* package (or *com.sun.java.swing.event* in Swing 1.0.x), listed in the following table.

Event	Event type	Listener	Listener method
Text insertion mark changed	`Caret- Event`	`CaretListener`	`caretUpdate()`

Document changed	`DocumentEvent`	`Document Listener`	`insertUpdate()`
			`removeUpdate()`
			`changedUpdate()`

List changed	`ListDataEvent`	`ListData Listener`	`intervalAdded()`
			`intervalRemoved()`
			`contentsChanged()`

List entry (de)selected	`ListSelection Event`	`ListSelection Listener`	`valueChanged()`
Data model of a table changed	`TableModel Event`	`TableModel Listener`	`tableChanged()`

Table column changed	`TableColumn ModelEvent`	`TableColumn ModelListener`	`columnAdded()`
			`columnRemoved()`
			`columnMoved()`
			`columnMarginChanged()`
			`columnSelection Changed()`

Table cell changed	`Change- Event`	`CellEditor Listener`	`editingStopped()` `editingCanceled()`

Data model of a tree changed	`TreeModel Event`	`TreeModelListener`	`treeNodesChanged()`
			`treeNodesInserted()`
			`treeNodesRemoved()`
			`treeStructureChanged()`

Tree entry opened or closed	`Tree Expansion Event`	`TreeExpansion Listener`	`treeExpanded()` `treeCollapsed()`
Tree entry (de)selected	`Tree Selection Event`	`TreeSelection Listener`	`valueChanged()`

Event	Event type	Listener	Listener method
Status changed	Change Event	ChangeListener	stateChanged()
Menu item changed	MenuEvent	MenuListener	menuSelected() menuDeselected() menuCanceled
Reversible opera-tion executed	Undoable EditEvent	UndoableEdit Listener	undoableEdit Happened()

After getting to know the theoretical fundamentals of event handling, we will now take a closer look at their practical realization. A Handler class that implements the Listener interface must be implemented for the handling of an event. You can do this in different ways:

1   By writing an open class that implements the Listener.

2   By locally defining the Handler class as an internal class.

3   By directly implementing the handling in the Listener registration.

Tip Since Swing, and particularly since Java 1.3, there has been an additional expansion. If you want to trigger the same action in several ways (e.g. by menu, toolbar, or Drag&Drop), it would be awkward to implement Listener for all possibilities that implement the desired behavior, and at the same time to influence the status of all components involved (e.g. status change to *disabled*). Using the `javax.swing.Action` interface, all affected components are treated in the same way.

8.4.1   Event handling using its own classes

In this approach, the Listener interface (in this case *FocusListener*) is implemented using its own class.

In the following, the Listener reacts to a text field being left and checks whether a five-figure zip code has been entered.

```
import java.awt.*;
import java.awt.event.*;
public class ZipcodeFocusHandler implements FocusListener
{
    // focusGained is called if
    // a control element gains the entry focus:
    public void focusGained(FocusEvent event) {}
    // focusLost is called if
    // a constraint loses the entry focus:
    public void focusLost(FocusEvent event)
    {
```

```
            TextField tf = (TextField) event.getSource();
            if (!checkZipcode(tf.getText())
            {  // invalid Zipcode: mark in red and set focus
               tf.setBackground(Color.red);
               tf.requestFocus();
            }
            else tf.setBackground(Color.white); //delete Marker
   }
   private boolean checkZipcode(String text)
   {
      // Zipcode is five-figure...
      if (text.length() != 5) return false;
      // ...and is numerical.
      for (int i=0; i<5; i++)
         if (!Character.isDigit(text.charAt(i)))
            return false;
      return true;
   }
}
```

> **Tip** For the sake of clarity, there is no check here on whether the control element in which this Handler was registered is actually of the *TextField* type.

Now the Handler must register as a Listener with the event source generating this event type. This is done in the example using the corresponding method addFocusEvent().

```
import java.awt.*;
public class AddressWindow extends Frame
{
   private ZipcodeFocusHandler handler;
   private TextField zipcode;
   [...] // additional control elements
   public AddressWindow()
   {
      // Create new instance of the listener class:
      handler = new ZipcodeFocusHandler();
      zipcode = new TextField(5);
      // Register handler:
   zipcode.addFocusListener(handler);
   [...] // additional initializations
   }
```

```
     [...]    // other methods
}
```

There are two small variants of this approach.

Variant I: implement Listener directly in container

If you only need the Handler class in one class and you cannot return it, then you do not need to write two classes, as the Listener methods can instead implement directly in the class in which the Listener is registered.

```
public class AddressWindow1 extends Frame
    implements FocusListener
{
    public void focusGained(FocusEvent event) {}
    public void focusLost(FocusEvent event)
    { [...] }   // Impl. As in ZipcodeFocusHandler
  public AddressWindow1()
    {
        zipcode = new TextField(5);
        // Register Handler:
    zipcode.addFocusListener(this);
    [...] // additional initializations
    }
    [...]    // other methods
}
```

> **Tip** Unlike the above case, you save one class. You don't need to register an extra object now, as the event handling can apply using the *this* reference.

Variant 2 : Using adapters

In the previous examples, you could see that you had to add the *focusLost* methods, although no logic is implemented in it. The effort here was justifiable, but in the case of *WindowListener*, for example, these can also be six unused methods.

In order to avoid the problem described in the last section, there is an associated Adapter class for each interface containing more than one method, which implements the corresponding interface. A class which implements the processing of a focus event, for example, can thus be derived from the *FocusAdapter* class, instead of implementing the *FocusListener* interface. Then the class derived from the Adapter class only has to implement the respective methods required. All others are inherited from the Adapter class, which implements methods defined in the interface using an empty method body. This saves the developer unnecessary programming time, particularly if not all of the methods defined in the interface are required for handling the events.

```
public class ZipcodeFocusHandler1 extends FocusAdapter
{
    // focusGained can be dropped.
    public void focusLost(FocusEvent event)
    { [...] }  // Impl. like ZipcodeFocusHandler
  private boolean checkZipcode(String text)
    { [...] }  // Impl. like ZipcodeFocusHandler
}
```

The use of Adapter classes increases the clarity in the case of Listener interfaces using many methods. However, the expansion of an Adapter class is not always a good solution as Java, as already mentioned, only allows simple inheritance. This can be a problem if you want to combine both variants, because the *Address Window* is already derived from *Frame* and not from *FocusAdapter*.

8.4.2   Event handling using internal classes

To cure the problems of multiple inheritance, internal classes (see Section 4.4.4) can be used as follows.

```
public class AddressWindow2 extends Frame
{
    class ZipcodeFocusHandler2 extends FocusAdapter
    { [...] }  // methods like ZipcodeFocusHandler1
    private ZipcodeFocusHandler2 handler;
    private TextField zipcode;
    [...] // additional control elements
    public AddressWindow2()
    { [...] }  // Impl. Like AddressWindow
    [...]     // other methods
}
```

The internal class *ZipcodeFocusListener2* is thus only visible within the *AddressWindow2* class immediately surrounding it. However, it has access to all variables and methods of the surrounding class and thus achieves the same functionality as in the other concepts for the implementation of event handling.

8.4.3   Event handling using immediate implementation

There is a short version in addition to the previously mentioned facilities for programming event processing. For this variant, neither inheritance of a class nor implementation of an instance is required. A newly instantiated *FocusListener* (or *FocusAdapter*) is simply passed to the addFocusListener() method, in whose execution block the event-processing methods are immediately implemented. However, the legibility of the programming code does suffer.

```
public class AddressWindow3 extends Frame
{
  public AddressWindow3()
    {
        zipcode = new TextField(5);
        // Register handler:
    zipcode.addFocusListener(new FocusAdapter()
        {
      public void focusLost(FocusEvent event)
            { [...] }  // Impl. like ZipcodeFocusHandler
      private boolean checkZipcode(String text)
            { [...] }  // Impl. like ZipcodeFocusHandler
        });
    [...] // additional initializations
    }
    [...]    // other methods
}
```

Tip Here we talk of *anonymous internal classes*, as a class is created implicitly, derived from the stated Adapter class. Instead of an Adapter class, you can also state the Listener interface here, but then – as usual – all of the contained methods must be implemented.

> **Tip** In Java 1.3 there is a more elegant solution for validating user entries. The new abstract class *javax.swing.InputVerifier* allows the user entry in a *JComponent* (Swing component, see Section 8.6.2) to be checked before the user is allowed to move the focus out from the control element.

8.5 Additional important AWT classes

In addition to classes for windows, control elements, LayoutManagers and event handling, the Abstract Windowing Toolkit also contains a number of additional classes dealing with the operating interface. These include the support of 2D graphics, the display of images and the use of the system clipboard.

First, to the subject of graphics:

8.5.1 The Graphics and Graphics2D classes

The graphics class

since	SE	ME	EE
1.0	x	-	x

The abstract class *java.awt.Graphics* provides the graphics primitive. You can define a font and character color, as well as issue lines, rectangles, circles and other graphic forms. Developers do not create a *Graphics* object themself, but have it placed from the context in which they want to draw.

> **Tip** This means that the *Graphics* class has no (public) constructor, but the classes of Component (and thus also *Frame, Applet* etc., see Section 8.2.1) as well as *PrintJob* (see Section 8.5.9) have a getGraphics()method, which returns a *Graphics* object. This then represents the character area of the applet, the inside of a window, or even a sheet of paper in the printer.

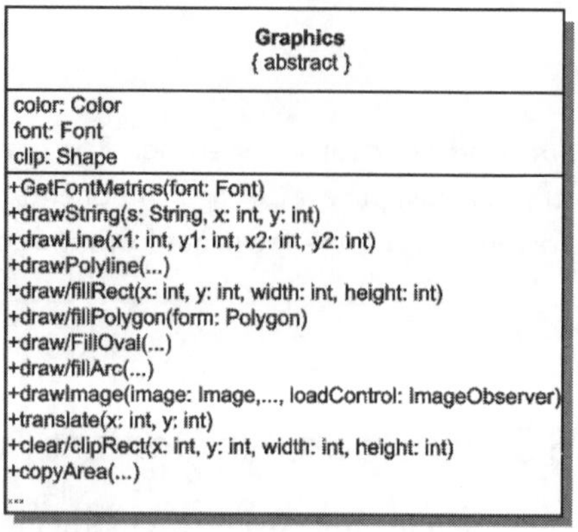

Figure 8.44 *The Graphics class*

Methods and attributes

You can define attributes such as font and character color (see Section 8.5.2) for the output of texts and graphic forms. Using `drawString()` you output a String to a certain position, `drawImage()` represents a bitmapgraphic (see Section 8.5.8). `drawLine()` outputs a line between two points, and `drawPolyline()` gives a course of a line with several reference points. Simple forms such as rectangles, ellipses or arcs can be output using `drawRect()`, `drawOval()` or `drawArc()`. If these are to be infilled, you use the corresponding `fill` method, such as `fillRect()` or `fillOval()`. However, the drawing facilities are rather restricted: there is only one thickness of line; there are no dotted lines or Bézier curves at all. This is not remedied until Java 2 with its 2D-graphics package *java.awt.geom*.

Frequently, not all fields have to be drawn, but only a section, called the *Clipping Area*, or Clip for short. You can set this using `setClip()`. Sections can be copied using `copyArea()` and deleted using `clearRect()` . `translate()` moves the original co-ordinate to the stated point.

The Graphics2D class

since	SE	ME	EE
1.2	x	-	x

The abstract class *java.awt.Graphics2D* expands the functionality of *Graphics* by transformations, line thicknesses, and style.

Methods and attributes

This class opens up practically unlimited opportunities for creating graphics. Using the `stroke` attribute, you can define line styles. This means that you can now create dotted, broken or normal lines in any thickness, as well as determine the appearance of the ends of lines and lines that abut.

`paint` expands the color model by the facility to use running colors or textures for filling geometric shapes. `transform` allows changes in the shape. There are also direct methods for some typical transformations such as rotate, move or scale. `composite` states how objects of different colors are to be overlain, and also allows soft color transfers (Anti-Aliasing).

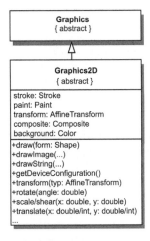

Figure 8.45 *The Graphics2D class*

Even the `draw` methods have been expanded. So you can draw any shape using `draw(Shape form)`; `drawImage()` supports different image types and `draw String()` allows the representation of handwriting in any style or direction.

```java
public void paint(Graphics g)          // e.g. in an applet
{
   Graphics2D g2 = (Graphics2D) g; // possible since Java 2
   Paint gp = Color.blue;
   g2.setPaint(gp);
   g2.fillRect(60, 60, 100, 80);   // blue rectangle
   g2.setComposite(AlphaComposite.getInstance(
     AlphaComposite.SRC_OVER, 0.5f)); // half transparent
   g2.setColor(Color.green));
   g2.fillOval(100, 45, 50, 50); // green circle
}
```

Tip The 2D-Graphics of Java 2 is very powerful. Unfortunately, it's not possible here to go into the graphics theory and all classes in greater detail; however, you can find a good example of how the classes can be used in Sun JDK under <JDK path>\demo\jfc\Java2D\Java2Demo.html. Apart from the *java.awt.Graphics2D* class, Java 2D covers API classes in the packages *java.awt.geom* (geometric shapes, paths and transformations), *java.awt.font* (txt setting), *java.awt.color* (color areas), *java.awt.image* and *java.awt.image.renderable* (bitmaps and filters) as well as *java.awt.print* (printing).

8.5.2   The Color class

since	SE	ME	EE
1.0/1.2	x	-	x

An object of the *Color* class represents a color in the RGB color scheme (see Figure 8.46). Since Java 2, additional color schemes have been supported. *Color* now implements both the new *Paint* interface (drawing color) and the two new classes *GradientPaint* (running color), and *TexturePaint* (bitmap as filling pattern).

Methods and attributes

A color object can be constructed from ratios of red, green and blue (in percentages as a *float* between 0.0 and 1.0 or as whole numbers between 0 and 255) or you can use the pre-defined color constants, such as `Color.red` or `Color.darkGray`. The *Color* class has methods for interrogating the color ratios, for lightening or darkening and for converting to other color models.

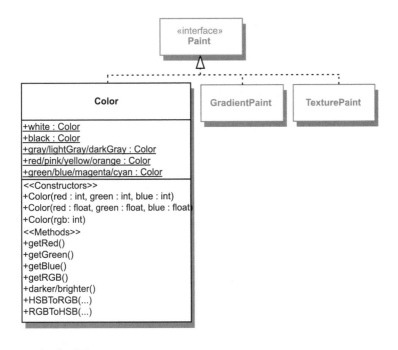

Figure 8.46 *The Color class*

8.5.3 The Font and FontMetrics classes

since	SE	ME	EE
1.0/1.2	x	-	x

Fonts are represented in the *Font* class. Runtime attributes such as the height of the lettering or the width of the Strings to be output in pixels depending on the font and size set can be determined using the *FontMetrics* class.

The font classes have been expanded in Java 2. In addition to new methods in both classes, there is now a *java.awt.font* package with classes for the analysis, manipulation, and output of fonts.

```
┌─────────────────────────────────────┐   ┌──────────────────────────────────┐
│                Font                  │   │           FontMetrics            │
│                                      │   │            {abstract}            │
├─────────────────────────────────────┤   ├──────────────────────────────────┤
│ +PLAIN: int                          │   │ +stringWidth(s: String)          │
│ +BOLD: int                           │   │ +charWidth(ch: char)             │
│ +ITALIC: int                         │   │ +getFont()                       │
├─────────────────────────────────────┤   │ +getHeight()                     │
│ <<Constructors>>                     │   │ +getWidths()                     │
│ +Font(name: String, style: int, size: int) │ +get[Max]Ascent()            │
│ +Font(attribute: Map)                │   │ +get[Max]Descent()               │
├─────────────────────────────────────┤   │ +getMaxAdvance()                 │
│ <<Methods>>                          │   │ +getLeading()                    │
│ +getName()                           │   │ +getStringBounds(str: String,    │
│ +getFamily()                         │   │               context: Graphics) │
│ +getSize()                           │   │ +getLineMetrics(str: String,     │
│ +getStyle()                          │   │               context: Graphics) │
│ +isPlain()                           │   │ ...                              │
│ +isBold()                            │   └──────────────────────────────────┘
│ +isItalic()                          │
│ +getAttributes()                     │
│ +Decode(font: String)                │
│ +GetFont(systemFont: String)         │
│ +DeriveFont(newStyle: int)           │
│ +CanDisplay(character: char)         │
│ ...                                  │
└─────────────────────────────────────┘
```

Figure 8.47 *The Font and FontMetrics classes*

Methods and attributes

A font is defined using the font name, for example "SansSerif" or "Dialog", the font size, for example 12 point, and a style. Pre-defined style constants are bold (Font.BOLD) and italic (Font.ITALIC). There are some standard fonts that exist on all Java systems (*Dialog, SansSerif, Serif,* and *Monospaced*). You can determine these using the AWT toolkit:

```
Toolkit.getDefaultToolkit().getFontList();
```

 If you want to output a String as a graphic and want to calculate the size in pixels to determine the output position, you can get a reference to a *FontMetrics* object by calling up the getFontMetrics on the *Graphics* object and calculate the size using stringWidth(outputString) and getHeight():

```
String outputString = "Demo";
Font f = new Font("Dialog", Font.PLAIN + Font.BOLD, 12);
graph.setFont(f);  // This is the Graphics object
                   // in the current context
FontMetrics fm = graph.getFontMetrics();
int widthInPixels = fm.stringWidth(outputString);
int heightInPixels  = fm.getHeight();
```

New methods

With Java 2, you can use all installed fonts and their styles. Instead of using the *Toolkit* class, you can now interrogate the fonts present locally using the *GraphicsEnvironment* class:

```
ge = GraphicsEnvironment.getLocalGraphicsEnvironment();
String[] fontNames = ge.getAvailableFontFamilyNames();
```

Using `getAllFonts()`, you can also get the variants of a font, for example a true (not calculated) italic or a variant for condensed type. For such a named font, you can instantiate a *Font* object using the `decode()` class method of the *Font* class. Using `derive()`, you can create a style variant for a stated font and, using `can-Display()`, you can determine whether the stated character can be displayed in the font used. This does not always have to be the case, because the Unicode font even contains Korean characters, for example, which cannot be represented using general fonts.

8.5.4   Dimensional information

since	SE	ME	EE
1.0	x	-	x

int values are used for most dimensional information. However, there are also frequently alternative formulation facilities using the classes *Dimension*, *Point*, and *Rectangle*.

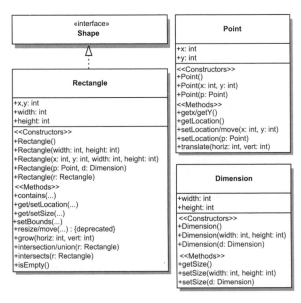

Figure 8.48   *The Dimension and Rectangle classes*

Methods and attributes

All `getSize` calls on control elements return an object of the *Dimension* class. In this class, the width (`width`) and height (`height`) are defined as public instance variables. If you ask a control element or a graphic shape for the rectangle surrounding it (using `getBounds()` or `getBoundingBox()`), then you will get an object of the *Rectangle* type. The class contains methods such as Content, Intersection, Association, and different manipulation functions.

```
Rectangle r1 = new Rectangle(100, 100, 200, 50);
Point corner = r1.getLocation();
Dimension size = r1.getSize();
corner.y = 140; size.width = 110;
Rectangle r2 = new Rectangle(corner, size);
Rectangle total = r1.union(r2);
```

8.5.5   The Shape interface and geometric shapes

since	SE	ME	EE
1.2	x	-	x

The *Shape* interface is implemented by the previous figures (e.g. *Rectangle, Polygon*) as well as by the new geometric shapes in the *java.awt.geom* package.

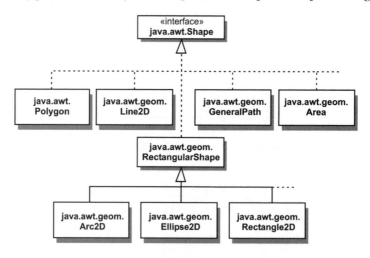

Figure 8.49   *The Shape interface and implementing classes*

The *java.awt.geom.GeneralPath* class represents open or closed courses of lines or curves.

Methods and attributes

`moveTo()` moves the cursor to the stated coordinate. `lineTo()` draws a line, `quadTo()` a quadrate curve (parabolic curve), and `curveTo()` a Bézier curve. `closePath()` draws a line to the coordinates of the last `moveTo()`.

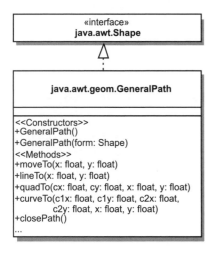

«interface»
java.awt.Shape

java.awt.geom.GeneralPath

<<Constructors>>
+GeneralPath()
+GeneralPath(form: Shape)
<<Methods>>
+moveTo(x: float, y: float)
+lineTo(x: float, y: float)
+quadTo(cx: float, cy: float, x: float, y: float)
+curveTo(c1x: float, c1y: float, c2x: float,
       c2y: float, x: float, y: float)
+closePath()
...

Figure 8.50 *The GeneralPath class*

8.5.6 The Cursor class

since	SE	ME	EE
1.1	x	-	x

You can also state the type of cursor in all windows and control elements that is to be displayed when it is over this element. Different constants are pre-defined in the *Cursor* class (see Figure 8.51).

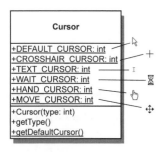

Cursor

+DEFAULT_CURSOR: int
+CROSSHAIR_CURSOR: int
+TEXT_CURSOR: int
+WAIT_CURSOR: int
+HAND_CURSOR: int
+MOVE_CURSOR: int
+Cursor(type: int)
+getType()
+getDefaultCursor()

Figure 8.51 *The Cursor class*

Tip Since Java 2, you can also use your own symbols for the cursor. To do this, use the `create-CustomCursor()` method of the *Toolkit* class (see Section 8.5.7, next).

8.5.7   The Toolkit class

since	SE	ME	EE
1.0	x	-	x

The *Toolkit* class – like *java.lang.System* - allows you to access system properties and resources but does, however, refer more strongly to the graphics subsystem.

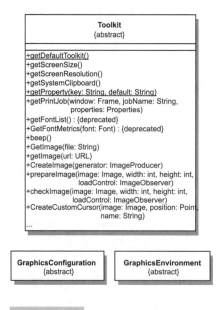

Figure 8.52 *The Toolkit class*

Methods and attributes

You can get a reference to the Toolkit using the `Toolkit.getDefaultTool-kit()` class method. Using this class, you can determine the resolution and size of the screen, which is important for centering windows. `getSystemClipboard()` gives a reference to the clipboard and `beep()` creates a beep. Using `getPrintJob()` you can generate a print order as we can see in Section 8.5.9.

Using `getFontList()`, you can get the standard fonts. However, since JDK 1.2 the method is deprecated and has been replaced by `getAvailableFontFami-`

lyNames() in the new *GraphicsEnvironment* class (see the Font and FontMetrics classes).

getProperty(<key>, <defaultValue>) interrogates runtime variables, which you can give to the Java Interpreter using the D<key>=<value> option.

The getImage() method loads an image from the stated source; standard formats are GIF and JPG. However, this image can often not be displayed immediately as it is still being loaded. A check on the loading and rendering process therefore takes place using the prepareImage() and checkImage() methods as well as the *ImageObserver* class (see Section 8.5.8).

The method createCustomCursor() has been available since Java 2 and allows you to define your own cursor (see Section 8.5.6).

```
Toolkit tk = Toolkit.getDefaultToolkit();
// Position window in screen center:
Dimension screenSize = tk.getScreenSize();
Dimension windowSize = win.getSize();
win.setLocation((screenSize.width - windowSize.width) / 2,
            (screenSize.height - windowSize.height) / 2);
// Read font from environment variable,
// if not stated, then "Dialog" will be used:
Font = new Font(tk.getProperty("Font", "Dialog"));
// Beep:
tk.beep();
```

8.5.8   Image classes

since	SE	ME	EE
1.0/1.2	x	-	x

The classes for image processing can be found in the *java.awt.image* package (see Figure 8.53). Using the *java.awt.Toolkit* class, you can load an image from a stated source (getImage(file/URL)). You will get back a *java.awt.Image* type object, which is immediately available. If you now output the image using drawImage(), it may be possible that the memory does not contain the complete image, particularly if you are loading it from the Internet. You can therefore monitor the load status of an object, whose class is implemented by the *java.awt.image.ImageObserver* interface. This is done, for example, by all AWT and Swing control elements. For simpler use in loading several images, there is also the *java.awt.MediaTracker* class. The additional classes in the *java.awt.image* package will allow you to scale, rotate, filter, and otherwise change the images. GIF and JPG are supported as image formats.

In Java 2, several classes appeared in the *java.awt.image* package and the new *java.awt.image.renderable* for the pixel-oriented creation and processing of images. The classes are closely related to the new 2D-graphics (see Sections 8.5.1 and 8.5.5) as well as to the color models (see Section 8.5.2).

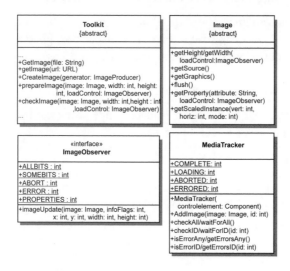

Figure 8.53 *Classes for displaying images*

```
Toolkit tk = Toolkit.getDefaultToolkit();
MediaTracker tracker = new MediaTracker();
Image image = tk.getImage("image.gif");
tracker.addImage(image, 0);
tracker.waitForID(0);
if (tracker.checkAll() && !tracker.isErrorAny())
{
    outputPanel.getGraphics().drawImage(
        image, 0, 0, outputPanel);
}
```

Tip In the Swing library, along with the *Icon* interface and the *IconImage* class there is further support for simple images, carrying out the loading process internally using *MediaTracker*.

8.5.9 The PrintJob class

since	SE	ME	EE
1.0/1.3	x	-	x

The print functionality in JDK 1.1 is not particularly convenient. It is based on a *Graphics* object; this is output to a sheet of paper instead of the screen. In this way, all AWT graphic elements can be used for the printout. However, expanded functions such as automatic page breaks are missing.

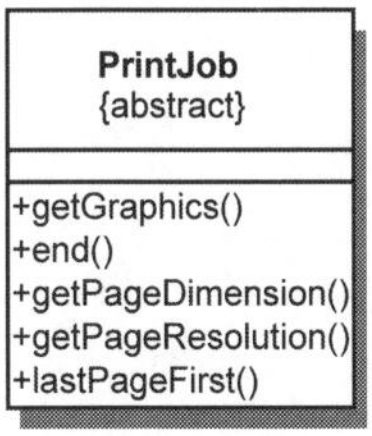

```
+---------------------------+
|         PrintJob          |
|        {abstract}         |
+---------------------------+
|                           |
+---------------------------+
| +getGraphics()            |
| +end()                    |
| +getPageDimension()       |
| +getPageResolution()      |
| +lastPageFirst()          |
+---------------------------+
```

Figure 8.54 *The PrintJob class*

Run

1   First you request a print order using the `getPrintJob()` method of the *Toolkit* class.

2   After that, a window appears for you to select the printer (see Figure 8.55). By selecting Setup, the properties of the print order can be set to this printer, for example portrait/landscape, resolution, paper format etc. If the user confirms the dialog, an object of the *PrintJob* class is returned, otherwise `null`.

3   From the *PrintJob* object, you get a reference to the *Graphics* object of the next page to be printed and you can draw on it.

4   Using the `dispose` method of the *Graphics* object, you send the page to the printer.

5   If you want to print further pages, you must obtain a new *Graphics* object from the *PrintJob* for each page.

6   `end()` closes the print job.

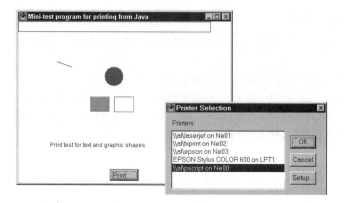

Figure 8.55 *Printing a window*

```
PrintJob pjob = getToolkit().getPrintJob(null,
                "Print-Test", (Properties) null);
if (pjob != null) // User has confirmed the job
{                  // and set options
   // obtain next page:
   Graphics page = pjob.getGraphics();
   if (page != null)
   {
      printAll(page);  // Contents on Graphics object
                       // draw
      page.dispose();  // close page
   }
   pjob.end();  // if there is no further page
}
```

Warning Printing from non-signed applets is not permitted and results in a *SecurityException*.

Tip In the package *java.awt.print* Java Version 1.2 contains classes (see Section 8.5.10) that let you work with different document types, and manage page layouts, formats and print jobs. Do not confuse the *PrinterJob* class with the previous *PrintJob*!

> **Tip** In Java Version 1.3, the *java.awt* package contains the two new classes *JobAttributes* and *Page-Attributes*, through which it is possible to interrogate and set the attributes of the print job and the printer, such as resolution, paper type, or duplex printing. A further variant of the `getPrintJob` methods is added to it in *java.awt.Toolkit*:
>
> ```
> public PrintJob getPrintJob(Frame window,
>     String jobName, JobAttributes jobAttributes,
>     PageAttributes pageAttributes)
> ```

8.5.10   PrinterJob and other printer classes

since	SE	ME	EE
1.2	x	-	x

The new Print-API can be found in the *java.awt.print* package. This works by page. You define a document (from the *Book* class or another implementation of *Printable*) and for each page you define a *PageFormat*. This is then passed to the *PrinterJob* object, which sends the correct number of print jobs to the selected printer. The end user can optionally set the formats.

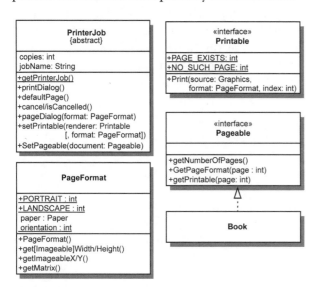

Figure 8.56   Print classes in Java 2

Methods and attributes

`getPrinterJob()` gives an object of the *PrinterJob* type. The user can select a printer and the number of copies in the selection window displayed using `printDialog()`. In order to be able to print an order, you first need one or more pages. In the simplest case, you can create standard pages using the `de-faultPage()` method (DIN A4, portrait). Alternatively, you can also select the user of the format in a selection window using `pageDialog()`. `set-Printable()` links a *Printable* object with the *PrinterJob* and `setPage-able()` sets a *Pageable* object. `print()` finally starts the printing.

The *PageFormat* interface contains the orientation (landscape/portrait), the size of the paper, as well as the printable area on the page.

The *Pageable* interface, on the other hand, represents the document with a number of pages. Each page can have its own *PageFormat*. The standard implementation is *Book*. This is used if you have documents with pages with different formats.

The *Printable* interface only has the `print()` method, which prepares a page for printing (rendering) and is used for print orders with a uniform format.

Printing from a class with a uniform format:
The Printable interface

`print(Graphics source, PageFormat format, int pageIndex)` is called using the `print` command of a PrinterJob object, which is associated with the *Printable* object – and in succession for all Page indices. If the method returns `PAGE_EXISTS`, then the page (in *PageFormat* format) previously drawn on the *Graphics* object `source` is printed out on the printer. If the method returns `Printable.NO_SUCH_PAGE`, then nothing is printed.

```java
import java.awt.*;
import java.awt.print.*;
public class PagesPrint implements Printable
{
   public static void main(String[] args)
   {
      PagesPrint pagesprint = new PagesPrint();
      PrinterJob pjob = PrinterJob.getPrinterJob();
      if (pjob.printDialog())   // Printer selection
      {
         PageFormat format =    // Pageformat
           pjob.pageDialog(pjob.defaultPage());
         pjob.setPrintable(pagesprint, format);
         try { pjob.print(); }  // Start printing
            catch (PrinterException e) { }
```

```
        }
    }
    public int print(Graphics g, PageFormat format,
            int index) throws PrinterException
    {
        if (index >3 ) return Printable.NO_SUCH_PAGE;
        g.setFont(new Font("Serif", Font.PLAIN, 48));
        g.drawString("Page: " +
                    String.valueOf(index), 100, 200);
        return Printable.PAGE_EXISTS;
    }
}
```

Printing from different classes or formats

If you are printing documents where the pages have different formats, you can implement the *Pageable* interface or use an object of the *Book* class, which files the *Printables* with its *PageFormat* in a *Vector* and has an append method.

Book() creates a new *Book* without entries. append() adds to the rear of the book a *Printable* page with associated *PageFormat*. By allocating a *Book* object to a *PrinterJob* and calling the print() method, the print methods of the individual *Printable* objects respectively are called up.

```
Book bk = new Book();
bk.append(Printable, job.defaultPage());
bk.append...
pjob.setPageable(bk);
try { pjob.print(); }
catch (PrinterException e) { /* handle Exception */ }
```

8.6 Swing

Using Java 2, an additional user interface library was added to AWT – *Swing*. This library, contained in the *javax.swing* package and a few subpackages contains numerous powerful classes, such as tree views, tables and notebook control elements. It is the main component of the *Java Foundation Classes*, so you often read the abbreviation *JFC* instead of *Swing*.

A comparison with AWT can be found in Section 8.1.1.

Tip Programming graphical user interfaces without any aids requires a good imagination. In addition, due to the volume and routine activities, programming is subject to errors and the code produced is hard to maintain. We therefore recommend using GUI editors, as can be found in many integrated development environments.

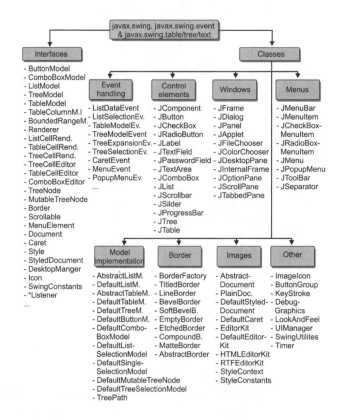

Figure 8.57 *Classes and interfaces of the Swing library*

8.6.1   Model-View-Controller design example

AWT manages all of the data to be displayed, even in the user interface control elements. So the elements of a list, for example, are contained both in the original source and as Strings in the *List* object. This dual management is obviously inconvenient, particularly if the data can change on both sides and therefore has to be synchronized.

Swing, on the other hand, uses the *Model-View-Controller* approach, which means the consistent separation of the data and the display. In the Model-View-Controller design example (MVC) there are three different sorts of application element:

→ *Model* (`data model`) – The status and functionality are stored in the data model. It can respond to enquiries from View on its status, and process status change requests from the Controller or other objects.

→ *View* (`Display, "Look"`) – The view knows little or nothing of the data model and simply graphically represents the data.

→ *Controller* (`control, "Feel"`) – Control represents a model of the real world and reacts to the user input via mouse, keyboard, or other entry devices.

In this way, a strict separation is obtained between the user interface and the program logic. However, Swing does not maintain this separation everywhere. Data and function models are indeed separated from the display (*View*) but the display also contains the user interaction (*Delegate*). However, with some control elements, you can release the controller components from the display (View) and replace them with others (such as the selection or editing of data).

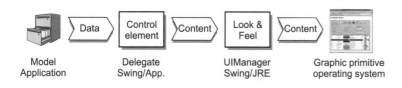

Figure 8.58 *Steps towards displaying in Swing*

Display proceeds in the following stages:

1 The control element only interrogates the model on those values which are currently visible.

2 This data is passed to a *UIManager*, which carries out the actual rendering. So, for example, a tree view can be represented in the way that is usual under Windows or Unix/Motif.

3 The implementing classes draw the user interface using the graphic primitive and output it to the target operating system.

8.6.2 The JComponent class

since	SE	ME	EE
1.2	x	-	x

Swing elements fall into two groups:

→ Windows (see Section 8.2.11), which are displayed directly by the operating system, e.g. *JFrame, JDialog* or *JApplet*. These are derived from the respective AWT components and are called heavy-weight components.

→ Control elements rendered by Java itself (light-weight components). These are subclasses of *JComponent*.

javax.swing.JComponent is derived from *java.awt.Container* and thus from *java.awt.Component* and so contains all of the methods described in Sections 8.2.1 and 8.2.9. As *Containers*, all of the *JComponents* in particular can also contain other *JComponents*.

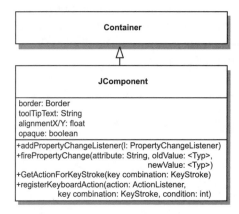

Figure 8.59 *The JComponent class*

Methods and attributes

Using the `border` property, a framework can be drawn around the components. There are different border classes for this, which define the appearance of the border. Examples include borders with a 3D-effect or with lettering incorporated in the border (see Figure 8.60). Some classes are included in the *javax.swing.border* package or in the platform-specific Look & Feel libraries.

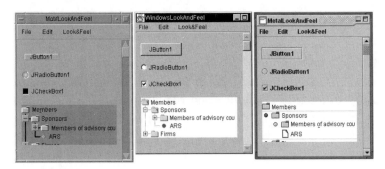

Figure 8.60 *Border variants*

Using *Tooltips*, a short description is overlain when the cursor rests for a moment over the component.

Mnemonics or KeyboardActions define key shortcuts and are used frequently, particularly in the case of menus. You can register an action and its associated key combination using `registerKeyboardAction()`.

> **Tip** In the language version 1.3, there are the two new Swing classes *InputMap* and *ActionMap* for the control of the keyboard. These are allocation tables that link key combinations with certain actions.

With Swing components, a *UIManager* can be stated, which determines the platform-specific appearance (*Look & Feel*).

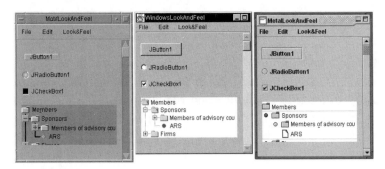

Figure 8.61 *Look & Feel variants of a Dialog window*

```
try
{  // Standard is Windows Look & Feel
   UIManager.setLookAndFeel(
     "com.sun.java.swing.plaf.windows.WindowsLookAndFeel");
}
catch (ClassNotFoundException e)
{  // Windows Look & Feel not found -> Platform L&F
   UIManager.setLookAndFeel(
}
```

Summary

Functionality	Description	Use
Framework	Definition and appearance of the border of a control element	`setBorder()` BorderFactory and Border classes
Tooltips	Help, if the cursor rests for a moment on the component	`setToolTipText()`

Keyboard navigation	Definition of key shortcuts	`registerKeyboardAction()`
		 `setAccelerator/setMnemonic()`
		 for some control elements

Display	Definition of layout restrictions	`setMinimumSize()`
		 `setMaximumSize()`
		 `setPreferredSize()`
		 `setAlignmentX()`
		 `setAlignmentY()`
		 `UIManager.setLookAndFeel()`

8.6.3   Overview of the Swing control elements

The following table is an overview of the most important functions of the Swing control elements that, together with the standard functionality of *JComponent* (see Section 8.6.2), are assumed to cover 90% of all application cases.

Tip The numbers in brackets refer to explanations following the overview.

Name	Description	Special properties	Methods	Events
JButton	Action button, pushbutton	text (not label!) actionCommand icon/pressedIcon enabled disabledIcon defaultButton	doClick(int)	action- Performed
JCheckBox	Control box	text (not label!) selected (not state!) icon pressedIcon disabledIcon	isSelected() setSelected (boolean) doClick(int)	itemState- Changed action- Performed
JRadioButton	Option switches (together with the ButtonGroup using the methods add and remove)	text selected icon pressedIcon disabledIcon	isSelected() setSelected (boolean) doClick(int)	itemState- Changed action- Performed
JLabel	Static text	text icon landscape/portrait Alignment	setText(String)	
JTextField, JPassword- Field	Datafield, single line text entry	text selectedText document columns editable landscapeAlignment echoChar (only with JPass wordField)	setText(String) cut/copy/paste()	action- Performed keyTyped caretUpdate
JTextArea	Datafield, multi-line text entry	text selectedText document columns rows lineWrap lineCount editable	setText(String) append(String) insert(String, int) cut/copy/paste() getCaret- Position() selectAll()	keyTyped caretUpdate

Name	Description	Special properties	Methods	Events
JSlider	Elevator	value minimum/maximum major/minor tab spacing orientation paintTicks/paint- Labels snapToTicks extent model	getValue() setValue(int)	stateChanged
JScrollBar	Scrollbars (horizontal and vertical)	value minimum/maximum block/unitIncrement orientation visibleAmount model	getValue() setValue(int)	adjustment- Value- Changed
JList	List field, list of Strings	model (1) selectionMode (2) selectedValue[s] selectedIndex first/lastVisibleIndex visibleRowCount selectionModel cellRenderer	ensureIndexIs- Visible(...) clearSelection() addSelection- Interval(...) isSelected- Index(int) isSelection- Empty() setListData(...) (1)	value Changed
JComboBox	Combination list, drop-down list	model editable selectedItem selectedIndex itemCount maximumRowCount cellRenderer	addItem(Object) insertItem- At(Object, int) remove[ItemAt] (int) remove- All[Items]() getItemAt(int)	itemState- Changed action- Performed

Name	Description	Special properties	Methods	Events
JTree	Tree view, browser display	model (3) editable editing/editingPath cellEditor cellRenderer selectionModel selectionPath min/maxSelection- Row selection- Count/Row[s] visibleRowCount	getRowFor Path() collapsePath/ Row(...) isCollapsed(...) expandPath/ Row(...) isExpanded(...) startEditing- AtPath(...) stopEditing() addSelection- Interval(...) addSelection- Rows(...) addSelection- Path[s](...) clearSelection()	treeCollapsed treeExpanded treeSelection- Events
JTable	Table	model (4) selectionMode selectedRow[s] selectedColumn[s] column/row- SelectionAllowed autoCreateColumns- FromModel cellEditor defaultRenderer showHorizontal- Lines showVerticalLines column/rowCount gridColor intercellSpacing selectionModel	getValueAt(int, int) setValueAt(...) editCellAt(int, int) add/remove- Column(...) moveCol umn(int, int) add/remove- Column/ RowSelection- Interval(...) selectAll() clearSelection() isCellSe lected(int, int) isRowSe- lected(int) isColumn- Selected (int) isCellEdit able(int, int)	

Name	Description	Special properties	Methods	Events
TableColumn	Table column	headerValue identifier cellRenderer cellEditor resizable width	sizeWidth ToFit() (5) getModelIndex()	
JToolBar	Function bar	floatable (6)	add/remove(...) addSeparator()	
JProgressBar	Scale, progress indicator	value minimum/maximum orientation visibleAmount model	getValue() setValue(int)	stateChanged
JPanel	Panel, window area for layout	layout components	add(Compo- nent) getCompo- nent[At](...) getComponent- Count() remove(...) removeAll()	component- Added component- Removed
JScrollPane	Part window with scrollbars	viewport horizontalScroll- Bar[Policy] verticalScroll- Bar[Policy] column/rowHeader-View	see JPanel! createHorizon- tal/ VerticalScroll- Bar()	see JPanel!
JSplitPane	2 Panels with split bar	orientation left/rightComponent bottom/topComponent [last]dividerLocation dividerSize	see JPanel! resetTo- PreferredSizes()	see JPanel!
JTabbedPane	Notebook	tabPlacement tabCount selectedComponent selectedIndexmodel	see JPanel! add/remove- TabAt(...) get/setTitleAt(...) get/setIconAt(...)	see JPanel! stateChanged

Name	Description	Special properties	Methods	Events
JTextPane (7)	Data entry using word processing functions	document/styled-Document page text contentType editable editorKit logicalStyle selectedText	cut/copy/paste() setPage(URL) getContent-Type() selectAll()	caretUpdate (7) hyperlink-Update
(JEditorPane	Superclass of JTextPane)			
JOptionPane (8)(9)	Messagebox or content for your own Messageboxes	messageType message icon optionType (9) value wantsInput inputValue initialValue initialSelectionValue	showConfirm-Dialog(...) showMessage-Dialog(...) showInput-Dialog(...) createDialog(...) getSelection-Values() selectInitial-Value()	property-Change
JFrame	Application window	title resizable size/location iconImage defaultClose-Operation menuBar/JMenuBar contentPane	setVisible (boolean) show() dispose() repaint()	window-Opened window-Closing window-Activated window-Deactivated
JInternal-Frame	Internal subsidiary window (MDI)	title resizable closable/closed maximizable selected iconifiable icon/frameIcon size defaultClose-Operation menuBar contentPane	setVisible (boolean) show() setClosed (boolean) setMaximum (boolean) setSelected (boolean) setIcon(boolean) repaint()	

Name	Description	Special properties	Methods	Events
JDesktop Pane	Window area containing internal subsidiary window (MDI)	componentsInLayer components-CountInLayer	getDesktop-Manager() setDesktop-Manager(...) getCompo nents() getComponent-At(...) getComponent-InLayer() moveTo-Back/Front(...) get/setLayer(...)	component-Added component-Removed
JDialog	Dialog window, message window	title resizable size modal defaultClose-Operation contentPane	setVisible(bool ean) show() dispose() repaint() toBack/Front() setLocation-RelativeTo()	window-Opened window-Closing window-Activated window-Deactivated
JApplet	Applet, application in web browser	appletContext codeBase documentBase appletInfo parameterInfo	see JPanel! start/stop() init/destroy() repaint() getParameter (String) getAudio Clip(URL) play() getImage(URL)	see JPanel!
JMenuBar	Menu bar	menuCount	add(JMenu) getMenu(int) remove(...)	
JPopupMenu	Context menu	label popupSize	add(JMenuItem) addSeparator() show(...)	popupMenu-WillBecome-Visible/In-visible popupMenu-Canceled

Name	Description	Special properties	Methods	Events
JMenu	Menu in a menu bar or as a submenu	text (not label!) actionCommand accelerator mnemonic icon itemCount menuComponent-Count selected	add(JMenuItem) addSeparator() insert/ remove(...) doClick(int) isSelected() isTopLevel Menu()	action-Performed itemState-Changed menuSelected menu-Deselected menuCanceled
JMenuItem	Menu item	text (not label!) actionCommand accelerator mnemonic icon pressedIcon disabledIcon	doClick(int) isSelected()	itemState-Changed action-Performed
JRadio Button-MenuItem JCheckBox-MenuItem	Menu item	text (not label!) selected actionCommand accelerator mnemonic selected icon selectedIcon pressedIcon disabledIcon	doClick(int) isSelected()	itemState-Changed action-Performed

Notes

The model for *JList* must implement the *ListModel* interface; *AbstractListModel* can be used as the derivation basis for the concrete (data) class; the class *Default-ListModel* contains an implementation as a *Vector*. If it is a matter of a simple static list, you can also do without the design of a model and instead allocate the data in the form of a *Vector* or Array using the `setListData()` method of the *JList*.

Modes of selection:

1 SINGLE_SELECTION – simple selection (one entry at most).

2 MULTI_INTERVAL_SELECTION – multiple selection (as many entries as you want).

3 SINGLE_INTERVAL_SELECTION – range selection (continuous interval).

4 The model for *JTree* must implement the *TreeModel* interface; *Default-TreeModel* can be used as the basis of derivation for the concrete (data) class. The individual nodes must implement the *TreeNode* or *Mutable-TreeNode* interfaces; the *DefaultMutableTreeNode* class contains a universal implementation, including navigation methods for tree structures.

5 The model for *JTable* must implement the *TableModel* interface; *AbstractTableModel* can be used as the basis of derivation for the concrete (data) class; the *DefaultTableModel* class contains an implementation from *Vector* objects nested inside each other.

6 The width is not adjusted automatically but must be initiated on changing the data displayed.

7 The use of free floating and movable toolbars does presuppose some adaptation work. In particular, *BorderLayout* should be selected in the parent window as the LayoutManager and the toolbar placed at the edge. The central field (CENTER) contains the client area. The other (Layout) fields may not be occupied as you would also be able to draw the toolbar into these fields and this would result in overlapping control elements.

8 The *JTextPane* is (unlike *JTextArea*) a complex control element for entering and displaying formatted text, such as in HTML or RTF formats. The cursor (text cursor) is used for positioning and selection.

9 *JOptionPane* is considered to be a simple message and entry window. It has a number of standard types, identified by different symbols (icons).

   - ERROR_MESSAGE

   - INFORMATION_MESSAGE

   - WARNING_MESSAGE

   - QUESTION_MESSAGE

   - PLAIN_MESSAGE (no symbol)

Icon Look & Feel	Error	Information	Question	Warning
Metal	⬡	ⓘ	ⓠ	⚠
Motif	⊘	i	ⓠ	❗
Windows	⊗	ⓘ	ⓠ	⚠

Figure 8.62 *Symbols for JOptionPane*

8.6.4 The JButton class

since	SE	ME	EE
1.2	x	-	x

Figure 8.63 *Display of JButtons*

Buttons, often also called *switches* or pushbuttons, are rectangular buttons that trigger an action when the user clicks on them. The *JButton* class is the equivalent for the AWT *Button* (see Section 8.2.3). The majority of the methods has already been defined in the *AbstractButton* superclass.

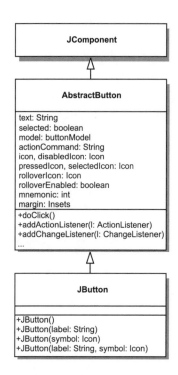

Figure 8.64 *The JButton class*

Methods and attributes

From the point of view of event handling, the *JButton* does not differ from an AWT *Button*. The `actionCommand` property is a String, which characterizes the button in the case of an *ActionEvent*. The event with the associated `action-Performed()` method is triggered when the button is pressed. If `actionCommand` is not set, then it is given the value of `text`; in the case of multi-language user interfaces, however, it can be sensible if the two values differ.

As described in the section on event handling (see Section 8.4), all classes that have to be reported when the button is pressed must register a *Listener* using `addActionListener()`.

Using the `mnemonic` property, you can define a key shortcut; the property for the label is now called a uniform `text` for all Swing components. Using the `do-Click()` method, you can simulate clicking on a button. You will find the design of the appearance to be significantly more flexible: you can state symbols for the different statuses of a button (`icon`, `pressedIcon`, `disabledIcon`, `rollo-verIcon`) and it is possible to define a border. For example, you can also integrate into a graphic a button that is completely borderless and shaded with an image.

The *ButtonModel* type model identifies the status of a *JButton*, such as *selected*, *pressed* or *rollover*. In addition, *EventListener* methods and keyboard control are required. The standard implementation is *DefaultButtonModel*.

```
JButton okButton =
    new JButton("OK", new ImageIcon("ok.gif"));
okButton.setActionCommand("OK");
okButton.addActionListener(eventHandler);
```

8.6.5   The JCheckBox and JRadioButton classes

since	SE	ME	EE
1.2	×	-	×

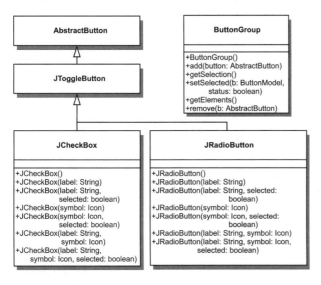

☑ Standard

🔆 with Icon (selected)

💡 with Icon (unselected)

┌─ Group of Radio Buttons ─┐
◉ Option 1

◯ Option 2
└─────────────────────────┘

Figure 8.65   *Display of JCheckBox and JRadioButton*

In Swing, round and angular option boxes are no longer combined in one class (compare with Section 8.2.4), but are represented by the two *JCheckBox* and *JRadioButton* classes. The allocation of mutually exclusive options to a group takes place through an object of the *ButtonGroup* class.

```
┌─────────────────────────────┐      ┌─────────────────────────────────┐
│      AbstractButton          │      │         ButtonGroup              │
└─────────────────────────────┘      ├─────────────────────────────────┤
              △                       │ +ButtonGroup()                   │
              │                       │ +add(button: AbstractButton)     │
┌─────────────────────────────┐      │ +getSelection()                  │
│      JToggleButton           │      │ +setSelected(b: ButtonModel,     │
└─────────────────────────────┘      │        status: boolean)          │
              △                       │ +getElements()                   │
              │                       │ +remove(b: AbstractButton)       │
                                      └─────────────────────────────────┘
┌────────────────────────────┐  ┌─────────────────────────────────────┐
│        JCheckBox            │  │           JRadioButton               │
├────────────────────────────┤  ├─────────────────────────────────────┤
│ +JCheckBox()               │  │ +JRadioButton()                      │
│ +JCheckBox(label: String)  │  │ +JRadioButton(label: String)         │
│ +JCheckBox(label: String,  │  │ +JRadioButton(label: String, selected:│
│        selected: boolean)  │  │        boolean)                      │
│ +JCheckBox(symbol: Icon)   │  │ +JRadioButton(symbol: Icon)          │
│ +JCheckBox(symbol: Icon,   │  │ +JRadioButton(symbol: Icon, selected:│
│        selected: boolean)  │  │        boolean)                      │
│ +JCheckBox(label: String,  │  │ +JRadioButton(label: String, symbol: Icon)│
│        symbol: Icon)       │  │ +JRadioButton(label: String, symbol: Icon,│
│ +JCheckBox(label: String,  │  │        selected: boolean)            │
│   symbol: Icon, selected: boolean)│                                 │
└────────────────────────────┘  └─────────────────────────────────────┘
```

Figure 8.66   *JCheckBox and JRadioButton*

Methods and attributes

JCheckBox and *JRadioButton*, like the *JButton*, have a `text` property, and in addition the `selected` status is important (not like `state` in AWT!). A change in the status is signalled by an *ItemEvent* (`itemStateChanged()`). However, you frequently do not react immediately to a change but only enquire of the current status of an option on starting an action. All significant methods are defined in the superclasses; you can find a description in the section on the JButton class.

The ButtonGroup class

JRadioButtons are summarized as a sequence of mutually exclusive options using a *ButtonGroup* object. By means of `add()`, you can add a RadioButton object to the group, and using `getSelection()` you can interrogate the currently selected option .

```
ButtonGroup options = new ButtonGroup();
JRadioButton option1 = new JRadioButton(
                          "Screen output",true);
options.add(option1);
JRadioButton option2 = new JRadioButton(
                          "Print output",false);
options.add(option2);
 [...]
boolean print = option2.isSelected();
ButtonModel selected = options.getSelection();
```

8.6.6   The JLabel class

since	SE	ME	EE
1.2	x	-	x

Figure 8.67   *Display of JLabels*

A *JLabel* is a static text used for labeling within windows. In addition to textual lettering, symbols are also possible. The class matches the AWT *Label* class (see Section 8.2.5).

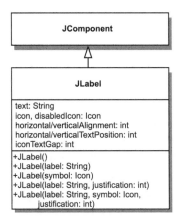

```
JComponent
                    △
                    |
                 JLabel

text: String
icon, disabledIcon: Icon
horizontal/verticalAlignment: int
horizontal/verticalTextPosition: int
iconTextGap: int

+JLabel()
+JLabel(label: String)
+JLabel(symbol: Icon)
+JLabel(label: String, justification: int)
+JLabel(label: String, symbol: Icon,
        justification: int)
```

Figure 8.68 *The JLabel class*

Methods and attributes

The displayed text is in the text attribute and can be modified using the set-Text() method. The justification can be selected as left justification (pre-setting, SwingConstants.LEFT), right justification (SwingConstants.RIGHT) or centered (SwingConstants.CENTER). In addition to the text, a symbol for the normal and switched-off status can also be stated (icon, disabledIcon). iconTextGap determines the distance between symbol and text, this is preset at 4 pixels.

```
Label labeling = new Label("a label");
labeling.setAlignment(Label.CENTER);
JLabel labeling = new Label("a text label");
JLabel symbolLabel = new Label("Label with symbol",
    new ImageIcon("euro.gif"), SwingConstants.LEFT);
symbolLabel.setIconTextGap(10);
```

8.6.7   The JTextField and JPasswordField classes

since	SE	ME	EE
1.2	x	-	x

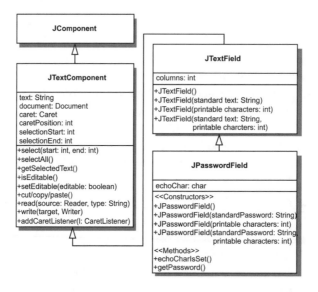

Figure 8.69 *Display of JText and JPasswordField*

A *JTextField* is a single-line input field and a *JPasswordField* is the field derived from this for the masked entry of passwords. Both are derived from the common *JTextComponent* basic class which provides the functionality such as select or edit.

The classes match the AWT classes *TextField* and *TextComponent* (see Section 8.2.6).

Figure 8.70 *The JTextField and JPasswordField classes*

Methods and attributes

Like *JLabel*, there is a `text` attribute. This text is generally editable in the case of input fields but you can switch this function off using `setEditable(false)`. The text can also be read in or written through Streams using the `read` and `write` methods.

Using different `select` methods, you can mark a text area and interrogate the marking. The `caretPosition` gives the input position, `getCaret()` gives the input cursor. Instead of the *TextEvents* usual under AWT, *JTextComponents* provide *Caret* and *KeyEvents*. `cut()`, `copy()`, and `paste()` are used to access the system clipboard.

`columns` states what the dimensions of the field have to be for dynamic layouts (see Section 8.3), so that there is room for the stated character number in the font stated.

In the case of *JPasswordFields*, there is additionally the `echoChar` attribute, which can be used to determine a replacement character; the standard is "*". In addition, `cut()` and `copy()` are blocked in the case of objects of this class.

```
JTextField userIDField = new JTextField(20);
JPasswordField passwordField = new JPasswordField(20);
[...]
String userID = userIDField.getText();
char[] password = passwordField.getText();
```

8.6.8   The JTextArea and JTextPane classes

since	SE	ME	EE
1.2	x	-	x

The JTextArea is a multi-line text field but without automatic scrollbars

The **JTextPane** supports *many* **Styles**

Figure 8.71   *Display of JTextArea and JTextPane*

Even the more complex text components are derived from *JTextComponent* (see Section 8.6.7). *JTextArea* is a multi-line input field but does not, however, have the functionality of *java.awt.TextArea* (see Section 8.2.6) which creates scrollbars if required (see Section 8.6.19). *JTextPane* is a complex control element for the input and display of formatted text. The control element resorts to the services of an *EditorKits*. So far, Rich Text Format (*RTFEditorKit*) and HTML 3.2 (*HMTLEditorKit*) have been contained as formats, but the full support of HTML 4.0. auxiliary classes and interfaces such as *Document*, *Style* or *EditorKit* are not yet available in the *javax.swing.text* package.

Methods and attributes

In addition to the `text` attribute, all text elements share the `document` model, which can describe a structured text with individual paragraphs and styles. The commands `cut()`, `copy()` and `paste()` allow simple access to the clipboard.

Non-formatted text

However, in a *JTextArea*, generally only non-formatted text is displayed. Using the option `lineWrap`, an automatic line break can be carried out, `tabSize` defines the character number standing for a tab. `columns` and `rows` states how large the field has to be in the case of dynamic layouts (see Section 8.3), so that there is sufficient room for the stated character number in the set font.

Warning Neither value has any influence on how many characters can actually be entered.

The multi-line *JTextArea* allows the text to be changed using `append()`, `insert()`, and `replaceRange()`.

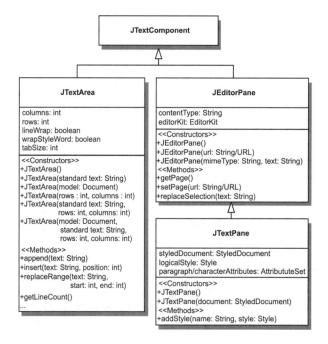

Figure 8.72 *The JTextArea and JTextPane classes*

Formatted text

The *JEditorPane* class and its subclass *JTextPane* allow you to display different types of text. These are stated as Internet MIME types (*contentType*): text/html, text/rtf, or text/plain. The documents are loaded either via HTTP (setPage(url)), a Stream (read()), or via the setText method. The parsing and editor functionality is contained in an *EditorKit* for the respective MIME type.

The use of styles based on paragraphs and characters is particularly marked in the *JTextPane* class.

```
JTextArea textInput = new TextArea();
textInput.setLineWrap(true); // activate line break
textInput.setTabSize(3);     // tab = 3 characters
textInput.setText("a multi-line text window.");
textInput.append("\nThe class is JTextArea.");
textInput.select(4, 29);
JScrollPane scroller = new JScrollPane(); // Scroll area
JEditorPane editor = new JEditorPane();
editor.setContentType("text/html");       // Type = HTML
scroller.getViewport().add(editor);       // for scrolling
try
{
   editor.setPage(url); // load HTML_Page
}
```

8.6.9   The JSlider, JScrollBar, and JProgressBar classes

since	SE	ME	EE
1.2	x	-	x

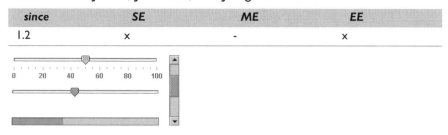

Figure 8.73 *Display of different elevators and displays*

In Swing, there are three control elements for entering and visualizing numerical values from a determined range:

→ *JScrollBar* - a simple scrollbar
→ *JSlider* - a complex elevator with a scale
→ *JProgressBar* - a progress display

All three support the *BoundedRangeModel* interface, which ensures access to the `value`, `minimum`, and `maximum` attributes, and the implementation of *ChangeEvents*.

Figure 8.74 *The JScrollBar, JSlider, and JProgressBar classes*

Methods and attributes

The *BoundedRangeModel* common to all three classes defines the current value as a whole number (value), minimum and maximum value, the range (extent) symbolized by the regulator, and a flag, which displays whether the value has just been set (valueIsAdjusting). All classes, however, contain the attributes defined in the model and important for the control element and, in addition, either a horizontal (HORIZONTAL) or vertical orientation (VERTICAL).

The *JScrollBar* class has an additional unitIncrement attribute for the increment taken on clicking on the arrow key (1 is standard), and blockIncrement for a mouse click on the white background of the scrollbar (10 is standard). For reasons of compatibility with AWT *Scrollbar* (see Section 8.2.7), the class implements the *Adjustable* interface and supports the *AdjustmentListener*.

The *JProgressBar* class is not able to be set by the end user, but indicates a progress in the procedure calculated in the program. You can also display a text in the bar (using setString() and setStringPainted()). Using getPercentComplete(), you can print out the value value as a percentage.

The *JSlider* class is an elevator with an optional scale. The scale divisions are called *Ticks* and come in two lengths: majorTicks and minorTicks. You can generate the lettering from the range as standard (createStandardTicks()) or state them yourself as a collection from *JLabels* (see Section 8.6.6).

```
JScrollbar controller = new Scrollbar(JScrollBar.VERTICAL);
controller.setValue(15);
controller.setUnitIncrement(2);
controller.setBlockIncrement(5);
controller.setVisibleAmount(30);
JProgressBar display = new JProgressBar (
   JProgressBar.HORIZONTAL, 0, 100);
display.setValue(35);
float percentComplete = display.getPercentComplete();
JSlider slider = new JSlider(JSlider.HORIZONTAL);
slider.setPaintLabels(true);
slider.setPaintTicks(true);
slider.setMajorTickSpacing(20);
slider.setMinorTickSpacing(5);
```

8.6.10   The JList class

since	SE	ME	EE
1.2	x	-	x

Figure 8.75   *Display of a JList*

The *JList* class is a list that allows the selection of one or more entries. Unlike the AWT match *List* (see Section 8.2.8), the objects are now managed in a model instead of in the user interface and now all types of object are allowed, as long as they can be depicted (i.e. can be rendered).

Methods and attributes

The *JList* is a typical example of the Model-View-Controller principle. In this, several models are available for the (*JList*) view. Most important are the data model of the *ListModel* type, the selection model (*ListSelectionModel*), and the class for depicting the entries (*ListCellRenderer*).

In addition to the model interface, the *JList* class includes the methods for representation such as for the cell height and width as well as to control visibility (getFirst/LastVisibleIndex(), ensureIndexIsVisible()).

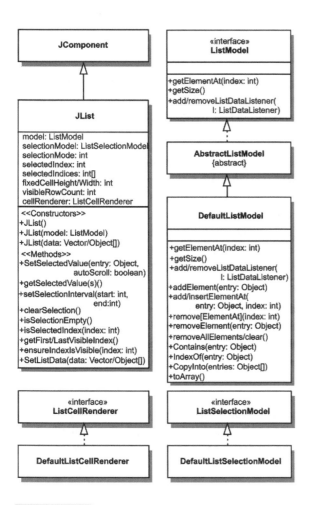

Figure 8.76 *The JList class and its models*

The functionality for the data management of the *JList* has been completely relocated to the `setListData()` method into *ListModel*. This interface between Model and View only contains methods that are required for communication between both of them: `getElementAt()` for interrogating a (visible) element, `getSize()` for the number of elements, and two methods for registering an EventListener, in order to be able to change the data immediately. The implementation is typical Swing. It gives an *AbstractListModel*, which contains only the event handling but leaves open the storing and manipulation of the data, and a *DefaultListModel*, which contains a simple implementation using a *Vector*.

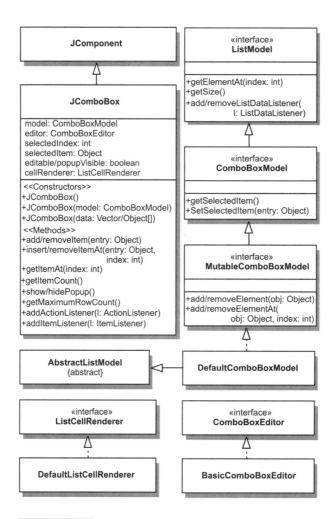

Figure 8.78 *The JComboBox class and its models*

Methods and attributes

The *JComboBox* is closely related to the *JList* (see Section 8.6.10) and shares the same display model (*ListCellRenderer*). The data model *ComboBoxModel* is derived from *ListModel* and extends it with methods for adding and deleting entries. In a *JComboBox*, you can only ever select one entry so the selection model does not apply.

In addition to the model interface, the *JComboBox* class includes methods for manipulating and selecting entries and controlling the drop-down list (`show/hidePopup()`, `get/setPopupVisible()`). The data model and the popup methods refer to the drop-down list of the *JComboBox*. If the ComboBox can be edited (`setEditable(true)`), there will be an additional entry field. Along with the *ComboBoxEditor* and the *DefaultComboBoxEditor* implementation, this has its own model.

```
JComboBox list = new JComboBox();
list.addItem("List entry 1");
list.addItem("List entry 2");
list.addItem("List entry 3");
list.setEditable(true);
list.addActionListener(ComboAddHandler);
[...]
/* Event handler for adding new list entries;
   is triggered on activating the return key after
   entering the value in the JComboBox */
public class ComboAddHandler implements ActionListener
{
   public void actionPerformed(ActionEvent e)
   {
     JComboBox cb = (JComboBox)e.getSource(); // Source
     Object newObject = cb.getEditor().getItem();  // Entry
     // if new entry -> add to list:
     if (cb.getSelectedIndex() == -1) cb.addItem(newObject);
   }
}
```

8.6.12 The JTable class

since	SE	ME	EE
1.2	x	-	x

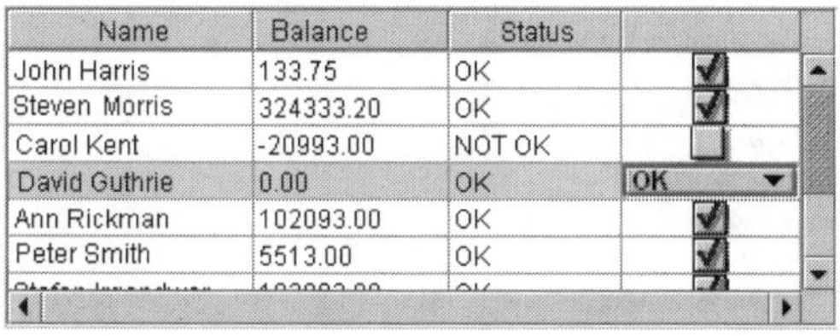

Figure 8.79 *Displaying a JTable*

The *JTable* is a complex table for presenting datasets. A *Renderer* class for displaying the cell content and an *Editor* class can be allocated to each column of the *TableColumn* type. Thus you can use symbols to represent certain values and drop-down lists for changes in the values (see Section 8.6.11). The data model for *JTable* must implement the *TableModel* interface; stated implementations are *AbstractTableModel* and *DefaultTableModel*.

Methods and attributes

A table can be constructed in two ways:

1 You can generate the *JTable* an add individual columns of the *Table-Column* type. Then you have to allocate a suitable data model.

2 You can select `autoCreateColumnsFromModel` and define the column headings in the data model.

Figure 8.80 *The JTable class and its models*

The table only interrogates those values (using `getValueAt()`) from the model that are currently visible. The functionality of the data management of the *JTable* is completely relocated to the *TableModel*. This interface between Model and View only contains methods that are required for communication between the two: `getValueAt()` for interrogating an element, `getRow/ColumnCount()` for the number of rows and columns, as well as the methods for registering an EventListener, in order to be able to display immediately any changes in the data. The implementation is typical Swing. There is an *AbstractTableModel*, which contains all of the methods up to the three just mentioned but leaves the storage and manipulation of the data open, and a *DefaultTableModel*, which contains a simple implementation based on *Vector* objects.

> **Tip** Thus the developer is given the choice of using the last model or deriving their own from *AbstractTableModel* . This is recommended, for example, if the quantity of data is very large compared to the section displayed or if loading takes place as required from files, databases or via the Internet.

The `autoResizeMode` of the *JTable* determines how the available width is distributed over the columns. Width adjustment is not, however, carried out automatically but has to be initiated using `sizeColumnsToFit()` after each change in the data displayed.

Renderers (see also Section 8.6.10) and Editors are generally defined based on columns. The table displaying a JTable shows a renderer for images in the last column as well as an editor with a *JComboBox*. A cell can be edited if the method `isCellEditable()` returns *true* from the TableModel.

```
public class AccountData extends AbstractTableModel
{
   private Vector data;
   private String[] columns = {"No.", "Balance", "Holder"};
 public TableData(Vector initData)
     { data = initData; }
   public int getColumnCount()
     { return columns.length; }
   public String[] getColumnName()
     { return columns; }
   public String getColumnName(int index)
     { return columns[i]; }
   public int getRowCount()
     { return data.size(); }
```

TAKE THAT!

```
    public Object getValueAt(int row, int column)
        { return ((Object[])data.elementAt(row))[column];}
}
[...]
JTable table = new JTree();
table.setAutoCreateColumnsFromModel(true);
table.setModel(new AccountData(accountVector));
```

8.6.13   The JTtree class

since	SE	ME	EE
1.2	x	-	x

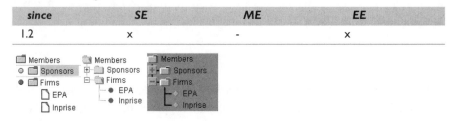

Figure 8.81   *Displaying JTree in different Look & Feel*

The tree display is based on a hierarchical data model. The model class for *JTree* must implement the *TreeModel* interface; the *DefaultTreeModel* implementation class is included in Swing. The individual nodes have to implement the *Tree-Node* or *MutableTreeNode* interfaces; the *DefaultMutableTreeNode* class contains a universal implementation including navigation methods for tree structures.

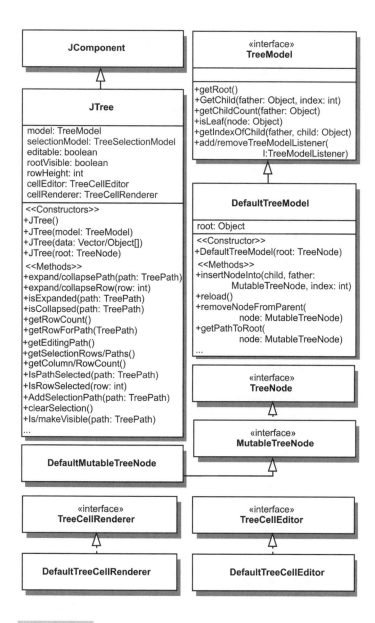

Figure 8.82 *The JTree class and its methods*

Methods and attributes

The *JTree* class represents a tree structure. Navigation in the tree takes place either via the index in the control element (row) or the path of father-to-child nodes. There are methods for selecting, dropping down, and putting away the individual subtrees.

The model implements the *TreeModel* interface, which describes a structure of nodes and pages. You can generate these using *DefaultTreeModel* type object. `root` represents the root and, using `insertNodeInto()`, you can add additional nodes.

Whilst the *TreeModel* still allows any objects as nodes, the *DefaultTreeModel* is tailored to the *MutableTreeNode* type. This represents a node and contains methods for interrogating and manipulating the data contained (`userObject`) as well as all neighboring nodes.

The Renderers (see also Section 8.6.10) for the nodes can be changed. As standard, a folder symbol is shown for inner nodes, and a dot or a sheet of paper is shown for pages (see Figure 8.81). If you make nodes editable using `setEditable(true)`, you can use a *TreeCellEditor*.

```
public class TreeData extends DefaultTreeModel
{
   public TreeData()
   {
      super(new DefaultMutableTreeNode("Members"))
      DefaultMutableTreeNode group1 =
         new DefaultMutableTreeNode("Firms");
      insertNodeInto(group1,
         (DefaultMutableTreeNode)getRoot(), 0);
      insertNodeInto(new DefaultMutableTreeNode(
         "Inprise"), group1, 0);
   [...]
   }
}
[...]
JTree tree view = new JTree();
tree view.setModel(new TreeData());
```

8.6.14 The JFrame and JDialog classes

since	SE	ME	EE
1.2	x	-	x

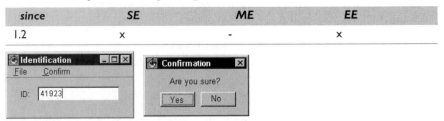

Figure 8.83 *Displaying JFrame and JDialog*

The Swing classes for main windows (*JFrame*) and Dialogboxes (*JDialog*) are derived directly from the corresponding ones in AWT *Frame* and *Dialog* (see Section 8.2.10) and therefore inherit all of their methods. The main difference is that now no more control elements are placed directly in the window but in a client container with the name `contentPane`. Now both classes can incorporate menu bars (*JMenuBar* type) and have specified values for the behavior on closing the window.

A *JFrame* object has a symbol, which appears when the window is minimized. A *JDialog* object can be modal in reference to its main window, which means that it is always in front of this window, and you cannot go back until the dialog box is closed.

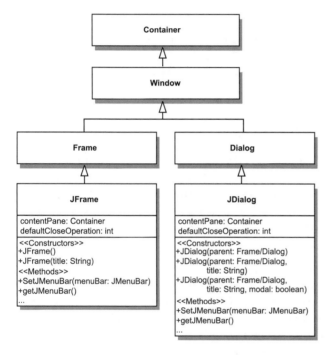

Figure 8.84   *The JFrame and JDialog classes*

Methods and attributes

The most important method is the method inherited from *Component*, `setVisible(true)` (or `show()`), as windows are not visible as standard. `dispose()` not only makes the window invisible, but also releases all associated resources. This is important as the life cycle of a window is controlled by the operating system, which does not recognize any automatic Garbage Collection. *WindowEvents* and its methods `windowOpened()` and `windowClosing()`, are also frequently used, in which an initialization or purge can be carried out. As a default value for `setDefaultCloseOperation()`, the following are permitted: `WindowConstants.DISPOSE_ON_CLOSE` (release resources); `WindowConstants.HIDE_ON_CLOSE` (make invisible); and `WindowConstants.DO_NOTHING_ON_CLOSE` (process `windowOpened()`).

Warning Unlike AWT, the method `add()` may no longer be used for adding control elements. Instead, it must be called `getContentPane.add()`.

Tip In addition, all common methods are of course available, which are defined in the superclasses *Frame* and *Dialog* (see Section 8.2.10), *Component* (see Section 8.2.1) and *Container* (see Section 8.29). In the case of *Container* objects, use is frequently made of LayoutManagers (see Section 8.3).

JFrame

A *JFrame* is a full-value window, as is generally used for applications. It has a frame with a title bar (`title` attribute) and can have a menu bar (*JMenuBar* attribute, unlike AWT!). `Resizable` states whether the use can change the dimensions of the window and `iconImage` is used to determine a symbol if the window accepts the status (`state`) `Frame.ICONIFIED`.

JDialog

One rather restricted variant of a window is *JDialog*. Each Dialog object has a clear owner (*owner*), which is generally the generating (*J*)*Frame* or (*J*)*Dialog* object. Unlike *JFrame*, there is no icon; unlike AWT a *JMenuBar* can now be allocated. An additional feature of the Dialogs is `modal`, through which you can state whether the dialog window has first to be closed before the user can again access the parent window, or whether both windows can be used simultaneously.

Tip In Java, there is no system modality as exists under Windows. Therefore, there can be no Java window that blocks all other windows on the screen.

```java
import javax.swing.*;
public class SwingWinDemo extends JFrame
{
    public static void main(String[] args)
    {
        SwingWinDemo win = new SwingWinDemo();
        win.setTitle("Identification");
        // even distribution of the control elements:
        win.getContentPane().setLayout(new FlowLayout());
        win.getContentPane().add(new Label("ID: "));
        win.getContentPane().add(new TextField(6));
        win.setDefaultCloseOperation(
            WindowConstants.DISPOSE_ON_CLOSE);
        // Positioning and displaying windows:
        win.setBounds(100, 100, 200, 80);
        win.setVisible(true);
    }
}
```

8.6.15   The JPanel class

since	SE	ME	EE
1.2	×	-	×

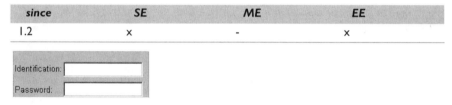

Figure 8.85   *Displaying a JPanel*

A *JPanel* is a window area in which other control elements can be placed (*Container*). The main task is the design and subdivision of user interfaces in window systems. The AWT match is called *Panel* (see Section 8.2.12).

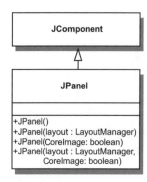

Figure 8.86 *The JPanel class*

A LayoutManager can be allocated through the inherited `layout` attribute. Several panels with different LayoutManagers are frequently nested within each other (see Section 8.3).

Tip The `CoreImage` (`isDoubleBuffered`) parameter shows whether double buffering is to be used for the components. This means that the *JPanel* should be indicated in the memory and in outputting only the memory area has to be copied in the screen output. Although this takes up more memory, it means a flicker-free display.

8.6.16 Further Swing containers

In addition to *JPanel* (see Section 8.6.15), *JFrame* and *JDialog* (see Section 8.6.14), quite a few Layout elements have been added, which can contain other containers or control elements, such as *JSplitPane*, *JScrollPane*, *JTabbedPane,* and *JOptionPane* (see Sections 8.6.18 to 8.6.21). In the case of windows, *JDesktopPane* and *JInternalFrame* have been added for implementing MDI applications (see Section 8.6.22).

Tip *MDI (Multi Document Interface)* is a type of application that is widespread under Windows, in which a main window controls several document windows linked to it. Examples are *Microsoft Word* or *CorelDraw.*

8.6.17 Swing menu classes

since	SE	ME	EE
1.2	x	-	x

Menus are used to select functions and options in applications. Menus can occur either in the form of *JMenuBars* on the upper edge of windows or as Popup menus at any place. Menus are often nested (compare with AWT menus in Section 8.2.13).

Figure 8.87 *Displaying different menu objects*

A menu is either embedded in a menu bar of a *JFrame* object (*JMenuBar* class) or appears on call as a context menu (*JPopupMenu* class). They contain either submenus (*JMenu* class) or menu items (*JMenuItem* class). The Swing menu classes show the inheritance hierarchy in Java (see Figure 8.88).

In addition to the key shortcuts (now called *Accelerators* instead of *Shortcuts*), the Swing variants of the menu classes also support *Mnemonics*. These are also key combinations formed from a meta-key (under Windows (ALT)) and a letter, and symbolized in a menu by an underline. In addition, you can link graphics into menus (see Figure 8.87).

Methods and attributes

All Swing menu items are derived from *AbstractButton* (see Section 8.6.4) and thus have a `text`, an optional symbol and generate an *ActionEvent* on being clicked. For menus, you can state key shortcuts using `setMnemonic()`. In addition, in *JMenuItem* objects, you can set an `accelerator`, i.e. a key combination that allows a menu item to be called without the user having to navigate through the menu.

As a variant of a *JMenuItems*, there is *JCheckBoxMenuItem* and *JRadioButton-MenuItem* for selectable options. All *JMenuItem* objects added to a *JMenu* object using `add` methods. In these menus and submenus, you can make subdivisions using separator lines (`addSeparator()`). You can incorporate *JMenus* into a *JMenuBar* or a *JPopupMenu* using `add()`.

```
JMenuBar menuBar = new JMenuBar();
```

Warning You must incorporate a *JMenuBar* object in a *JFrame* (or *JDialog*) using setJMenu-Bar() (see Section 8.6.14). *JFrame* has inherited the method setMenuBar() from *Frame* but this only supports AWT menus!

```
JMenu fileMenu = new JMenu("File");
fileMenu.setMnemonic('D');  // Alt+D opens file menu
menuBar.add(fileMenu);
win.setJMenuBar(menuBar);
JMenuItem new = new JMenuItem("New",
                    new ImageIcon("newfile.gif"));
new.setMnemonic('N'); // Alt+N selects "New"
// Ctrl+N activates "New":
new.setAccelerator(KeyStroke.getKeyStroke(
                KeyEvent.VK_N, Event.CTRL_MASK));
new.addActionListener(eventHandler);
fileMenu.add(new);
open JMenuItem = new JMenuItem("Open",
                    new ImageIcon("openfile.gif"));
open.setMnemonic('f'); open.setAccelerator(KeyStroke.get-
KeyStroke(
                KeyEvent.VK_O, Event.CTRL_MASK));
open.addActionListener(eventHandler);
fileMenu.add(open);
```

Figure 8.88 *The Swing menu classes*

Toolbars

Using the *JToolBar* class (see Figure 8.89), you can create toolbars containing buttons. You generally use them together with the LayoutManager *BorderLayout* (see Section 8.3.1), with which they are applied to the top and left-hand side of an application window. By setting the `floatable` property, you can also create floating toolbars, which are not fastened to a window like menu bars but are placed like a popup menu in their own small windows.

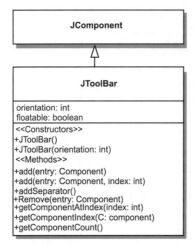

Figure 8.89 *The JToolBar class*

8.6.18   The JSplitPane class

since	SE	ME	EE
1.2	x	-	x

Figure 8.90   *JSplitPane*

This control element divides an area into two parts, separated by a horizontal or vertical separator. Using this *Divider*, the user can divide up the available space between the two zones.

```
splitPane = new JSplitPane(JSplitPane.HORIZONTAL_SPLIT);
splitPane.add(leftTextArea, "left");
splitPane.add(rightTextArea, "right");
```

8.6.19   The JScrollPane class

since	SE	ME	EE
1.2	x	-	x

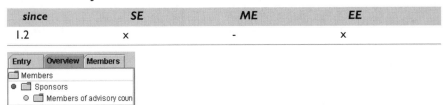

Name	Balance	Status	
John Harris	133.75	OK	✓
Steven Morris	324333.20	OK	✓
Carol Kent	-20993.00	NOT OK	
David Guthrie	0.00	OK	OK ▼
Ann Rickman	102093.00	OK	✓
Peter Smith	5513.00	OK	✓

Figure 8.91 *JTable in JScrollPane*

The *JScrollPane* container allows the display of a section of a component. For example, the text in a *JTextArea* object can project over the edge (see Section 8.6.8). The *JScrollPane* object then lets you to move the displayed section over the whole image, using overlain scrollbars as required. The visible section is called Viewport and is set up using the `setViewport()` and `setViewport-View()` methods. Whether the scrollbars are always shown, never shown or shown as required can be stated using policies.

> **Tip** By adding a *JTextArea* (see Section 8.6.8) in a JScrollPane, you can obtain behavior similar to the AWT *TextArea* (see Section 8.2.6).

```
JScrollPane scroller = new JScrollPane(); // Scroll area
JTextArea editor = new JTextArea();
scroller.getViewport().add(editor);        // for scrolling
```

8.6.20 The JTabbedPane class

since	*SE*	*ME*	*EE*
1.2	x	-	x

Figure 8.92 *JTabbedPane*

A *JTabbedPane* object allows the display of several containers, which can be accessed using tabs (Tabs). The page number currently selected is in the `selectedIndex` property, the container located on this page in `selectedComponent`.

```
JTabbedPane notebook = new JTabbedPane();
notebook.insertTab("Entry", null, page1, null, 0);
notebook.insertTab("Overview", null, page2, null, 1);
notebook.insertTab("Members", null, page3, null, 2);
notebook.setSelectedIndex(1);
```

8.6.21   The JOptionPane class

since	SE	ME	EE
1.2	x	-	x

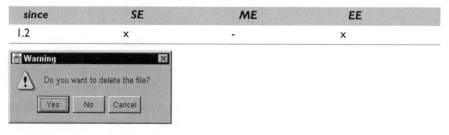

Figure 8.93 *JOptionPane*

This container is generally not used for including components but with its different `show` methods offers the facility to open a message window. In this, depending on the type of dialogs, different symbols, buttons or an input field can be displayed in addition to `message`.

The `optionType` attribute can assume the values of:

→ DEFAULT_OPTION
→ YES_NO_OPTION
→ YES_NO_CANCEL_OPTION
→ OK_CANCEL_OPTION

However, they can also provide their own set of options using `setOptions()`.

The `messageType` recognizes the following standard types, identified by different symbols (icons):

→ ERROR_MESSAGE
→ INFORMATION_MESSAGE
→ WARNING_MESSAGE
→ QUESTION_MESSAGE
→ PLAIN_MESSAGE (no symbol)

Look & Feel \ Icon	Error	Information	Question	Warning
Metal	⬢	ⓘ	？	⚠
Motif	⊘	i	？	!
Windows	✖	ⓘ	？	⚠

Figure 8.94 *Look and feel of symbols*

```
JOptionPane.showConfirmDialog(win,
    "Do you want to delete the file?", "Warning",
    JOptionPane.YES_NO_CANCEL_OPTION,
    JOptionPane.WARNING_MESSAGE);
```

8.6.22   The JDesktopPane and JInternalFrame classes

since	SE	ME	EE
1.2	x	-	x

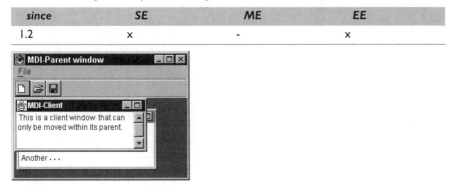

Figure 8.95 *JDesktopPane and JInternalFrame*

In the Windows environment there are many *MDI* applications. The *Multiple Document Interface (MDI)* centered on the program intends that each file or each document is displayed with its own window within the program's main window. The menus are in the main window; the inner windows cannot leave this but can be minimized and maximized within this. Examples of such applications are *Microsoft Word* or *CorelDRAW.*

Using the Swing class *JDesktopPane*, a *JFrame* object can be expanded for management of MDI clients. The clients must be derived from the *JInternalFrame* class, whose functionality to a large extent corresponds to that of *JFrame*.

```
JDesktopPane mdiParent = new JDesktopPane();
win.getContentPane().add(mdiParent, "Center");
// MDIClient is a subclass of JInternalFrame:
JInternalFrame mdiClient = new MDIClient();
mdiParent.add(mdiClient);
```

8.6.23   Chooser classes

since	SE	ME	EE
1.2	x	-	x

Analogous to *FileDialog* under AWT (see Section 8.2.11) there are also two dialogs under Swing, which are intended for the selection of files (*JFileChooser*) or colors (*JColorChooser*) by the user.

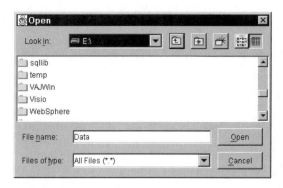

Figure 8.96   *The JFileChooser class*

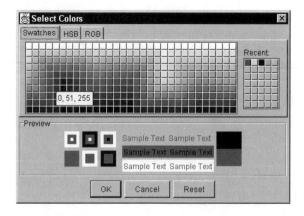

Figure 8.97   *The JColorChooser class*

Applets – Java in browsers

9

9.1 Applets – java.applet

The *java.applet* package is a small but important package for clients. It contains the *Applet* class, which is the only class that can be displayed in browsers.

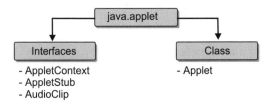

Figure 9.1 *The java.applet package*

9.2 Principles

All applets are derived from the *Applet* superclass or a subclass of it.
One subclass of Applet is *javax.swing.JApplet*, which in turn is used as the basic class for its own applets that use Swing.

The *Applet* class covers many methods that the programmer can use or override. As the *Applet* class does not do anything visible, you have to derive its own subclass from it, which then displays the desired behavior, such as making graphic outputs. The declaration of a new class to work as an applet is as follows, for example:

```
public class DateApplet extends java.applet.Applet
```

Run

With an applet, the class is not given to a Java Interpreter as a parameter, rather it is embedded in a HTML file that is loaded into a Java-capable web browser . This then takes on the loading and control of the applet. In this, the browser informs the applet of user action, just like the visibility or maximization of the applet or the browser.

Applications and applets

You can also write applications that are used both as applications and applets. These must also be derived from the *Applet* class and must, in addition, contain a `main()` method (for use as an application).

9.2.1   The Applet class

since	SE	ME	EE
1.0	x	-	x

The programming of applets consists of the addition of new methods to the derived Applet class and the overriding of the inherited methods that are automatically called by the browser in certain situations at runtime.

paint method

The most important method for graphical output in a web browser is `paint()`, which draws the surface which the applet takes up on the web page. Using the graphic primitive (see Section 8.5.1), you can draw on this surface, display a collection of control elements as a form, display an image (see Section 8.5.8), and so on.

The method is as follows:

```
public void paint (Graphics g)
```

The method has a *Graphics* object (see Section 8.5.1) as a parameter and is not called by the developer in the code but by the browser. By overriding this method, you can only create an applet, for example, that outputs a text or presents a simple graphic. However, there are other methods that are used for certain tasks and that are called automatically at very particular times by the browser. You can override these methods. It is worth knowing what the run of an applet in a web browser looks like.

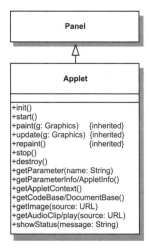

Figure 9.2 *Important methods in the Applet class*

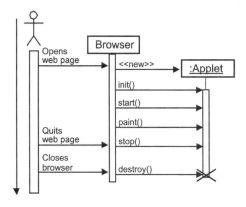

Figure 9.3 *Life cycle of an applet*

1. Loading

    When the user loads a HTML page into the browser, which contains a Java applet, first of all the class is loaded that is stated in the `<applet>` tag. This class must be a subclass of *Applet* .

2. init()

    On first loading the applet, the `init()` method is called by the browser. The method can be overrided by the programmer, in order to carry out initializations.

3. start()

    Then it's the turn of the `start()` method. This method is newly called each time the user makes the applet visible if, for example, the applet was not previously visible on scrolling the web page, or if the web page was quit.

4. paint()

The paint () method is called automatically by the browser to draw the applet. This method is practically always overridden by the developer. It is not called directly. If the necessity of redrawing arises from the application itself, you should use repaint () instead.

5. update()

If there are changes which require redrawing in whole or in part, then the browser calls the update() method. It deletes the output surface (the panel) as standard and calls paint () (see Figure 9.4).

6. repaint()

If the programmer wants to obtain a redrawing, they will not directly call either paint () or update(), but the repaint ()method, which instructs the browser to initiate an update as soon as possible.

7. stop()

If the applet is invisible, the stop() method is executed (as a match to *start*) .

8. destroy()

destroy () is finally the match to the init ()method in deleting the class or in closing the browser.

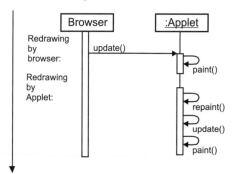

Figure 9.4 *Redrawing an applet*

The majority of these methods are only seldom overrided; only the paint () method is frequently adapted by the programmer. Because the applet of *Panel* – i.e. an AWT *Container* – is derived, you can also add any number of control elements.

Additional methods

Using getParameter(), you can interrogate the value of one of the parameters named in the HTML page. getCodeBase() supplies the URL of the applet and getDocumentBase() that of the HTML document, in which the applet is linked. showStatus() outputs a message from the status line of the browser; using getImage() or getAudioClip(), you can load resources from the server. You can override getAppletInfo(), so that information on the applet can be output in the Java console of the browser.

```java
import java.awt.*;
import java.awt.event.*;
public class LogonApplet extends java.applet.Applet
    implements ActionListener
{
    private Button logonButton;
    private LogonDialog logonDialog; // own subclass
                                     // of java.awt.Dialog
    public void init()
    {
      setLayout(new FlowLayout());
      add(new Label("LogonDemo"));
      logonButton = new Button("LogonWindow");
      logonButton.addActionListener(this);
      add(logonButton);
    }
    public void actionPerformed(ActionEvent e)
    {
      if (e.getSource() == logonButton)
      {
        if (logonDialog == null)
           logonDialog = new LogonDialog();
        logonDialog.setVisible(true);
      }
    }
}
```

9.2.2   The JApplet class

since	SE	ME	EE
1.2	x	-	x

This *JApplet* class is not in the *java.applet* package but in *javax.swing* (see Section 8.6), but is does belong logically to the applets. It expands the applets with typical Swing characteristics, as addressed in the section on *JFrame* (see Section) 8.6.14).

Warning Unlike *Applet*, where you can add control elements using `this.add()`, you have to use `this.getContentPane().add()` in the case of *JApplet*!

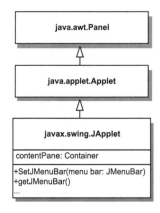

Figure 9.5 *The JApplet class*

9.2.3   The AppletContext interface

since	SE	ME	EE
1.0	x	-	x

Using the `getAppletContext()` method of each applet, you can access the applet context in the web page. The reference to the type of *AppletContext* interface is mainly used for communication between the applet and the web browser and/or other applets.

```
          «interface»
          AppletContext

+showDocument(source: URL)
+showDocument(source: URL,
              target frame: String)
+showStatus(message: String)
+getApplet(name: String)
+getApplets()
+getImage(source: URL)
+getAudioClip(source: URL)
```

Figure 9.6 *The AppletContext interface*

Methods and Attributes

For example, you can access other applets using

`getAppletContext().getApplets()`

or

`getAppletContext().getApplet("Appletname")`

and in the last call an applet must be equipped with a name using the tag

`<APPLET CODE=... NAME="Appletname" WIDTH=...>`

With the reference to the applet, its methods can now be accessed.

The `showDocument()` method loads a web page into the browser in which the applet is running. We have already shown this method in dealing with the *URL* class (see Section 7.2.4). The frame in the browser, in which the page is loaded, can also be stated as an optional parameter, e.g. `"_self"` (current frame), `"_parent"` (surrounding frame), `"_top"` (top-level frame), `"_blank"` (new frame) or frame given an explicit name.

Using `showStatus()`, a message can be displayed in the status line of the web browser. `getImage()` and `getAudioClip()` are used to load resources.

Tip GIF and JPG are supported as image formats (see Section 8.5.8); the *Java Media Framework* expansion is available for additional image processing functions. Java Sound supports the following audio file formats: AIFF, AU, WAV, MIDI, RMF at a sample rate of 22kHz in 16-bit stereo.

Two steps are necessary to play sound:

→ Using the `getAudioClip()` method, you get an object that implements the *AudioClip* interface.

→ You can play the sound file by means of play(), loop() or stop() from *AudioClip*.

9.3 Applets and security

9.3.1 Restrictions

(Unsigned) applets are subject to some security restrictions, which do not exist with applications. We speak of the Sandbox principle. We start with the premise that any Java code that is installed on the local computer can be viewed as being secure and everything that comes from outside is insecure. All local data and resources must be protected against manipulation and information transfer by this potentially dangerous code. This includes, in particular:

→ The applet may not read or write, delete or rename any files or request any information on files.

→ No new directories may be created and neither may information on directories or their attributes be ascertained or changed.

→ The transfer of information on the system and the users, such as computer or user names, is forbidden.

→ Apart from the existing connection to the web server from which the applet was loaded, the applet may not create any new network connections.

→ No local programs may be started (such as format.com) and no native libraries (DLLs) may be linked.

→ No "foreign" Threads may be influenced. These are all Threads that do not belong to the Thread group of the applet.

→ The classes of the Java system class library (*java.**) may not be overwritten by other classes or versions. Otherwise, the above restrictions can easily be switched off by overwriting the Security classes.

→ No output to a printer is permitted.

Monitoring restrictions

These restrictions are monitored by different mechanisms during compilation, the downloading of classes, linking, and during the runtime.

9.3.2 Signed applets

One special problem of applications distributed in Inter/Intranets is that the user often does not take into account that hazards can lurk in malicious or faulty applications when just selecting a web page. Unlike locally installed programs, which can be evaluated in a test environment before being released, Java applets start immediately and automatically. Even a firewall is of no help here, because the downloaded code is executed locally. You can only block all applets and thus you will also lose all utilities.

Fortunately, the developers of Java knew about this problem and introduced mechanisms to protect the client from unknown or even undesired code from an insecure, untrustworthy ("untrusted") source. However, the Sandbox principle has shown itself to be too restrictive and, little by little, has been further developed.

Signed applets

The Sandbox restrictions were very rigid. For example, it was impossible to write a Java applet for the "safe" Intranet, which can print and store files locally. In the newer versions of Java, and in particular since Java 2, there is now the facility to lift parts of the restrictions for "safe" applets (signed or trusted applets).

In addition to the safe local code and the insecure code from the Internet, there is now also code from a trustworthy source ("trusted code"). For example, this can be a web server in the Intranet. For this code, you can now grant rights, such as "printing is allowed for all applets coming from the www.linkfont.co.uk Intranet server".

Digital signatures

You must ensure that this code with its additional authorization really comes from a trustworthy source. All necessary classes and resources (e.g. images) are packaged with this proof in a Java archive file (JAR) and this is signed digitally. The digital signature here refers to the data contained in the file and it is obvious when classes are changed or damaged in transmission. In order to be able to have a digital signature, the signer must register with an authorized certification authority, which will confirm their identity.

When these applets are downloaded from a secure host that also supplies a cryptological certificate, and the user trusts this company or the certificate, they can release certain directories for writing, or to a printer, for example. However, they must do this explicitly so that no unnoticed intrusion is (should be) possible.

Problems in practice

Unfortunately, this security model only has a restricted function, as the market leaders in web browsers, Netscape and Microsoft, offer their own proprietary security models. In addition, it is relatively time consuming to obtain a certificate. One additional problem of the Java 1.1 security model was a restriction under the motto "all or nothing". A signed applet automatically had all entitlements.

Java 2

This problem was tackled in Java 2. It is now possible to define detailed access rights via *Policies* for any Java code, not just for applets from the Internet. For individual resource accesses, there are special access rights, *Permissions*. Examples of these would be read/write access to a certain file on the local computer or network connections to a certain computer (host + port number).

```
grant signed by "Addison-Wesley",
  codeBase "http://www.nittyGritty.com/*" {
  permission java.io.filePermission "c:\\temp\\*", "read";
  permission java.io.SocketPermission
          "dbserver.nittyGritty.com:8000", "connect";
};
```

However, the most important expansion is a finely granulated issuing of authorization for code from any source. When the code is executed, a secure runtime environment is created, called a *Protection Domain*. This code can contain requests for access to certain resources. Using the source (URL) and the certificates carried, a comparison is made with the local policies and a decision is made whether a request is to be permitted. If not, the program is informed of this through an exception.

9.4 Linking to a HTML page

Applets can be displayed directly using the *Applet-viewer* of the JDK and above all using a Java-capable web browser. In both cases, the applet must be linked to an HTML page (Hypertext Markup Language).

`<applet>` Tag

The class of the applet is linked using the `<applet>` tag. One very simple example is:

```
<HTML>
<HEAD><TITLE>a Java example page</TITLE></HEAD>
<BODY>
<H1>An applet to display a date</H1>
<APPLET CODE="DateApplet.class" WIDTH=300 HEIGHT=100>
    Please use a Java-compatible browser!
</APPLET>
</BODY>
</HTML>
```

Paths

A condition for starting is that the class is within the same directory as the HTML file. If you want to manage Java code in another directory, you can give an alternative path using the CODEBASE parameter:

```
<APPLET CODE="DateApplet.class" CODEBASE="../applets"
WIDTH=300 HEIGHT=100>
```

Java archive

With Java archives (JAR files), using the ARCHIVE directive you can state the archive in which the class is contained under CODE. The archive is then loaded as a whole and the corresponding class started. In addition, you can also state other archives in which classes used by applets will be searched at runtime.

```
<APPLET CODE="DateApplet.class" ARCHIVE="date.jar"
WIDTH=300 HEIGHT=100>
```

Parameter transfer

With applets, there is another mechanism for transferring parameters as the string array in applications. They are defined in the HTML file using PARAM tags and interrogated in the applet using the `getParameter(String name)` method.

```
<APPLET CODE="AppletDate.class" WIDTH=300 HEIGHT=100>
 <PARAM name=delay value=100>
 <PARAM name=backgroundimage value="java.jpg">
  Please use a Java-compatible browser!
</APPLET>
```

Interrogation in the applet:

```
String imageFile img = getParameter("backgroundimage");
int delay = Integer.parseInt(getParameter("delay"));
```

Additional important libraries

In this chapter, I will present the component model of JavaBeans, the Security classes and the *java.security* package, which is used as a pool of different types of classes, from time and date to Collections.

10.1 Mixed – java.util

java.util is the "mixed" category of the standard libraries.
It contains Collection classes, classes for date, time, and multilingual applications, some classes for event handling as well as additional ones which do not fit any other category (see Figure 10.1). In addition, there are the *java.util.zip* and *java.util.jar* subpackages, which contain the classes for the zip compression algorithm, which is important, above all, for the Java archive (JAR files, see Section 4.10.5).

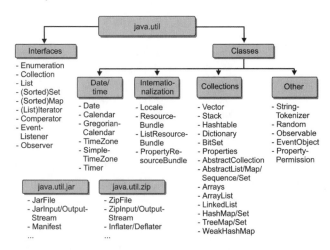

Figure 10.1 *The classes of the java.util package*

10.1.1   Date and time

The *Date* class internally manages time and date values as whole numbers. Using the *java.text.DateFormat* class, it can make both formatted and country-specific outputs; the *Calendar* class allows access to subcomponents such as day, month, or hour.

10.1.2   The Date class

since	SE	ME	EE
1.0	x	x	x

The *Date* class contains date and time functions. However, since Java 1.1 it has forfeit lots of its functionality as it is not optimized for international display differences and was unsuitable for the management of years after 2000; for example, the year 2001 had to be coded as 101. Most methods were therefore declared as obsolete (*deprecated*) and transferred to the *Calendar* class. There remained a date and time functionality in the **Date** class itself, which is based on a time model in milliseconds since 1. 1. 1970. It is used as the basic class of the SQL classes *java.sql.Date*, *java.sql.Time* and *java.sql.Timestamp* (see Section 7.3.7).

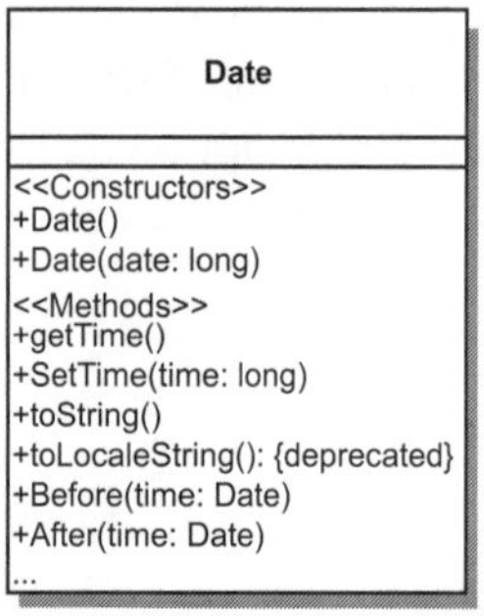

```
                    Date

<<Constructors>>
+Date()
+Date(date: long)
<<Methods>>
+getTime()
+SetTime(time: long)
+toString()
+toLocaleString(): {deprecated}
+Before(time: Date)
+After(time: Date)
...
```

Figure 10.2 *The Date class*

Methods and attributes

The boolean methods `before()` and `after()` are used to compare *Date* objects. `toString()` outputs the date in a long format, for example:

```
Mon Apr 26 13:12:22 GMT+02:00 1999
```

Of course, this is not the generally desired format. Using `toLocaleString()`, you can obtain an output using the current *locale*, which is the country settings for language and country (e.g. en_US):

```
Apr 4, 1999 1:12:22 PM
```

> **Tip** `toLocaleString()` is deprecated and is best replaced using *java.text.DateFormat*, which allows more exact control of the output.

10.1.3   The DateFormat class

since	SE	ME	EE
1.1	x	-	x

The *DateFormat* class is not contained in *java.util*, but in *java.text*. It is used for formatting time and date values.

Methods and attributes

Using `getDateInstance()`, you can obtain an instance for the formatting of date values, `getTimeInstance()` for time values, and `getDateTimeInstance()` for a combined input/output. As an option, you can state a style and a locale (see Section 10.1.5).

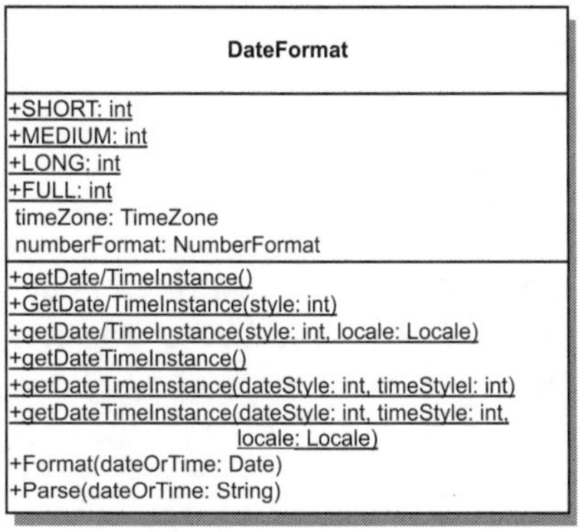

```
                         DateFormat
+SHORT: int
+MEDIUM: int
+LONG: int
+FULL: int
 timeZone: TimeZone
 numberFormat: NumberFormat
+getDate/TimeInstance()
+GetDate/TimeInstance(style: int)
+getDate/TimeInstance(style: int, locale: Locale)
+getDateTimeInstance()
+getDateTimeInstance(dateStyle: int, timeStylel: int)
+getDateTimeInstance(dateStyle: int, timeStyle: int,
                   locale: Locale)
+Format(dateOrTime: Date)
+Parse(dateOrTime: String)
```

Figure 10.3 *The DateFormat class*

The following are permitted as styles:

→ `SHORT: 14/06/00 - 10:53 (UK)`
       `6/14/00 - 10:53 AM (US)`
→ `MEDIUM: 14-Jun-00 - 10:53:35 (UK)`
       `Jun 14, 2000 - 10:53:35 AM (US)`

→ LONG: 14 June 2000 - 10:53:35 GMT+02:00 (UK)
          June 14, 2000 - 10:53:35 AM GMT+02:00 (US)
→ FULL: 14 June 2000 - 10:53:35 o'clock GMT+02:00 (UK)
          Wednesday, June 14, 2000 - 10:53:35 AM GMT+02:00
          (US)

The `format()` method outputs a *Date* value in the set format; the `parse()` method reads a *String* in this format and supplies a *Date* object.

We used this in our date example in Section 7.1.2:

```
String timestamp =
  (new Date(curFile.lastModified())).toLocaleString();
```

A clean solution (without *deprecated* methods) can be achieved using the *Date-Format* class:

```
java.text.DateFormat df =
  java.text.DateFormat.getInstance();
String timestamp =
  df.format(new Date(curFile.lastModified()));
```

The result is identical apart from the missing seconds:

```
26.04.99 13:12.
```

10.1.4   The Calendar class

since	SE	ME	EE
1.1	x	x	x

The *Calendar* class has to a large extent replaced *Date* (see Section 10.1.2) since Java 1.1 and provides a functionality for setting time zones and for interrogating individual fields, such as the weekday. In addition, it contains a number of constants for months, days, etc.

```
+-----------------------------------------+
|                Calendar                 |
|                {abstract}               |
+-----------------------------------------+
| +YEAR: int                              |
| +MONTH: int                             |
| +WEEK_OF_YEAR: int                      |
| +DAY_OF_MONTH: int                      |
| +DAY_OF_WEEK: int                       |
| +DAY_OF_YEAR: int                       |
| +HOUR: int                              |
| +MINUTE: int                            |
| +SECOND: int                            |
| +ZONE_OFFSET: int                       |
| +MONDAY...SUNDAY: int                   |
| +JANUARY...DECEMBER: int                |
+-----------------------------------------+
| +getInstance()                          |
| +GetInstance(locale: Locale)            |
| +GetInstance(time zone: TimeZone)       |
| +toString()                             |
| +Get(attribute: int)                    |
| +Set(attribute: int, value: int)        |
| +set(year: int, month: int, day: int)   |
| +setTime(d: Date)                       |
| +setTimeZone(zone: TimeZone)            |
+-----------------------------------------+
```

Figure 10.4 *The Calendar class*

For example, this is what an access to the year of a Calendar object looks like:

```
Calendar cal = Calendar.getInstance(); // Instance with
          // current time zone and country setting
cal.setTime(new Date());  // today
int year = cal.get(Calendar.YEAR);
```

10.1.5 Internationalization

since	SE	ME	EE
1.1	x	-	x

In addition to the time zone, which is implemented in the *TimeZone* class and is based on the time zones relative to Greenwich Mean Time (GMT), and the *Localeclass*, which codes the language (e.g. en for English) and the country (e.g. US for the USA), the *ResourceBundles* model is also important here. These allow you to write international applications, whose Strings are dynamically loaded and displayed using the current country settings.

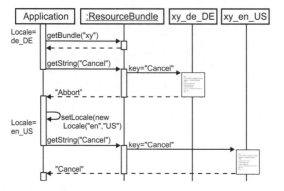

Figure 10.5 *String call from ResourceBundles*

ResourceBundles

The application is very simple. Instead of creating a String constant directly in the code, you load each String using the `getString(key)` method from a *ResourceBundle*. In this, the bundle can be either a file or a class. Then you just have to state the source in starting the application or in initializing the applet:

```
ResourceBundle b = ResourceBundle.getBundle(bundlename);
                        // bundlename without country suffix
String cancelButtonLabel = getString("Cancel");
```

The application looks for a suitable bundle according to the following plan:

→ `bundlename_<current language shortcut>_`
  `<current country shortcut>.class`, e.g. **xy_en_US.class**
→ `bundlename_<current language shortcut>.class`,
  e.g. **xy_en.class**
→ `bundlename_.class`, e.g. **xy.class**

If none of the classes can be found you will get a *MissingResourceException*. In this, the application is completely independent of the language and it does have to be changed if a new language is added. In this case, just a new *ResourceBundle* class has to be added. This has the following structure:

```
public class xy_en_US extends java.util.ListResourceBundle
{
   static final Object[][] contents =
   {
      // Pairs of key and localized String
      {"Cancel", "cancel"},
      {"Help", "Help"}
```

```
        }
        protected Object[][] getContents() { return contents; }
}
```

10.1.6   Collection classes

Java 1.1 contains a few small but very important classes for managing objects –
the Collections (see Sections 10.1.7 to 10.1.11). In Java 2, the selection has been
greatly expanded. For example, there are added quantities (*Set*), sequences
(*List*), *Maps* and sorted variants (see Sections 10.1.12 to 10.1.18).

10.1.7   The Vector class

since	SE	ME	EE
1.0	x	x	x

Vector is a class that displays a sort of array, with the difference being that the
length of an object of the *Vector* type does not have to be determined from the
start. A *Vector* object represents a linear list of objects of any class (i.e. instances
of *java.lang.Object*), which means that each element has a fixed position.

Methods and attributes

The addElement() method adds a reference to a new object at the end of the
vector, and insertElementAt() adds it to a particular point. Using copy-
Into(), all elements of the *Vector* object can be copied into the transferred array.

Using contains(), you can check how the object is contained in the vector,
and using elementAt() you can interrogate an element; indexOf() and
lastIndexOf() supply the position of an object in the vector and size()
gives its size.

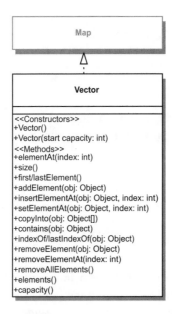

Figure 10.6 *The Vector class*

Warning Do not confuse `size()` with `capacity()`! The latter states how many elements have a place in the Vector object, without an (automatic) size adjustment being made.

Objects are removed from the vector using `removeElement()` or `removeAllElements()`.

Tip Since Java 2, a few methods have been added to *Vector*, so that the *List* Collection interface can be implemented (see Section 10.1.15).

Comparison with arrays

	Array	Vector

Creation	`Object[] field = new`
	`  Object[10];`
	`String[] str = new`
	`  String[100];`
		`Vector vector = new`
		`  Vector();`

Access to
i element
	`Object o  = field[i];`
	`String os = str[i];`
		`Object o  = vector.`
		`  elementAt(i);`
		`String os = (String)`
		`  vector.elementAt(i);`

Attach
object o
	`for(int i=0; i<field.length;`
	`i++)`
	`    if (field[i] == null)`
	`      { field[i] = o; break;`
	`}`
		`vector.addElement(o);`

Search for
position of o
	`for(int i=0; i<field.length;`
	`i++)`
	`    if (o.equals(field[i]))`
	`      { pos = i; break; }`
		`pos = vector.indexOf(o);`

Number of elements	`field.length`	`vector.size()`
Disadvan- tages	laborious programming, no flexible size adjustment	no strict type checks, casting neces- sary, not for elementary data types

10.1.8 The Enumeration interface

since	SE	ME	EE
1.0	x	x	x

Classes such as *Vector* or *Hashtable*, which contain a list of elements that you can run through in sequence, offer the possibility of running through the elements using *iterators*.

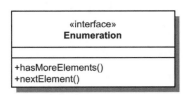

Figure 10.7 *The Enumeration interface*

Methods and attributes

Access to elements referenced by an iterator takes place using the *Enumeration* interface using the two methods hasMoreElements() and nextElement(). The *Vector* class provides an *Enumeration* object through the elements() method.

```
Enumeration list = source.elements();
while (list.hasMoreElements())
{
    Object elem = nextElement();
    // elem casting and use...
}
```

10.1.9   The Hashtable and Properties classes

since	SE	ME	EE
1.0/1.2	x	(x)	x

A *Dictionary* is a number of elements that are identified using a key value. Generally, you use the concrete class *Hashtable*, derived from the abstract *Dictionary* class, which presents the most important methods of put(), get() and contains(). Derived from this is the *Properties* class, a set of key value pairs that can also be loaded and written using Streams.

Tip Since Java 2, some methods have been added to *Hashtable*, so that the *Map* collection interface can be implemented (see Section 10.1.17).

Tip In the Java Micro Edition, there is only the *Hashtable* class, which is derived directly from *Object*.

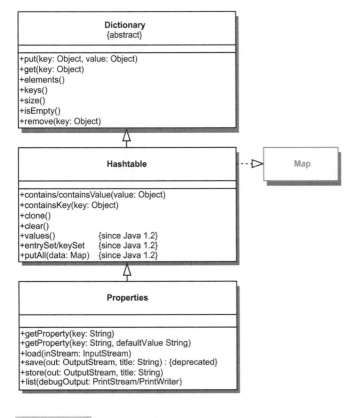

Figure 10.8 *The Hashtable and Properties classes*

10.1.10 The Stack class

since	SE	ME	EE
1.0	x	x	x

One subclass of *Vector* is the *Stack* class, which implements a last-in-first-out stack. The most important methods are push() and pop().

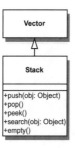

Figure 10.9 *The Stack class*

10.1.11   The BitSet class

since	SE	ME	EE
1.0	x	-	x

BitSet is a number of boolean flags (bits), which can be linked using operations such as and(), or(), or xor().

Figure 10.10 *The BitSet class*

10.1.12   Java 2 collections

The previous implementations are generally sufficient in most cases. However, sometimes you have different requirements of an implementation, and therefore want to separate abstract collection types such as sorted lists from the concrete implementation. You can then go for a different algorithm for an application case with relatively stable data but which has many search accesses than for data with an increased frequency of change.

The Collections Framework, available since Java 1.2, contains such Collections as *Set* (a list without duplicated elements) and *SortedSet*, *List* (replaces *Vector*), *Map* (replaces *Hashtable*) and *SortedMap*.

You can implement your own *Comparator* interfaces, in addition to natural ordering, and sort according to them.

The names of the access methods are abbreviated (list.set(index, object) instead of vector.setElementAt(object, index).

TAKE THAT!

The *java.util* package contains the following interfaces, amongst other things:

Abstract Collection	Description	Implementation
Collection		no implementations
List	like *Vector*	*ArrayList, LinkedList, Vector*
→ Set	list without duplicated elements	*HashSet*
→ SortedSet	sorted *Set*	*TreeSet*
Map	access via keys	*HashMap, Hashtable*
→ SortedMap	*Map*, sorted by keys	*TreeMap*

According to the Collections Framework, the interfaces (as general as possible) and not the implementations in the methods should be passed over as input values.

10.1.13 The Collection interface

since	SE	ME	EE
1.2	x	-	x

The *Collection* interface forms the basis of all new Collection classes and interfaces and contains general management functions.

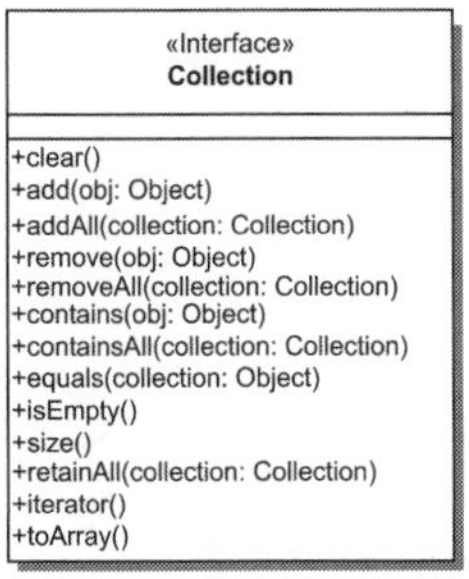

```
          «Interface»
          Collection

+clear()
+add(obj: Object)
+addAll(collection: Collection)
+remove(obj: Object)
+removeAll(collection: Collection)
+contains(obj: Object)
+containsAll(collection: Collection)
+equals(collection: Object)
+isEmpty()
+size()
+retainAll(collection: Collection)
+iterator()
+toArray()
```

Figure 10.11   *The Collection interface*

Methods and attributes

The *Collection* interface contains the (self-explanatory) methods of isEmpty(), contains(), and containsAll(). The *boolean* methods add(), addAll(), remove(), removeAll(), and retainAll() return *true*, when the Collection has been changed by the operation.

The command c1.addAll(c2) adds all elements from c2 to c1. The command c1.retainAll(c2)... means that all elements from c1 not contained in c2 are deleted.

The following single-liner removes all occurrences of the e object from a c collection (`Collections.singleton(e)` creates an unchangeable set using only one element)

```
c.removeAll(Collection.singleton(e));
```

10.1.14   The Iterator interface

since	SE	ME	EE
1.2	x	-	x

Iterator (replaces *Enumeration*) allows, amongst other things, the deletion of elements from its Collection.

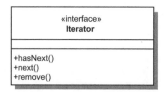

Figure 10.12   *The Iterator interface*

The following example removes all objects from a Collection, which do not meet the cond condition:

```
static void filter(Collection c)
{
    for (Iterator i = c.iterator(); i.hasNext(); )
        if (!cond(i.next()))
            i.remove();
}
```

10.1.15   The List interface

since	SE	ME	EE
1.2	x	-	x

A *List* is a Collection with objects in a fixed sequence. Using an index, you can access all elements. *java.util ArrayList* (= an array of adjustable size), *LinkedList* (a double linked list), and the *Vector* adapted class contain implementations for lists. *ArrayList* is the quickest implementation for most applications: it is quicker than *Vector*, but not synchronized for it.

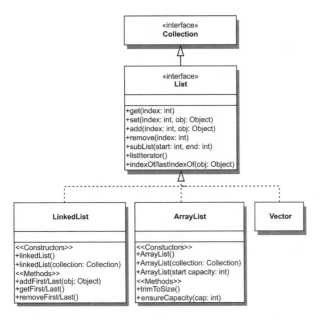

Figure 10.13 *The List interface and implementing classes*

Methods and attributes

The *List* interface adds the following functionality to the functionality inherited from Collection:

`get()` and `set()` allow index-based access to an entry. Using `indexOf()` or `lastIndexOf()`, you can search for the index of a list element. The range-view operation `subList(start, end)` creates a view of the list, which exclusively contains the elements from the `start` to the `end` of the index, inclusive. All *List* operations can be applied to the sublist and influence the original list, if necessary.

The following example creates a new list, in which list2 is attached to list1:

```
List list3 = new ArrayList(list1);
list3.addAll(list2);
```

> **Tip** When using the *ListIterators* , make sure that the index is always between two elements: if, for example, the index is at 1, `next()` will supply the second element, and `previous()` will supply the first element in the list.

Replacing all occurrences of the `val` object in a list using `newVal`:

```
public void replace(List l, Object val, Object newVal)
{
  // l, val and newVal are <> 0
  for (ListIterator i=l.listIterator(); i.hasNext(); )
    if (val.equals(i.next())) i.set(newVal);
}
```

10.1.16   The Set interface

since	SE	ME	EE
1.2	x	-	x

A *Set* is a quantity in which no duplicated entries can occur. *Set* has the same methods as *Collection*. Standard implementations for *Set* are the unsorted *HashSet* (= an array of adjustable size) and the sorted *TreeSet* (= binary tree).

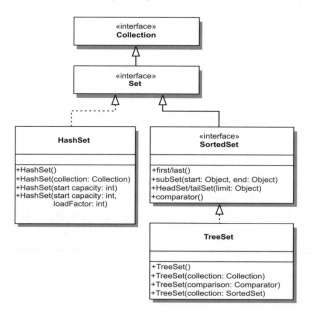

Figure 10.14   *The Set interface and implementing classes*

Methods and attributes

`equals()` returns *true* if two sets contain the same elements – no matter how the sets are implemented. In a *SortedSet*, the entries are comparable according to a comparison model (*Comparator*, see Section 10.1.18) and are available sorted.

The following example uses a *Set* in order to remove duplicates from a Collection:

```
Collection noDups = new HashSet(c);
```

10.1.17 The Map interface

since	SE	ME	EE
1.2	x	-	x

A *Map* is a number of objects that are accessed using keys. Each key (*Key*) is allocated exactly one value (*Value*).

Standard implementations are *HashMap* and *HashTable* (= size-adjustable array, see Section 10.1.9) and *TreeMap* (= sorted binary tree).

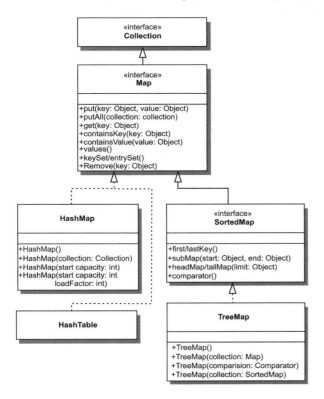

Figure 10.15 *The Map interface and implementing classes*

Methods and attributes

As in the previous *Hashtable* (see Section 10.1.9) put (key, value) creates a new entry or overwrites the previous one if the key already exists. get (key) returns the entry allocated to the key. `contains(value)` has been renamed `containsValue(value)` for the sake of better legibility.

In the following examples, keys and values are mixed; the *Map* manager allocates each employee to his manager. The following routine ascertains all employees who are not managers:

```
Set simpleEmployee = new HashSet(manager.keySet());
simpleEmployee.removeAll(managers.values());
```

In this way, you release all employees who are allocated to a `bill` manager:

```
manager.values().removeAll(Collections.singleton(bill));
```

In this operation, it can happen that some employees no longer have a manager (namely if one of those just released is a manager). The following (rather complicated) code returns all employees whose manager no longer works for the company:

```
Map m = new HashMap(manager);
m.values().removeAll(manager.keySet());
Set employeeWithoutManager = m.keySet();
```

10.1.18 The Collections class

since	SE	ME	EE
1.2	x	-	x

The *Collections* class is an auxiliary class using class methods for operations on quantities as well as for compatibility with the old Collection classes of Java 1.2.

Tip Equally, there is an *Arrays* auxiliary class for operations using arrays (fields).

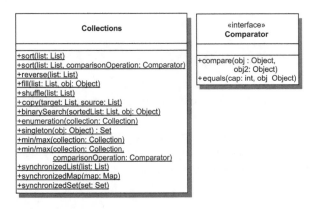

Figure 10.16 *The Collections class*

Methods and attributes

`sort()` sorts the list, and using the *Comparator* interface, you can arrange the sort sequence to be other than alphabetical. `shuffle()` permutes the list in a random manner, `reverse()` turns it around. `fill()` fills all elements with the stated object. `copy()` copies the second list to the first. `binarySearch()` only functions in sorted lists and supplies the index of an object. `singleton()` creates an unchangeable set, which only consists of the object.

For reasons of compatibility with the *Enumeration* interface (see Section 10.1.8), you can create an implementing object using the `enumeration()` method. The `synchronized` methods each respectively create a thread-safe variant of the stated Collection.

The following program supplies the values transferred on being called in a random sequence:

```java
import java.util.*;
public class Shuffle
{
    public static void main(String args[])
    {
        List l = Arrays.asList(args); // an auxiliary class
                                      // for arrays
        Collections.shuffle(l);
        System.out.println(l);
    }
}
```

10.2 References – java.lang.ref

since	SE	ME	EE
1.2	x	-	x

In addition to the usual references, there have been a few more specialized types since JDK 1.2 that print out the status of objects within an automatic memory purge. Soft, weak, and phantom references give information on the extent to which these objects have actually already been removed from the memory. This can be useful if you want to write a caching mechanism.

10.3 Reflection – java.lang.reflect

since	SE	ME	EE
1.1	x	-	x

The classes of this package are not normally of importance for the developer unless you want to write a development environment or a code generator. You can analyze classes using them. The *java.lang.Class* class is used as a basis in this (see Section 6.1.3), whose methods return objects of the *Constructor*, *Method*, *Field*, etc., type, defined in the *java.lang.reflect* package.

10.4 JavaBeans – java.beans

JavaBeans is the component model of Java. These components have a more exact and, for programming tools, more comprehensible interface definition than Java classes. The interfaces and classes required for describing and analysis are found in the *java.beans* package. They work very closely with the classes for the runtime analysis of Java classes in the *java.lang.reflect* package. The interface of *JavaBeans* is called *Features*; it consists of three parts:

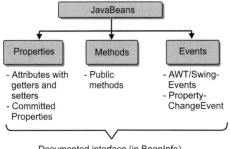

Documented interface (in BeanInfo)

Figure 10.17 *The JavaBean features*

1 The public attributes or characteristics of a JavaBean are called *Properties*. Using these properties, Beans can be adapted to suit the ideas of the programmer without him/her having to change the source code or having to access it in any way. This adaptation is called *Customizing*.

2 The public methods, i.e. functions, which a Bean can execute are called *Methods*.

3 A Bean creates *Events*. This mainly happens when their properties change.

These three sorts of features are documented in the *BeanInfo* interface; the *PropertyEditor* interface is used to customize JavaBeans.

Figure 10.18 *The BeanInfo interface*

In addition to the implementing class, each component is also supplied with a *BeanInfo* class, which describes the features of the Bean, for example an *AnimationListBeanInfo.class* to *AnimationList.class*. The explicit intention of the *BeanInfo* class is to analyze graphic development environments to compile individual components in an application. The tools also generally offer convenient opportunities to generate your own JavaBeans and to generate the *Bean Info* class using Wizards and generators.

10.5 Encryption – *java.security*

You can find classes and interfaces for the encryption of data and the creation and checking of codes and certificates in the *java.security* package.

In the applets environment (see Chapter 9), we have already dealt with the problem of unwanted and hazardous code from an unknown source, and Java's response in the form of the Sandbox principle and signed applets. Classes and interfaces are provided for the encryption and signature in the *java.security* package (see Figure 10.19)

10.5.1 Encryption using Security classes

Encryption and code generation takes place by means of public-key procedures according to *Java Cryptographic Architecture* (JCA). However, only the interfaces for the use of the procedure are determined in the *java.security* package, but not the procedure (implementation) itself. Just the use of one-way-hash functions is defined. These produce a fixed-length output String (hash or digest). These algorithms are therefore also called Message Digest Algorithms.

Those classes that implement the abstract *MessageDigest*, *KeyPairGenerator* and *Signature* classes are called Engine classes. Sun provides MD5 and SHA-1 as Message Digest Algorithms and DSA as a Signature Algorithm.

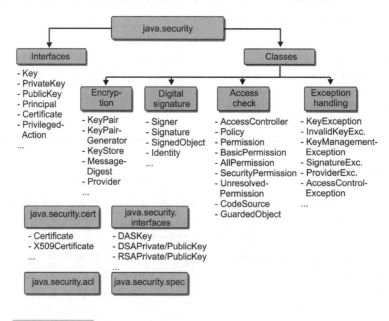

Figure 10.19 *Classes in the java.security package*

Crypto-extensions

APIs for encoding and decoding are supplied together with some implementations in an external packet called JCE (*Java Cryptography Extension*), which may not, however, be used outside the USA for legal export reasons.

10.5.2   Java 2 – Protection Domains

In Java 2, the security model has been refined and the security packages expanded. So it is now possible, for example, to define access rights via *policies* (*java.security.Policy*) for any Java code, and not only for applets from the Internet. These security regulations are filed in the policy database, and the *AccessController* class, which replaces the *SecurityManager* from Java 1.1, checks that they are adhered to.

Policies and Permissions

A policy consists of a number of *Permission* objects, which represent access rights to resources. Examples are read/write access to a certain file on the local computer (see Section 7.1.14) or network connections to a certain computer (host + port number, see Section 7.2.6). You can compare this to the access control in network operating systems such as Windows NT or OS/2, but in Java the rights are not granted to a user or a user group, but rather to one or more websites (e.g. the "local intranet zone" in Internet Explorer). For example, one policy may state what degree of access Java code is given by an origin (e.g. web server).

Certificates

To solve the certification problem, namely that every person who wants to have a digital signature has to possess a recognized form of identification, there is now support from the X.509 V3 standard, which will make the creation of digital signatures more easy through a hierarchy of certification authorities (CAs). The classes for this are contained in the *java.security.cert* package.

Protection Domain

The most important expansion is a finely graded issuing of entitlements for code from any source. As soon as the code is executed, a secure runtime environment is created, called a *Protection Domain*. This code can contain requests for access to particular resources. Using the source (URL) and any certificates that are also sent, and on comparing with the local policies, a decision is made whether a request is to be permitted. If not, then the program is informed of this by an exception.

Part II

Go ahead!

Exception handling

The third and last part of this book gives advice on which problems you can solve using which technologies, and tips on the practical use of the language and libraries. In Chapter 11 you will find an introduction to fault handling in Java. Chapter 12 is devoted to the aspect of how you can accelerate your applications and the thirteenth and last chapter brings together different architectures and gives tips on which technologies are best suited for which purpose.

11.1 Introduction

Exception handling is a language concept taken over from C++.
Exception handling is a very effective and simple concept for handling runtime errors. At the point of error, an *exception* is "thrown" up (see Figure 11.1), which is "trapped" by a *handler* defined for this purpose and processed. "Throwing" is the transfer of a specially generated *exception* object with information on the error to an error handling routine.

The background to this mechanism is as follows: a software developer who implements a class library, for example, knows when errors occur. On the other hand, the developer does not know how the users of this class library wants to react to this error.

Conversely, the users of the library well know how they want to react to the error, but they do not have an overview of the places at which errors can occur.

The solution is simple using the exception handling mechanism: the module developer creates exceptions at the places of error; the users can process these exceptions using their own handler functions.

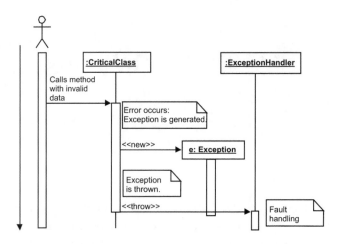

Figure 11.1   *Error handling using exceptions*

11.2 Comparison with return codes

With traditional programming languages, you generally use function return values as return codes. If, for example, a function call returns a value not equal to zero, then an error has occurred there. The value is used as a key. Unfortunately, it has been shown in practice that, for the sake of simplicity, many developers either report the error code directly to the end user ("Error 4711 has occurred") or summarize all possible return codes of a function call as a single one and report it. In doing so, much information on the real reason for the error gets lost. In particular, the person with whom the error at long last appeared generally has no documentation to convert the error numbers into a description.

11.3 Implementation in Java

For this reason, we use exceptions, which through their names give a clue to the error and, in addition, give information on the type and historical origin of the error through a detailed description and a call-stack extract. Exceptions are Java objects that have inherited these characteristics from their superclasses (e.g. *java.lang.Exception*, see Section 6.1.1).

11.3.1 try-catch construct

The user of a fault-critical method embeds the code to be monitored in a `try` {...} statement. Everything included in this block is processed regularly if no error occurs. However, if an *exception* to the normal run occurs in the case of a statement in the *try* block, the block is quit immediately and a search is made for the exception that has occurred according to the following *catch* statements.

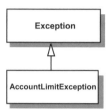

Figure 11.2 *Example of an exception*

Let's assume that an *AccountLimitException* could occur in the `setBalance()` method of our Account class (see also Section 4.4.2). Directly after the *try* statement, an exception handler is defined for this field, which handles the *AccountLimitException*.

```
public void withdraw (double amount)
{
   // non-monitored area up to here
   try
   {                                    // This area
      setBalance(balance - amount);     // should be
   }                                    // monitored.
   catch (AccountLimitException e)
   {
               // Exception handler:
               // User of the method will react.
      System.out.println("Payout impossible."+
                     "Withdrawal exceeds account limit");
   }
   // Continuation of the non-monitored area

}
```

In your experiments with Java, you have possibly had some exceptions occur that were reported by the runtime system. If you started the faulty application, you would have seen "Uncaught exception" in the command line. This means an exception that was not handled using *catch*. This output follows the stacktrace, which states what methods were called before the error occurred.

> **Tip** You can obviously write more legible code using this way of separating error handling from the point of origin. You formulate the normal case within a *try* block; all irregularities are excluded at this point. Those who later have to maintain the source code will now be able to understand the rule more quickly, as 80 – 90% of error handling covering source code is excluded.

11.3.2 Obligatory code – finally

There are certain actions that have to be carried out no matter whether the *try* block is successful or not, or whether the execution was interrupted by an exception (obligatory code). For example, open files should be closed whether the reading was successful or not. In order not to have to write the obligatory code in several places, there is an optional *finally* block.

```
try
{                        // This area
    [...]                // should be
}                        // monitored.
catch (Exception e)
{  [...]  }              // Exception handler
finally
{                        // This block must be executed
    [...]                // in all cases.
}
```

The code in the *finally* block is carried out in all cases, no matter whether the *try* block was successful or not.

11.3.3 Your own exceptions

As exceptions are no longer objects of Exception classes, you can also define your own types. You must derive these from an existing exception:

```
public class AccountLimitException extends Exception
{
    public AccountLimitException() {;}
    public AccountLimitException(String error message)
    {
        super(error message);
    }
}
```

The new class contains no additional methods but its name indicates the type of error. As an option, you can add a detailed description with the second constructor.

11.3.4   throws and throw

One method in which such an exception can occur declares this in the header with `throws <exception name>`. This ensures that a possible exception has to be handled using a *try-catch* construct. A newly generated object of the Exception class is "thrown" using *throw* .

```
public void setBalance(double amount)
    throws AccountLimitException
{
    if (amount > 0)
        balance = amount;
    else
        // Error message
        throw new AccountLimitException(
                "No overdraft allowed.");
}
```

Warning There are a few exceptions whose occurrence does not have to be announced with *throws*. These include all exceptions of the *RuntimeException* or *Error* types, and classes derived from these. In this, no reminder is sent on the handling of the exceptions by the compiler in using the methods in which they could occur. The reason for this is that some errors can occur in almost any situation, for example an *OutOfMemoryError* or a *NullPointerException* (subclass of *RuntimeException*), so that they have to be announced or handled in use in practically all methods using *throws*.

Re-throw

Exception handling in Java is based on errors being handled at the place where there is sufficient knowledge for the removal of the problem. This means that if an exception cannot be handled at its origin – i.e. in the called method – it is passed to the calling method using *throw*. However, if it cannot be handled by that method at that moment, but only by a *try-catch* construct lying further out, the exception can again be thrown using a renewed *throw* (*re-throw*).

11.3.5 Throwable and error

In addition to the *Exception* class, there is also the *Error* class (see Section 6.1.11). Both derive from the *Throwable* superclass (this is a class and not an interface, in spite of the name). Errors are *fatal errors*, which generally make it impossible to continue running an application. Errors refer to the system; conversely, exceptions refer to applications or data. One example of an error is a lack of memory (*OutOfMemoryError*), an example of an exception is an incorrect file name (*FileNotFoundException*).

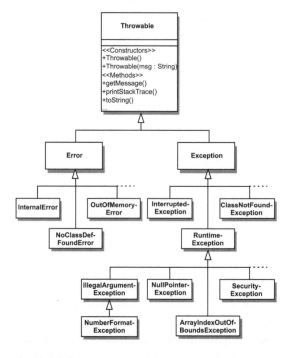

Figure 11.3 *Exceptions and errors in java.lang*

The methods have already been presented in Section 6.1.11.

Tip The `printStackTrace()` method outputs a Call Stack excerpt to the standard output (or another stream). This excerpt is an enumeration of the method calls that led to the error, and thus gives information on the history of the origin of the exception.

Exceptions in java.lang

A number of exceptions are defined in the *java.lang* package. A small section is shown in Figure 11.3.

However, many other exceptions are not contained in this package but instead are in the packages in whose classes they typically occur, for example, the *EO-FException* (file end) and the *FileNotFoundException* are in the *java.io* package (see Section 7.1.13).

> **Tip** The classes are not *final*, so you can therefore derive your own exception classes from them. Also, you should really do this, as application-specific exceptions are more individual and can be clearly allocated and handled. In particular, by stating *throws*, you can even force handling of the error.

Catching all exceptions in the `main` method is inelegant. Using the following piece of code, you can escape the effort of error handling but in the event of an error you will not get any acknowledgement – the program will simply terminate:

```
public static void main(String[] args)
{
    // not this way!!!
    try  // Try block around all code
    {
        [   ]... // Application task
    }
    catch (Throwable e)  // only catch most general
                         // cases of error
    { ; }                // ignore all errors
                         // or output standard
                         // error message
}
```

In other methods, such a handling of errors is even more serious, as the application or the applet is then continued without consideration of the error status.

Tuning 12

How can you accelerate a Java application? On the one hand, there are naturally good algorithms, but also different virtual machines or techniques for avoiding or optimizing the loading of classes via the network.

12.1 Possible influences

Algorithms

Of course, nothing is more important than efficient algorithms and data structures. However, it is becoming increasingly more difficult for developers to influence this themselves. Due to the current size and complexity of programs, you are dependent on all sorts of libraries whose internal implementation is often unknown.

Even the developers of the Java class libraries have learned something new. Formerly, many classes were programmed to "play it safe" and were strictly synchronized ($\rightarrow$ thread-safe). This security does, however, often require a great performance and this protection was often therefore removed in Java 1.2 and 1.3 or only functioned after an explicit request (example: Swing, Collection classes).

Memory management

As memory management in Java is to a large extent passed to the runtime system, the manufacturers of virtual machines are in demand here. If needs be, you can at an early stage set to *null* references to objects no longer required to signal to the memory management that the objects can be removed.

Since Java 1.2, you can also use the reference library *java.lang.ref* (see Section 5.4) to create object caches that allow access to objects that were released for deletion but have not yet been removed.

Communications connection

Here, you should ensure that you keep small the quantity of data to be transmitted. In using RMI and in the case of serialized data in general, you should not transmit unnecessary class attributes (fields) or class attributes that are easy to reconstruct, but identify them using the *transient* modifier. You can compress and unpack the actual objects to be transmitted using, for example, the classes *java.util.zip.ZipOutputStream* and *java.util.zip.ZipInputStream*.

Loading and storing classes

Even with applets, with which the classes are initially loaded over a network, it is important to transmit these efficiently and then only load them when they are required. Instead of having to create a connection to the web server for each class, it is better to pack them in (compressed) Java archives (see Section 4.10.5) and load them at one go.

However, this can also "start back to front" if the archive contains very many classes and resources that are not actually required by the applet. Targeted packaging is needed here. If individual functions are seldom needed in an application, you should first dynamically load the associated classes using `Class.forName()` (see Section 6.1.3). Then the classes will not be immediately provided on loading the applet but when they are actually needed (→faster start-up time).

Class libraries that are regularly used should be present locally. The Java standard library has grown enormously since Java 1.0; many earlier expansions are now present in each runtime environment as standard. You can permanently instal additional Java extensions in the <jre>\lib\ext directory. In version 1.3, you can now have versions of these extensions. An applet can now also recognize whether a necessary extension is already present in a suitable version or whether it has to be reloaded. The use of this functionality is simplified using the *WebStart* tool from Sun. Here, for example, the applet can accurately define which expansions are required in which version, and load them, if they are not already present, from a stated server and cache them locally for the future.

Multithreading

The use of several threads often significantly accelerates applications, as wait times can be used efficiently. With all dialog-oriented applications, such as applets, servlets or graphical user interfaces, you frequently have to wait for user inputs, and, in the case of server applications, many sessions are often open but only a few actually simultaneously active.

Database access

In this area, there are different facilities such as the caching or pre-fetching (pre-offloading of the presumed subsequent data of an access) of data, which is not directly to do with Java, but whose use is important for good performance. You can only avoid the time-consuming making and breaking of connections to a database server by using Connection Pools. Java application servers and Java persistency frameworks offer good support in this field.

Runtime environment

Finally, the virtual machine is also an important factor, and is described in the section.

12.2 Garbage Collection

In Java, the Garbage Collector looks after memory purging. If the last reference to an object disappears, it can delete this independently. You can also explicitly set references to *null*, to facilitate an early Garbage Collection.

A few questions arise:

→ When does a reference disappear?
  A reference defined in a block ({...}), for example a local variable, loses its validity on reaching the end of the block.
  A reference to an instance variable becomes invalid when the object is deleted.

→ When is the memory released?
  This is decided by the Garbage Collector, which runs parallel to the application. It is generally active when the program does not have anything to do (for example, when it is waiting for an event).

→ What happens when two or more objects mutually reference themselves?
  The Garbage Collector recognizes *circular references*. If the last reference disappears in this "island", the Garbage Collector can delete all objects. In Figure 12.1, the solution can then take place when the list reference is deleted.

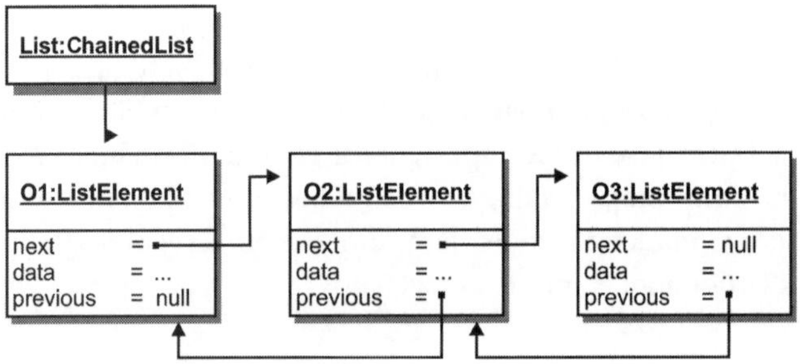

Figure 12.1 *Circular references*

12.3 Packaging

The aim is to find an arrangement of classes that is very likely to be required by the application and to transmit this compressed.

In the case of locally installed *applications* this is not so critical, as memory space on the hard disk is cheap and it is therefore all the same whether a few kilobytes or megabytes of class files and resources are stored that are not required at runtime.

In the case of *applets*, it is really a matter of only transmitting via the Internet or Intranet the data that is actually necessary. Java offers very good facilities for this, as the *ClassLoader* actually loads only the classes that are required. You can therefore simply give access on the web server to all classes that are possibly required (as byte code).

However, this procedure has two disadvantages:

→ A network connection must be created for each class, which costs a lot in performance in the case of several hundred or thousand classes, as a lot of protocol overhead is created.

→ You cannot used any signed applets (see Section 9.3.2), as individual classes cannot be signed.

You should therefore provide the classes and resources in the form of a *Java archive* (jar file, see Section 4.10.5) as a single compressed packet. You can then sign this digitally.

However, there is conversely no danger that this archive will contain many classes that are not used at all and would thus be transmitted superfluously.

The optimum middle way is as follows:

→ The archive (or the archives) contain the classes that are absolutely required for any application case.

→ All other classes are provided on the server and are loaded as required using dynamic classloading (see Sections 6.1.3 and 12.1).

The application should be designed with reference to this architecture. Ask yourself how many functions the user practically always uses, and which are only seldom used by special user groups.

Tip In Section 4.10.5, the creation of Java archives and the contained manifesto are explained in more detail. Since Java 1.3, information for the required extensions can also be contained in this manifesto (see Section 12.1). Information on the signing of archives can be found in Sections 9.3.2 and 10.5 as well as on the Sun Java security homepage (http://java.sun.com/security/index.html).

Tip Java archives to be loaded are stated in the applet tag of a HTML page (see Section 9.4):
`<APPLET CODE="HomeBanking.class"` **`ARCHIVE="Banking.jar"`** `WIDTH=300 HEIGHT=100>`
(Locally instaled) applications can use classes from Java archives explicitly stated in the CLASS-PATH variable (**just the directory that contains the jar-file is insufficient!**). Since JRE 1.2, you can state an archive on calling the *Java* interpreter java using the *-jar* option

12.4 Runtime environment

Finally, in addition to the optimization on the part of the application development, there are also approaches for accelerating the runtime environment.

Efficient virtual machines

Manufacturers are always looking to develop more efficient virtual machines . In the Windows field, several free Java VMs are competing for the customers' favor, for example those from Sun, IBM, and Microsoft (just to name the largest).

Runtime compiling

Just-in-time compilers (JIT) convert the byte code after downloading the applet or after the start of an application into machine code and execute it. JIT compilers are today contained in almost all runtime environments and web browsers.

HotSpot: analysis and compilation at runtime

The *HotSpot* virtual machine from Sun analyzes the code at runtime and concentrates the compilation and optimization on methods that are used particularly frequently. Additional information is available, for the purpose of optimization, from real execution behavior.

> **Tip** HotSpot has been available since JRE 1.2 in a server variant and since JRE 1.3 it has been available as the standard virtual machine from Sun for client variants.

Compilation at development time

As in other programming languages, there are native compilers for Java that produce platform specific machine code. These are available in development environments (e.g. IBM VisualAge for Java Enterprise Edition, WebGain Visual Café). However, this is a last resort and is generally only sensible for server environments, as one of the most important advantages of Java, namely platform independence, is lost in the case of a native compilation.

Architectures

13.1 Overview

The first basic question that you should ask yourself is whether the application runs just by itself (stand-alone) or exchanges data with a server.

Stand-alone applications

There are two variants here:

→ A *Java application* demands a locally installed Java runtime environment. If you have this under your own control (e.g. in a company Intranet), you can have free choice in the selection of the Java version and can have unrestricted use of all functions. However, the application must first be instaled and configured as necessary (e.g. set CLASSPATH).

→ An *applet* runs in the browser (see Chapter 9). You do not need to instal it or worry about new versions, as the applet is reloaded from the server on each call. The disadvantage is that, on the one hand, the browsers often also supply an obsolete virtual machine (Microsoft Internet Explorer 4/5, Netscape Communicator 4), so that you are severely restricted in the design of the user interface, for example, or have to risk long download times. On the other hand, applets are subject to security restrictions (see Section 9.3.1), which can only be lifted after time-consuming signing.

Servlets

Servlets are Java applications that run purely on the web server and generate dynamic HTML (similar to CGI scripts). The necessary class libraries are a part of the Java 2 Enterprise Edition (see Section 5.2.3). These avoid the disadvantages of applets regarding security and language versions, but can only send documents (generally HTML pages) to the client. This means that there is no continuous connection and any change results in a newly generated web page.

Communication

You have connection-oriented communication when two applications on the client and server sides exchange data over a network. In Java, you can choose from *Sockets*, *Datagrams*, *RMI* and *CORBA* (or sometimes *Enterprise JavaBeans*). These technologies are described in Chapter 7.

Integration of Enterprise systems

On the server side, there is often a problem that very many non- object-oriented backend systems have to be linked (e.g. relational databases, or transaction systems). You can encapsulate this system particularly well using *Enterprise JavaBeans*.

Combination of technologies

Often the solution can be found in a combination of different technologies. For example, HTML clients can communicate with Enterprise JavaBeans via servlets.

13.2 K.O. criteria

Wide public

Your application should be able to be used by everyone in the Internet and HTML is insufficient for control.

→ Avoid new language functions (from Java 1.2 or 1.3)!

Reason: Microsoft Internet Explorer 4/5 and Netscape Communicator 4 only support Java 1.1. The Java plug-in is one solution but there are often administrative problems.

Restrictive firewalls

A firewall only lets HTTP traffic through and all other ports are blocked.

→ Avoid Sockets, RMI and CORBA!

Reason: these technologies are based on TCP/IP and use other ports. Consider whether servlets could offer a solution.

Complex graphical user interfaces

You have a lavish user interface with tree views, Drag&Drop, etc.

→ Avoid servlets!

Reason: HTML does not offer this functionality.

Little memory

Poor computer hardware equipment.

→ Avoid Swing, CORBA and Enterprise JavaBeans!

Reason: these technologies are very memory-intensive.

High degree of scalability, fail-safe

You have a lot of requests. The servers run as a cluster or multi-processor machines. The clients should continue to run without a changeover in the case of a server failure.

→ Avoid Sockets and RMI!

Reason: these technologies are not designed for changing servers. All services for load distribution, localization and security have to be implemented themselves. Use CORBA or Enterprise JavaBeans.

Index

Pushbutton 214, 283